22

P9-CKW-066

SOUP CLASSICS

KNACK®

SOUP CLASSICS

Chowders, Gumbos, Bisques, Broths, Stocks, and Other Delicious Soups

LINDA JOHNSON LARSEN

Photographs by Debi Harbin

KNACK®
MAKE IT EASY

Guilford, Connecticut
An imprint of Globe Pequot Press

DISCARD

Library Resource Center
Renton Technical College
3000 N.E. 4th St.
Renton, WA 98056

To buy books in quantity for corporate use
or incentives, call **(800) 962-0973**
or e-mail **premiums@GlobePequot.com.**

Copyright © 2010 by Morris Book Publishing, LLC

ALL RIGHTS RESERVED. No part of this book may be reproduced or transmitted in any form by any means, electronic or mechanical, including photocopying and recording, or by any information storage and retrieval system, except as may be expressly permitted in writing from the publisher. Requests for permission should be addressed to Globe Pequot Press, Attn: Rights and Permissions Department, P.O. Box 480, Guilford, CT 06437.

Knack is a registered trademark of Morris Publishing Group, LLC, and is used with express permission.

Editor in Chief: Maureen Graney
Editor: Katie Benoit
Cover Design: Paul Beatrice, Bret Kerr
Text Design: Paul Beatrice
Layout: Melissa Evarts
Cover photos by Debi Harbin
Interior photos by Debi Harbin with the exception of p. 5 (right): tobik/Shutterstock; p. 6 (right): Courtesy of Rival/Crock-Pot; p. 7 (left): Courtesy of Rival/Crock-Pot; p. 7 (right): Courtesy of Rival/Crock-Pot; p. 8 (left): © Hixson Dreamstime.com; p. 8 (right): Courtesy of Cuisinart; p. 19 (left): Rudyanto Wijaya/Shutterstock; p. 19 (right): Tatiana Popova/Shutterstock; p. 20 (right): © Nickr | Dreamstime.com; p. 21 (left): Traveler/Shutterstock; p. 21 (right): Courtesy Hamilton Beach; p. 30 (left): Courtesy OXO Good Grips Food Mill

Library of Congress Cataloging-in-Publication Data

Larsen, Linda Johnson.
  Knack soup classics : a step-by-step guide to favorites for every season / Linda Johnson Larsen ; photographs by Debi Harbin.
    p. cm.
  ISBN 978-1-59921-775-8
  1. Soups. I. Title. II. Title: Soup classics.

  TX757.L37 2009
  641.8'13—dc22
                                    2009019050

The following manufacturers/names appearing in *Knack Soup Classics* are trademarks:
Crock-Pot®, Cuisinart®, OXO Good Grips®, Hamilton Beach®, Rival®

The information in this book is true and complete to the best of our knowledge. All recommendations are made without guarantee on the part of the author or Globe Pequot Press. The author and Globe Pequot Press disclaim any liability in connection with the use of this information.

Printed in China

10 9 8 7 6 5 4 3 2 1

641.813 LARSEN 2010

Larsen, Linda Johnson

Knack soup classics

Dedication
To my dear husband Doug, my best friend and love.

Acknowledgments
Thanks to my family, especially my parents Marlene and Duane, and to my sisters Lisa and Laura. Thanks also to my agent Barb Doyen for supporting me through thick and thin, and to the staff at GPP. I'd also like to thank Debi Harbin, the wonderful photographer for this book, for bringing the recipes to life so beautifully.

Photographer Acknowledgments
Special thanks to: Diane DeBrosse, Tina Jones, and Michelle-Sibley Feeser. They shopped, chopped (many tearful pounds of onions), and assisted me on the photography in *Knack Soup Classics*!

—Debi Harbin

CONTENTS

INTRODUCTION

Soup: the word conjures up images of comfort and home. It is a universal food, loved by cultures around the world. Soup can be simple or complex; it ranges from a flavorful broth to a complicated one-dish meal. But how many people have enjoyed a true homemade soup instead of one reconstituted from a box or can?

Soup is not difficult to make. Most of the best soups require two things: good ingredients and time. But the actual time you must invest in a good soup is minimal. Most of the time is spent letting the food bubble away on the stove, in the oven, or in a slow cooker or pressure cooker.

A soup can be as simple as a combination of lentils, water, and a few vegetables, or as complicated as a gumbo with twenty ingredients. The magic happens when the ingredients simmer together, for minutes or hours. The flavors blend and are accentuated by herbs and spices.

And soup is so good for you! Chicken soup, sometimes known as "Grandma's penicillin," contains proteins that can help lower blood pressure and anti-inflammatory ingredients that stop the release of chemicals that make you feel sick.

Soup recipes are very tolerant; that is, they will still be delicious no matter what you add to or subtract from the recipe. You can change the vegetables out entirely, use different meats, add more herbs, or change the proportions, and the soup will still be delicious. Measuring accurately is only important with seasonings. Other ingredients can be added in greater or lesser amounts without negatively affecting the recipe.

The basis for all of the best soups is a good broth or stock. These are the easiest soups to make, and the time and effort spent in making a rich and flavorful broth will pay you back many times over. Once you have good broths on hand, you can make every soup in the world.

Soups, chowders, and bisques vary mostly in their

ingredients, texture of the finished soup, and thickness. A soup is usually made of a clear broth and ingredients added for flavor, color, and texture. Chowders are a thicker soup, with added cheese and dairy ingredients. And bisques are thickened with milk and egg yolks, sometimes pureed for a velvety texture.

The soups in this book were selected for their classic appeal and timelessness. Once you understand how to make them, you can vary the ingredients and create something brand-new. Soup is a very forgiving food; you can change almost all of the ingredients and it will still taste wonderful.

You can enjoy soup any time of the day or night. Some soups are delicious for breakfast, lunch, dinner, and snacks. Soup can be the perfect treatment for a cold or an elegant first course to start a formal dinner.

Soups are a great choice for your lunchbox, too. A well-made insulated thermos is essential for packing cold or hot soups. To prepare the thermos for hot soups, rinse it out with boiling water, then immediately add the simmering soup. Seal the thermos; it should stay hot up to 6 hours.

For cold soups, rinse the thermos with very cold water, then add the already chilled soup. Don't expect a hot or cold thermos to be able to heat or chill soups; they'll just hold them at a safe and palatable temperature.

There are quickly made soups, then there are soups that simmer for hours, either in the slow cooker or on the stove. Soups don't have to cook for a long time to be of high quality. Some quickly made soups include Beer Cheese Soup, fruit soups, and egg drop soup. The key to short-cooking soups is to use a full-flavored broth; that makes the soup taste as if it cooked for hours.

Soups that require a long cooking time include stocks and broths, bean soups, and some vegetable beef and chicken soups. The long simmering time creates complex flavors and aromas.

When you make a stock or broth, or a long-simmering soup, foam or scum may rise to the surface. This is just protein from the bones or meat, forming bubbles as the mixture cooks. Just skim off this foam and discard it; it doesn't add anything to the soup.

It's important to have good equipment to make the best soup. A heavy, high-quality stockpot, sauté pans, whisks, strainers, sturdy tongs, sharp knives, and heavy-duty spoons and spatulas all make creating the best soups easier. These items don't have to be expensive; they just have to be sturdy and well made.

Take care of your equipment, and it will last you a lifetime. Don't let soups sit in metal pots and pans; transfer them to hard-sided containers, refrigerate or freeze them immediately, and then wash the pot with hot soapy water right away. Don't wash your knives in the dishwasher, because that can dull them and dry out wooden handles. Store them in a knife block, not in a drawer, for safety and to keep them in top condition. And learn how to sharpen knives using a knife steel.

The ingredients you use must be the best quality, too. A soup is only as good as its ingredients. Never use wilted vegetables or fruits or poor-quality meats. Long-cooking soups, especially, concentrate the flavor of the ingredients. Poor-quality ingredients make a poor-quality soup.

Canned, frozen, and fresh ingredients are equally good in soup. Don't be afraid to use canned or frozen produce in your soup recipes. These products are processed very soon after harvesting, so they can retain even more vitamins and minerals than fresh produce that's been shipped across the country or around the world.

Preparing ingredients for soup is simple. Most meats and produce are just peeled and chopped, sliced, or diced, then added to the soup at different times according to how long they take to cook. For a quicker cooking soup, cut everything into a small dice. For long-cooking soups or soups made in a slow cooker, cut the ingredients into larger pieces.

Soups are found in every ethnic cuisine and culture in the world. This makes it easy for you to alter a soup recipe just by adding and subtracting a few ingredients. For instance, the Greek cuisine features lemons, oregano, feta cheese, and olives. Add these ingredients to a basic broth for a Greek soup. The Creole cuisine relies on peppers, both hot and sweet; rice; and earthy flavors like cumin and chili powder, along with seafood and spicy sausages like andouille and boudin.

For a Tex-Mex slant, add some roasted poblano or Anaheim peppers, baby corn, chipotle chiles, adobo paste, chili powder, black beans, and corn. And to make an Italian soup, add pasta, both plain and stuffed; herbs like oregano and basil; and grated Parmesan, Asiago, or Romano cheeses.

When you serve your homemade soup, make sure that the hot soup is served hot and the cold soup served cold. Use the appropriate serving utensils and bowls or plates, too—heatproof bowls for hot soups and glass or metal bowls for cold soups.

You can purchase a collection of lovely soup plates and dinnerware as sets or find them over time at antiques stores and estate sales. Match your dishes to the occasion. A hearty Tex-Mex chili is fun to eat in rustic stoneware bowls, while a delicate egg drop soup looks beautiful in plain bone china.

Enjoy these soup recipes and enjoy creating your own wonderful variations. Have fun using your favorite foods in these delicious and classic recipes.

SOUP BASICS

Once you understand the basics for making soup, the sky's the limit

Soup is only as good as its ingredients. The best soup is made using high-quality ingredients, carefully cooked together to bring out all of the flavor. This doesn't mean it has to simmer for hours or be full of complicated and expensive foods.

Soups can be served hot or cold, be savory or sweet, and be smooth or chunky with vegetables.

Most good soups start with the same thing: an excellent broth or stock. A broth is made with meat or vegetables and no bones. A stock is made with meat and vegetables and uses bones. Bones give the stock a richness and depth of flavor impossible to achieve with any other ingredient.

You can make a soup out of plain water and a few other

Soup Definition

- A soup is made of solid and liquid ingredients. The solids include meats, vegetables, and fruits.

- The quality of the liquid part of the soup, or the broth or stock, is crucial to the soup's taste. A rich and well-rounded broth elevates plain soup into a feast.

- Use the best-quality stock or broth you can find, or make your own using any recipe.

- Commercial stocks and broths are available canned, frozen, and boxed. The boxed soups usually have the best flavor.

Soup Base

- Sautéing vegetables in butter or some type of oil forms the base of most savory soups.

- This method softens the vegetables and introduces flavor into the fat, which carries it throughout the soup.

- Don't skip this step, and watch the ingredients carefully. Stir often to prevent burning and so the vegetables cook evenly.

- You can make soup base ahead of time; freeze it in one-cup portions for a quick start to any soup.

ingredients. Some of the best soups in the world, such as vichyssoise and fruit soups, are really this simple.

There are several ways to cook soup. The stovetop is the obvious method, but soups also cook well in slow cookers, pressure cookers, and the microwave. There are also soups that can be made in the food processor or blender.

Soups are popular in every culture around the world. They have nourished populations for generations. Enjoy this collection of delicious and easy soups.

········· GREEN ● LIGHT ·········
Enjoy experimenting with soups to create your own masterpiece. Soups are among the most tolerant and variable of recipes. You can add just about anything or subtract ingredients and the soup will still be delicious. Add your favorite vegetables, meats, or cheese to any soup recipe.

Cooking Techniques

- There are quite a few ways to cook soup. One of the best is with a slow cooker.

- The flavors of the soup blend beautifully when cooked in this appliance. There's almost no evaporation, but all the flavors concentrate.

- You can also simmer soup on the stovetop. This is a much faster method; you can usually make a soup in about thirty minutes.

- An immersion blender or food processor is another necessary tool to make pureed soups and bisques.

Best Ingredients

- The best ingredients for soup are the freshest you can find. Don't use old or shriveled vegetables, thinking you can "save" them.

- Plump free-range chickens, good cuts of beef and pork, and the freshest seafood are all essential.

- The water you use is also very important. Filtered water provides the cleanest taste.

- Good cheeses, herbs, and spices are also essential to the best-tasting soup.

TYPES OF SOUP
Soups are classified by ingredients, texture, and thickness

Soup is usually defined as a combination of broth or stock and solid ingredients. It can be chunky or pureed smooth. There are chowders, bisques, chilis, and stews, too.

The types of soup in this book include soups, chowders, bisques, and gumbos. Both hot and cold soups are featured. None of these soups are as thick as a chili or stew, although using slurries, roux, and reductions, you can make soup as thick as you like.

Clear soups are the simplest. A homemade broth or stock can be a perfect first course or a soothing treatment for a cold. Float a few herbs and chopped vegetables in the broth for garnish and appearance. Egg drop soup is a good example of a clear soup taken one step further.

Chowders are thicker than soups. They are usually, but not always, based on seafood, with some milk or other dairy products included in the recipe.

Soup

- A good soup starts with a good base. Use the best broth, vegetables, meats, and dairy products.

- When you're serving a clear broth, it's important to use the best ingredients. Such a simple recipe has to be high quality.

- Quick soups can be made in thirty minutes, while consommés and stocks take hours to cook.

- When you serve hot soup, make sure it's hot, at least 140°F. And cold soups should be well chilled.

Chowder

- Classic chowders are made of seafood, but they can be made with any meat or as a vegetarian soup.

- The soup is thickened with milk and cheese and almost always uses potatoes, both for flavor and thickening.

- Most chowders begin with a base of crisply cooked bacon. This adds lots of smoky flavor.

- The best chowders are made with fresh seafood and a homemade seafood or chicken stock.

Bisques are soups for a more formal occasion. They are thickened with egg and cream and usually pureed. Bisques can be served hot or cold.

Gumbos are the thickest soups. Classic gumbos are made with a roux, or mixture of cooked flour in oil, and filé powder for thickening.

All well made soups are delicious and easy.

••••••••••••••••• GREEN ● LIGHT ••••••••••••••••

Whenever you make soup, save the fruit and vegetable trimmings to make compost for your garden. Don't use meat scraps or kitchen grease, but vegetable peelings, fruit skins and seeds, eggshells, spoiled fruits and veggies are all candidates for the compost pile.

Bisque

- A bisque is the richest of soups. Almost always pureed, it is made from meat and vegetables and thickened with cream and eggs.

- The flavor of a bisque is quite intense; the ingredients used to make it should be top quality.

- Like chowders, bisques are usually made with seafood, although they can be made with any meat.

- A bisque, served in small quantities, is an elegant appetizer or first course for a formal dinner.

Gumbo

- Gumbo is the country cousin of soups. It originated in the Gulf Coast area of the United States.

- Gumbos always start with the "holy trinity" of vegetables sweated in a saucepan.

- These include celery, bell pepper, and onion. The soup usually includes sausage and seafood, mostly shrimp.

- Classic gumbos begin with a roux, a mixture of flour and oil cooked until brown. This thickens the soup and adds a deep flavor.

STOCKPOTS
Stockpots, by their shape and size, make a superior soup

You can make soup in everything from a saucepan to a Dutch oven, but a stockpot offers some superior qualities.

Because most stockpots are deep and narrow, with straight sides and a well-fitting cover, they help soup cook without losing too much liquid to evaporation.

A good stockpot has to be made of sturdy material. Make sure yours has a very heavy bottom so the soup doesn't scorch or burn over the long cooking time. Stockpots are usually made of cast iron, stainless, or aluminum. The newest types of "hard-anodizing" aluminum are harder than stainless steel and great conductors of heat.

Conductivity is an important property of stockpots. The pot has to be able to evenly transmit heat from the stovetop to the food. The soup at the bottom of the pot shouldn't cook at a hotter temperature than the soup at the top.

A handle made of heatproof material is a good option.

High, Narrow Stockpot

- A high and narrow stock-pot is useful for making broths, stocks, and other long-simmering soups and chowders.

- Because the pot is narrow, there is less surface area for evaporation of liquid.

- The liquid also undergoes more convection, or move-ment, in a high and narrow stockpot so cooks more evenly.

- Of course storage space is a consideration with any large utensil. Make sure your stockpot fits easily into a cupboard or pantry.

Low, Wide Stockpot

- For a thicker soup, a low and wide stockpot is ideal. More surface area means more evaporation.

- This type of stockpot is also good when you start a soup with lots of pan frying, browning, and sautéing.

- The ingredients spread out over a larger surface area, so they will brown and caramelize. It's also easier to see how the ingredients are cooking.

- If ingredients are crowded together during the brown-ing process, they will steam instead of brown.

Sometimes soups are baked in the oven; a handle made of the same material as the rest of the pot lets you do this with ease.

Stockpots range in size from 5 to 20 quarts. A good all-purpose stockpot is 10 to 12 quarts.

ZOOM

Stockpots made of copper are considered the best, but they can cost more than $500. A sturdy stockpot of steel or anodized aluminum should cost around $100 to $150. Consider it an investment in your kitchen, much as you would a new appliance.

Dutch Oven

- A Dutch oven is a large cooking pot with a tight-fitting lid. Some have legs for use in a fireplace.

- Dutch ovens can be used on top of the stove, in the oven, or even on a campfire.

- They can be made of cast iron, enameled steel, cast aluminum, or ceramic.

- Some Dutch ovens come in nesting sets. These can be useful for making different soups and help alleviate the storage issue.

Pot and Pan Sets

- Most pots and pans come in sets. While this can be a great way to stock a kitchen, it's usually not the best way to buy a stockpot.

- Most pot and pan sets usually include only one stockpot, about around 6 to 8 quarts.

- Sometimes you can find a set of stockpots in the 8- to 12-quart sizes. These sets can be good bargains.

- Make sure the sets are well made, with tight-fitting lids and solidly attached handles.

SLOW COOKER
The slow cooker is the perfect appliance for cooking soup

A slow cooker or Crock-pot is a wonderful appliance to make soup. There is little or no evaporation, and flavors concentrate as they cook in a sealed environment, preserving aromas and vitamins.

Because there is virtually no evaporation when cooking in a slow cooker, broths and stocks have to be at regular concentration when added to the appliance. Meats, vegetables, and fruits will add their flavor to the broth. It is possible to get some reduction by evaporation by leaving the lid off the slow cooker for the last thirty to forty minutes.

A slow cooker consists of an outer metal heating element, with a ceramic or metal insert. The newer slow cookers have a removable insert, which makes cleanup easy. There are usually just two cooking levels: low and high. At low, the temperature gets to about 200°F; on high, 300°F. This is well above the necessary temperature for meat doneness, which ranges

Large Slow Cooker

- Large slow cookers range from 5 to 8 quarts. These appliances are good for cooking large quantities of stock.

- It's important to keep the lid on the slow cooker while it's cooking and to be sure it's seated against the insert.

- A slight pressure builds up as the lid seals to the insert and steam is produced.

- Each time you lift the lid you need to add twenty minutes to the total overall cooking time.

Triple Slow Cooker

- You can serve soup right out of your slow cooker, especially with this triple model that is made for entertaining.

- This appliance is great for a buffet; it's a casual and inexpensive way to entertain.

- Be sure to look for individual controls on these multiple slow cookers. It's nice if they have a "keep warm" feature.

- Keep the lid on the cookers. You can remove them at serving time, but they should be covered while they stand.

from 145°F to 180°F, so you don't have to worry about safety.

Fill your slow cooker one-half to three-quarters full for best results. If there is less food, it may scorch or burn. Too much food means the ingredients may not cook through in the allotted time.

· · · · · · · · · · · YELLOW ● LIGHT · · · · · · · · · ·

The newer slow cookers tend to cook hotter than older appliances. Where an older slow cooker may have taken 7 to 8 hours to cook chicken breasts, they are now done in 5 to 6 hours in the new appliances. If you are using older recipes with a new slow cooker, take this into account.

Programmable Slow Cooker

- Programmable slow cookers give you a lot more versatility in cooking times.

- With these slow cookers you can delay the start of cooking up to 2 hours and keep the food warm 2 hours after cooking is done.

- For food safety be sure you never exceed these times.

- You can also program in different cooking temperatures. For instance, start a chicken dish on high for 1 hour, then reduce the heat to low for 3 to 4 hours.

Timers and Controls

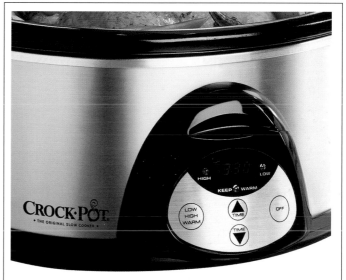

- Some of the newer models have alarm systems that will let you know if the power went off during cooking or standing times.

- If the slow cooker has an alarm and it lets you know the power was off less than 2 hours, you can serve the food.

- If you don't know how long the power was off, don't serve the food.

- These controls can be very sophisticated; be sure you read the manufacturer's directions before use.

PRESSURE COOKER
For homemade soup in minutes, a pressure cooker is key

Pressure cookers have come a long way from the unwieldy old-fashioned appliances with a stopcock and tendency to explode. The newer pressure cookers have lots of built-in safety features and can make a complicated soup in minutes rather than hours.

Electronic pressure cookers don't even need a stovetop. Older pressure cookers had to be cooked over high or medium heat on a burner, making it difficult to regulate the temperature and pressure. If you want to cook soup in a pressure cooker, look into the new electronic models.

One of the best things about making soup in a pressure cooker is its ability to cook dried beans and peas quickly and evenly. Even after overnight soaking, these products sometimes don't get soft enough with regular cooking methods. The pressure cooker eliminates that problem.

Whichever type of pressure cooker you use, be sure to fol-

Basic Pressure Cooker

Electronic Pressure Cooker

- Old-fashioned pressure cookers have to release steam before they can be opened. This is done two ways.

- The pressure cooker is placed in a sink and cold water is carefully poured over it. The water can't enter the steam valve.

- Or the pressure cooker can be left alone to cool down naturally: this takes twenty to thirty minutes.

- Store your old-fashioned pressure cooker with the lid off so off flavors and mold don't develop.

- The electronic pressure cooker is very easy to use. You just fill it up, choose the pressure (high, about 9 psi, or low, about 5 psi) and time, and turn it in.

- These appliances have self-locking lids and automatic pressure release.

- The lid won't open until the pressure is reduced to a safe level.

- Some of these newer pressure cookers can also be used as a slow cooker and rice cooker.

low the manufacturer's instructions to the letter. The pressure cooker can't be opened until the pressure is reduced through the release of steam. Always use care around the pressure cooker: steam can burn.

Timing is important when cooking in a pressure cooker. Vegetables can overcook in the time it takes some meats to cook, so the size of food put into the appliance is important.

• • • • • • • • • • • • • • • RED ● LIGHT • • • • • • • • • • • • • •

Don't buy used pressure cookers at garage sales or consignment stores. There's no way to know if they can still be safely used. An accident can cause severe injuries. Everything about the pressure cooker has to be in top condition, including the gaskets, vent tubes, seals, and stopcock.

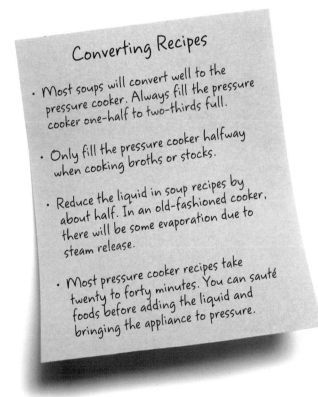

Converting Recipes

• Most soups will convert well to the pressure cooker. Always fill the pressure cooker one-half to two-thirds full.

• Only fill the pressure cooker halfway when cooking broths or stocks.

• Reduce the liquid in soup recipes by about half. In an old-fashioned cooker, there will be some evaporation due to steam release.

• Most pressure cooker recipes take twenty to forty minutes. You can sauté foods before adding the liquid and bringing the appliance to pressure.

Releasing Pressure

• The pressure that builds up inside a pressure cooker brings the liquid to a higher temperature than the boiling point of 212°F.

• This is what cooks the food more quickly, usually reducing cooking time by 60 to 70 percent.

• Any pressure cooker you use must have a backup safety valve that will release pressure if it gets too high.

• Follow the manufacturer's directions to release pressure, and do so carefully, using mitts to protect your hands and arms.

FOOD PROCESSOR

A food processor is an essential tool for making pureed soups and bisques

Food processors not only speed up the preparation of the food that goes into the soup, they can make a cold soup from start to finish.

For soups like gazpacho and chilled pea or melon soups, just coarsely chop the ingredients, peel when necessary, and add to the processor. A few pulses and you can serve the soup immediately or chill to let the flavors blend.

Processors are also used to puree hot soups. But use care when pureeing boiling hot mixtures. And never fill a food processor more than two-thirds full of a cold liquid or solid.

Some soups are partially processed; that is, some of the solid ingredients are pureed in a food processor and then re-

Large Food Processor

- A large food processor can make everything from pureed soup to chocolate mousse.

- The capacity of large food processors ranges from 8 to 14 cups. Mini–food processors range from 2 to 4 cups.

- Check reviews on Internet shopping sites carefully to make sure the food processor has the capacity and versatility you need.

- You might want to consider buying more than one bowl for the food processor so you don't have to wash the bowl during cooking.

Mini–Food Processor

- A mini–food processor can be a very good buy. They are much less expensive than the larger food processors and are easier to store.

- With a mini–food processor, you can chop an onion, mince garlic, puree beans, and chop mushrooms.

- Some large food processors have mini-bowls to chop and mince smaller amounts of food without dirtying the big bowl.

- Even the mini–food processors have feed tubes and shredding and slicing disks.

turned to the soup. This thickens the soup naturally, without the use of roux or slurries of flour or cornstarch.

Another advantage of the food processor is that it easily chops food all the same size so it cooks evenly. And you're more likely to make soups from scratch if you know the ingredients can be prepared quickly. Food processors come in large and small sizes. Large processors are good if you make a lot of cold soups; miniprocessors can be enough if you just chop vegetables.

YELLOW ● LIGHT

Be careful of that food processor blade—it's very sharp. It must be razor thin to easily chop and mince vegetables and puree food. Handle it by the bottom plastic piece, never by the blades. And watch out for it when you put it in the dishwasher for cleaning.

Ladle Soup into Processor

- Use a large, sturdy ladle or a measuring cup with an integral handle to pour soup into the food processor.

- Hot liquid will expand with the heat and pressure, so never fill a food processor more than half full of a hot liquid.

- You will probably have to process separate batches at one time. Pour the pureed part into a fresh pan or pot.

- For more safety, you can let the soup cool for ten to fifteen minutes before processing.

Puree Soup

- Cover the top of the food processor with a folded kitchen towel to protect your hands.

- Start at a low speed and just pulse the soup at first. If the soup pushes against the lid, remove some of the soup, then continue.

- The soup can be heated after being pureed. Often cream or cheeses are added at this time.

- Put your finger in the hole in the bottom of the processor bowl to hold the blade as you pour the puree out.

Library Resource Cen
Renton Technical Co
3000 N.E. 4th St.
Renton, WA 98056

LADLES & SPOONS

Ladles of different sizes and materials make creating soups easier

Ladles and spoons are essential to the soup-making process. Have a large supply of different types of spoons and ladles on hand at all times. Make sure the utensils are sturdy, with long handles to keep you safe from bubbling soups and steaming broths.

Ladles are different from spoons. They have a larger bowl that is deeper and wider, and the bowl is attached to the handle differently. The handle should be perpendicular to the bowl. One-piece ladles are generally sturdier than those with an attached handle. Some one-piece ladles have a rubber or silicone handle cover so you don't burn yourself using the utensil.

Ladles range in size from 2-inch bowls to 4-inch bowls. The capacity of the ladle ranges from 3 to 6 ounces. A larger ladle can make transferring soup to another container or a food processor easier.

Metal Ladle

- The best metal ladles are made with 18/10 or 18/8 stainless steel.

- That number means the percentage of nickel and chromium used to make the metal. The first number is the amount of chromium, the second is nickel.

- Chromium is used for strength, and nickel is used for shine. Both of those numbers indicate good quality.

- If the utensil isn't marked, it's probably 18/0, which is a lower quality. Avoid these; the utensils may not stand up to repeated use.

Silicone Ladle

- Silicone ladles are nonstick. The handle won't transfer heat to your fingers and is comfortable to use.

- Since silicone is bendable, the ladle has to have a rigid core. These utensils are heat resistant up to 500°F.

- Silicone is a great choice to use on nonstick cookware, since it won't scratch no matter how hard you rub.

- Choose a ladle with a long handle. Some of the bowls have lips that make pouring easier.

Some ladles and spoons come with a hook or hold on the end so you can hang them on a pegboard or wall hook. This keeps the utensils close at hand so you don't have to dig through a drawer while you're cooking.

Hold the ladles and spoons in your hand before you buy them. Make sure they are well balanced and comfortable to use and hold.

•••••••••• GREEN ● LIGHT ••••••••••

Once you've found utensils that are good quality, think about fun ways to store them. You can dress up your kitchen by choosing a decorative container to hold your spoons and ladles. This not only looks nice, but it keeps the utensils right at your fingertips.

Wooden Spoon

- Wooden spoons are also safe for nonstick cookware. They come in two varieties: a round bowl and a bowl with a flat top.

- The flat-top spoon, usually called a wooden turner, is useful for scraping the bottom of pans to remove drippings and stuck-on food.

- The best spoons are made from beech wood with an oil finish to keep them from splitting.

- Wash your wooden spoons in the sink; the dishwasher's harsh environment will dry them out.

Slotted Spoon

- You can find slotted spoons in wood, nylon, steel, and silicone. They are useful for removing solids from a soup for pureeing.

- The bowl of the spoon has slots literally cut into the material. This lets liquid run off from the solids when you lift the spoon.

- If you have nonstick cookware, be sure to get nylon, silicone, or wooden slotted spoons.

- Slotted spoons range in size from 9 to 16 inches; get the one best suited to your needs.

FAT SEPARATORS

Some soups need to have fat removed; this is how to do it

When making stocks and broths you may want to remove the fat before freezing. This is also something you'll do to drippings when making a pan gravy.

There are several ways to remove the fat from soups. You can chill the soup, use a fat separator, or skim the fat off the top using a flat spoon.

Chilling soups to remove the fat takes time. To remove fat by skimming, you have to have a clear broth or stock that hasn't been combined with a slurry or roux for thickening. Manual fat separators are the quickest way to accomplish this task.

The fat in a broth or stock will always rise to the top as the soup cools. When you chill a soup overnight, in the morning you'll find a layer of fat has risen to the top and solidified. You can easily remove the fat and discard it.

Skimming broths and stocks manually can take some time.

Chill Soup

- To chill soups safely, transfer them while still hot to a large, fairly shallow container.

- The larger surface area will help the soup cool quickly to get it through the danger zone of 40°F to 140°F.

- When the soup is cold, you'll find a solid layer of fat on the surface.

- Gently break the fat and peel it off. If there's a thicker clear layer under the fat, keep that; it's gelatin, which thickens the soup.

Top Fat Separator

- These fat separators are often called gravy separators because they're commonly used to make gravy.

- Pour the broth or stock into the cup. The fat will rise to the surface into a visible layer.

- The utensil has a stopper that prevents the fat on top from being poured out with the defatted stock.

- Some of these separators also have strainers to remove small bits of solid material as they separate the fat.

The fat will appear as clear puddles on top of the liquid; scoop it off carefully using the side of a spoon.

Manual separators are an essential piece of equipment if you make lots of stocks and broths. They're easy to use and inexpensive.

ZOOM

When you're making chicken broth and remove the fat by chilling the mixture, you can reserve the fat, called schmaltz, to make matzo balls or chopped chicken liver. The fat can be used for other purposes too; divide it into small portions and freeze up to one month.

Skim Fat

- It takes a steady hand and some practice to be able to skim fat off the surface of soup.

- This method only works when no flour or cornstarch has been added to the soup. Those ingredients bind the fat in a suspension in the liquid.

- The fat will look like clear, shiny puddles on the surface of the soup.

- Gently, using the side of a spoon, skim off the fat puddles, trying not to include much of the broth.

Bottom Fat Separator

- This type of separator removes the fat from the broth in a different way.

- You pour the broth or stock into the utensil in the usual way and let stand until the fat separates.

- But then a lever on the handle lets you remove the stock from the bottom without disturbing the fat layer.

- Just stop pouring when all the stock is out and only the fat remains in the bowl.

SOUP MUGS & BOWLS
Serve your delicious soup in fun mugs and bowls

Once you've made your soup, how are you going to serve it? A plain soup can be elevated to gourmet status simply by the type of bowls and serving utensils you use and by adding a little garnish like fresh herbs or a lemon slice. And rustic soups can be heartwarming served in mugs that guests can cradle in their hands.

Always make sure the bowl or mug you are going to serve the soup in is heat resistant; you especially need to do this with antique bowls. Place the bowl in a sink and fill it with boiling water; let stand for 5 minutes. If the bowl doesn't leak or crack, it's safe to use. Soup bowls range from sturdy ceramic or stoneware pieces to delicate bone china and glass. A sturdy soup like chowder or gumbo is best served in a sturdy piece of china, while broths and delicate soups like egg drop look wonderful in china or glass bowls.

It's also fun to collect soupspoons from antiques stores or

Ceramic Bowls

- Ceramic bowls can be manufactured or handcrafted and are found in all types of colors and styles.

- When you buy ceramic or stoneware bowls, be sure they are microwave and dishwasher safe and 100 percent lead free.

- Follow the manufacturer's directions for care and washing of these bowls. Some aren't dishwasher safe.

- You can warm these bowls before adding the soup to keep your soup piping hot longer.

Classic Mugs

- A good soup mug has a generous capacity, holding at least 16 ounces, or 2 cups. The mug should be balanced and feel comfortable in your hand.

- Mugs should be dishwasher and microwave safe, with sturdy handles.

- Some of these mugs are oven safe, too, so you can warm them in the oven before adding the soup.

- Match the mugs to your decor, or try something fun and wild for eating soup at a picnic.

garage or estate sales. You can often find beautiful silver plate or sterling silver utensils at these locations.

However you choose to serve your soup, enjoy mixing and matching soups and bowls to make eating soup even more enjoyable.

•••••••••••• RED ● LIGHT ••••••••••••

Be aware that older bowls and mugs may contain lead paint or solder; that means that hot, acidic foods can leach lead into your soup. It's best to use newer bowls and mugs to serve soup; you can have the older bowls tested. There isn't a safe threshold for lead consumption.

GADGETS

Soup and Cracker Mug

- Soup and cracker mugs are a great way to serve soup for a casual occasion.

- Kids, especially, will enjoy eating their soup this way. After all, part of the enjoyment of food is the visual presentation.

- Another specialty soup mug is the French onion soup mug, which has small handles attached to the side.

- You can often find matching soup bowls or mugs paired with a large tureen for a beautiful presentation.

Fancy Bowls

- You can turn soup into an elegant first course by serving it in bone china or tempered glass.

- These bowls are sometimes called soup plates, because they are flat and shallow.

- This shape makes it easier to eat soup at a formal occasion, because there's lots of surface area from which to scoop a spoonful.

- Pair these fancy bowls with sterling or silver plate spoons. A good soupspoon has a large, shallow bowl.

STRAINERS & SIEVES

Broths, especially, benefit from a trip through a strainer or sieve

A strainer is an essential piece of equipment for making soup. Whether you are making a broth or removing some of the solids from a soup for pureeing, a strainer makes the job so much easier.

Strainers are better than slotted spoons for many tasks just because they have a larger capacity. Look for nested strainers or sieves made of stainless steel with sturdy attached handles.

There are several different types of strainers and sieves. Some are handheld with a sturdy handle; others are made to sit in the sink or a large bowl. There are collapsible strainers and nested strainers.

The strainers can be made of plastic, silicone, or metal. The handheld models usually have a small hook on the end opposite the handle; this lets you place the sieve on a bowl and keep it in place while you pour liquid through it.

Nested Steel Strainers

- These strainers are heavy-duty and well made and will strain the smallest particles out of broth or stock.

- While these strainers are easy to use, they can be a bit difficult to clean. It's best to rinse them immediately after using them.

- If you don't rinse them or immerse them in water immediately after use, food can stick to the small holes.

- Store them nested together to save cupboard and pantry space.

Silicone Strainer

- These fun strainers come in many colors, so they're decorative too. They pop open to use, then fold flat.

- Silicone can handle temperatures up to 500°F, so don't worry about their durability.

- These strainers are easier to clean than fine-mesh strainers because they are flexible.

- Because they fold flat to store, they take up less room and store much more easily than metal or plastic strainers and sieves.

Colanders are different from strainers. They are made to sit in the sink and have larger holes. This equipment is usually used to drain cooked pasta or vegetables.

Take care of your strainers, sieves, and colanders and they will last a long time. Be sure to completely dry the metal strainers and sieves so they don't rust or corrode.

········· GREEN ● LIGHT ·········

Funnels are another piece of equipment useful when making soups. It's very easy to package soup in solid freezer containers with a funnel. And some funnels come with an attached strainer, which lets you eliminate a step in processing the soup. Clean these utensils carefully and thoroughly.

Chinese Strainer

- These strainers are very inexpensive and versatile. They almost always have a bamboo handle.

- Besides being earth friendly and renewable, bamboo keeps the handle cool while you handle hot food.

- Chinese strainers are made of wire woven together; the holes are much larger than those of a sieve or even some colanders.

- The strainers come in sizes ranging from 3 inches up to 7 or 8 inches. It's a good idea to have different sizes for flexibility.

Colanders

- Colanders are usually made of plastic, steel, or melamine. They come in fixed or collapsible versions.

- They can also be used in food preparation; their size and shape are ideal for rinsing items like strawberries and mushrooms.

- Keep the colanders clean by rinsing and removing food right after use.

- Even if you put the colander in the dishwasher to clean, rinse it first so food doesn't get stuck in the holes.

BLENDERS & WHISKS

An immersion blender is a great tool for pureeing soups

There will be many times when you'll need to use a blender or a whisk when making soup. There's no better utensil to use when making a roux than a whisk. And a stand blender and immersion blender will help you to make purees perfectly and easily.

Whisks are made of wire, silicone, or nylon. There are balloon whisks or ball whisks; all will help blend sauces and ensure that your soups are smooth and velvety. If you use non-stick pans, buy a silicone or nylon whisk so it won't scratch the finish.

Whisks are easy to clean; just plop them into the dishwasher or rinse under hot running water. Buy more than one, in different sizes, and keep them on hand.

Immersion blenders are so easy to use and perfect for the ardent soup maker. Also called hand blenders, they are easily held in the hand. The bottom part contains a blade that will

Immersion Blender

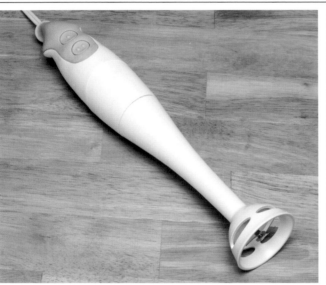

- Look for an immersion blender with a blade guard that will eliminate spattering as it works.

- Many immersion blenders have variable speeds, letting you do everything from whipping cream to chopping foods.

- Buy a blender with a removable blending attachment to make it easy to toss into the dishwasher.

- Be sure to hold the blender before you buy it. It should be lightweight but sturdy, with easily accessible controls.

Balloon Whisks

- Balloon whisks are an essential part of your kitchen utensil drawer.

- Nothing reaches into the corners of pans better. When you add flour to fat to make a roux, the flour must be evenly dispersed.

- Only a whisk will help you blend the roux so your soup is velvety smooth.

- Make sure that the balloon whisk is stable and not too large or heavy for your hand. You'll reach for it again and again.

puree soups in seconds. Clean in the dishwasher or by running the blade in soapy water.

And then there are stand blenders, staples of the kitchen. There are new-generation blenders with "dual wave action" that work much better than the old blenders. They puree soups and make pesto in seconds.

· · · · · · · · · · GREEN ● LIGHT · · · · · · · · · ·

When looking for an immersion blender, make sure you buy one that has a powerful motor and a long shaft. The best measure is at least twelve inches to keep your hands and arms away from the simmering soup. And because steam can burn, a blender that works in seconds will keep you safer.

Wire Ball Whisk

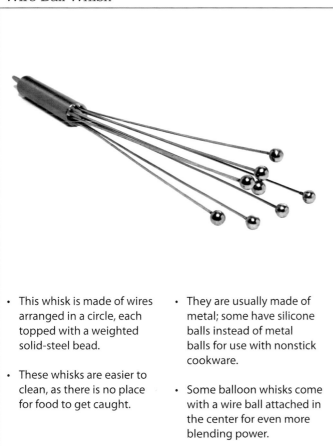

- This whisk is made of wires arranged in a circle, each topped with a weighted solid-steel bead.

- These whisks are easier to clean, as there is no place for food to get caught.

- They are usually made of metal; some have silicone balls instead of metal balls for use with nonstick cookware.

- Some balloon whisks come with a wire ball attached in the center for even more blending power.

Wave Action Blender

- A blender that sits on the countertop should be as large and powerful as you can afford.

- The glass jars range in size from 4 to 6 cups. A 6-cup blender will be more versatile and can puree soups faster.

- The newer blending systems force the food down into the blades so you don't have to shake or rock the blender.

- Blenders are easy to clean; just fill with soapy water, blend, then rinse.

THERMOSES
Thermoses keep hot food hot and cold food cold

Everyone remembers the classic thermoses of the 1970s, which featured your favorite cartoon hero or band. They can't compare to the thermoses of today, which are high tech and beautiful.

Thermoses use a vacuum to maintain temperature. Two walls create an airless vacuum that doesn't transfer heat and keeps the food at the same temperature for hours. The walls of the thermos are doubled, so heat can't transfer from the food to the outside. Old-fashioned thermoses used to be lined with glass. Some of the modern varieties still are, but for ultimate safety, look for a thermos lined with stainless steel. Some are made with plastic so they aren't breakable.

Don't give glass thermoses to children; they can break or crack. Plastic or steel is much safer, and these materials hold heat as well as glass does.

A good quality thermos can keep soup hot up to 10 hours

Individual Thermos

- Small thermoses range in size from 1 to 3 cups. These thermoses usually don't have a cup attached; you can eat directly from them.

- They will keep foods in addition to soups cold or hot for hours. Pack small sandwiches or hot chocolate into the thermos.

- These thermoses are just the right size for tucking into a lunchbox or backpack.

- Look for different colors to match your child's outerwear or pencil box.

Large Thermos

- Large thermoses can be used to carry foods for a picnic or a gathering on a boat or in a park.

- Never fill a thermos right to the top. Always leave a headspace of an inch or two.

- The lid extends into the thermos for a tight seal. If you fill it to the top, the soup will spill over when you tighten the lid.

- Always follow manufacturer's instructions for cleaning and storing thermoses.

or keep it cold up to 24 hours. Be sure to warm or cool the thermos before adding the soup.

Once you have the basics down, it's time to have fun. Thermoses come in every color of the rainbow and every shape and size. And you can still find thermoses emblazoned with cartoon characters or stars from TV shows, too.

· · · · · · · · · · · · · · RED●LIGHT · · · · · · · · · · · · · ·

Be careful when opening a thermos, particularly one that contains hot soup. Open the lid gingerly, and make sure it's pointed away from your face or other people. If you hear a very loud noise, retighten the lid and don't open the thermos; there could be a problem with the liner.

GADGETS

Heat Thermos

- For better heat retention and temperature control, always preheat a thermos before filling.

- You can simply rinse the thermos with hot water from the tap or add boiling water.

- Let the thermos stand with the hot or boiling water for a few minutes to let it warm up. Then dump out the water and add the soup.

- Screw the lid on as soon as possible to keep the heat in, so the soup stays hot.

Chill Thermos

- You can chill a thermos several different ways. If the thermos is lined with steel, you can add ice and let stand for a few minutes.

- Never add ice to a glass-lined thermos, because that temperature contrast can make the glass crack.

- You can put the thermos in the fridge for twenty to thirty minutes with the lid off to chill.

- You can also rinse the thermos with very cold water and immediately add the cold soup.

ROUX

A roux is a mixture of flour and fat used to thicken soup

Roux, the French word for "red," is a classic way to thicken soup, as well as the basis for recipes like gumbo. It's simply a combination of flour and fat, heated so the starch in the flour expands to absorb liquid. A roux stabilizes the soup too so it won't "break."

Roux comes in different colors: white, blond, brown, and dark brown. A white roux is made by cooking the flour for a short period of time; just until the mixture bubbles and

smells toasted. A blond roux develops more color, and brown and dark brown roux are used to make gumbo and other Cajun dishes.

A wire whisk is an essential tool for making a roux. It's almost impossible to make a smooth roux without it.

The proportion of roux is usually one part fat to one part flour. The fats can be bacon fat, butter, olive oil, peanut oil, or schmaltz. The flour used is almost always all-purpose white.

Ingredients

- ¼ cup butter
- ¼ cup flour

Basic Blonde Roux

- In medium saucepan, melt butter over medium heat. Add flour and stir with wire whisk.

- Cook over medium-low heat, stirring constantly with whisk, until mixture bubbles. Cook and stir for 15 minutes.

- Now you can add the roux to the soup, or add liquid to the roux to thicken. This amount will thicken 6 to 8 cups of liquid.

- Gradually add part of the soup's liquid to the roux, stirring until the liquid thickens, then stir into the soup.

You can make a quantity of roux, then refrigerate or freeze it. This is a great shortcut tip if you make lots of dark and rich stews and gumbos. The mixture may separate as it sits; just whisk it for a minute and it will recombine.

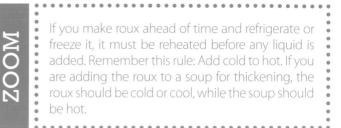

ZOOM

If you make roux ahead of time and refrigerate or freeze it, it must be reheated before any liquid is added. Remember this rule: Add cold to hot. If you are adding the roux to a soup for thickening, the roux should be cold or cool, while the soup should be hot.

Melt Butter

- Melt the butter until it starts to bubble; don't let the butter brown or burn.

- You can use clarified butter if you're making a quantity of roux. Melt the butter slowly; skim off the foam and pour off the clear liquid.

- This liquid is clarified butter. There will be solids in the bottom of the pan; just discard those.

- Clarified butter doesn't burn easily, so it's great for making roux.

Cook until Bubbly

- A white roux is cooked for 5 minutes, just to remove the raw taste of the flour.

- A blond roux is cooked for 10 to 15 minutes until the flour is slightly toasted. It will smell like popcorn.

- Brown roux is used in gumbos and chowders.

- It's cooked for 25 to 30 minutes, until it is the color of peanut butter.

- Dark brown roux is cooked for 40 to 50 minutes. The flour starts to lose its thickening power as the roux is used for flavor.

SLURRIES

A slurry is a mixture of cornstarch or flour and a liquid

A slurry is a good way to quickly thicken a soup at the last minute. It is made from a combination of broth or water and cornstarch, potato starch, arrowroot, or flour.

The thickening ingredients have to be mixed with a cool or cold liquid. You don't want to start cooking the flour or cornstarch when it's first mixed with the liquid; you just want to dissolve the thickening agent.

Make sure that the slurry is well stirred, preferably with a wire whisk, so that there are absolutely no lumps in the finished slurry.

The ratio of thickening agent to soup is about 1 tablespoon for every 2 cups soup. If you like a thicker soup, or are making a chowder, you can increase that to 1 tablespoon for every 1 cup liquid. But don't go beyond that proportion or the soup will be too thick.

After the slurry is added to the soup, it should heat for 10

Ingredients

· 2 tablespoons cornstarch

· 1/4 cup water or broth

Cornstarch Slurry

- In a small bowl combine cornstarch with cold water or broth, stirring with wire whisk until blended.

- Add all at once to the soup, stirring constantly with wire whisk to avoid lumps.

- You can also make a slurry from flour and other liquids.

Try soy sauce for Asian soups, or use chutney with cornstarch or flour for curried soups.

- The liquid has to be cool for the cornstarch to work properly. Only simmer soup after adding a slurry; don't boil.

to 20 minutes. You can simmer the mixture, but don't let it boil hard, or the thickening power will be reduced. A slurry is always added at the end of the soup's cooking time.

Potato starch is a good choice for kosher foods, while arrowroot can be used by people with wheat or corn allergies.

········· YELLOW ● LIGHT ·········
Always make the slurry just before you add it to the soup. A slurry that stands may start to thicken, and the flour or cornstarch will settle to the bottom and form a thick layer. You can stir the slurry to reincorporate the flour or cornstarch, but it's best to just make it right before it's needed.

Cornstarch Slurry, continued

- If you added cornstarch directly to the soup, it would be very difficult to make a lump-free soup.

- The water or broth dissolves the cornstarch so it combines easily with the liquid in the soup.

- If you are using a juice to make the slurry, add half more cornstarch, since the acids in the juice will reduce the thickening power.

- Cornstarch slurry is also used to thicken fruit pies and seal the edges of egg-rolls and pastries.

Flour Slurry

- Use double the amount of flour than cornstarch called for when making a flour slurry.

- Flour's thickening power is half that of cornstarch. This holds true when you make a slurry using citrus juices.

- The flour will taste raw unless it's well cooked. Let the soup simmer at least 10 minutes.

- Taste the soup. If you can taste flour, let it simmer 5 to 10 minutes longer until that taste disappears.

REDUCTION
Thicken a soup by reducing it to concentrate flavors

Reducing a soup makes the texture thicker and also concentrates the flavor. This is the easiest method for making a soup thicker, and doesn't add any more fat. It will increase the calories of the soup, though, just because there is less water.

Reduction does take a bit of time. Bring the soup to a fast simmer, but not a boil, and cook with the cover off for anywhere from 30 minutes to an hour or two. Stir the soup occasionally to make sure it isn't burning on the bottom.

Taste the soup. If it tastes rich and you like the texture, you're done! If not, keep simmering until the soup looks and tastes how you want it.

You can reduce soups on the stovetop, obviously, but also in the oven and in the slow cooker. In the oven, bake the soup with the lid off for 1 to 2 hours. In the slow cooker, remove the lid and turn the heat to high. Cook for 30 to 40 minutes, until the soup is reduced.

Water Evaporates

- The steam coming from the soup is the water evaporating, which is the definition of reduction.

- You shouldn't leave the soup alone longer than 15 minutes while it's reducing, or it may scorch or reduce too much.

- Stir the soup gently as it simmers and reduces. You don't want to break up the solids in the soup.

- To reduce the soup more slowly, partially cover the pan as it simmers on the stove.

Before Reduction

- There is a limit to reduction. If the solid ingredients in the soup simmer too long, they can become too soft.

- You can, if the broth tastes weak, remove the solids using a strainer or sieve, then reduce the broth.

- Put the solids in another pan. When the liquid has reduced to the state you want, pour it over the solids in the other pan.

- Hold off on seasoning a soup that you are going to reduce until after it is done.

You can use the power of reduction to improve a canned broth or stock, too. Just add some chopped vegetables and a bit of water to a canned soup and simmer until it's reduced and rich.

· · · · · · · · · · YELLOW ● LIGHT · · · · · · · · · ·

Watch out for seasoning when you reduce soup. The seasoning, as well as the flavors of the vegetables and meat, becomes more intense as it reduces. Hold back some of the salt and spices if you're going to reduce the soup and add them at the end when you correct the seasoning.

Simmer Soup

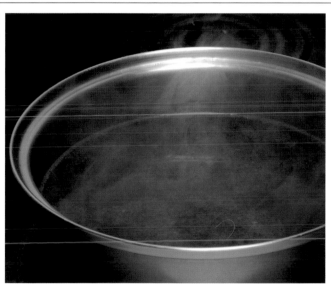

- Unless you're cooking a broth or stock that needs to reduce quickly, don't let the soup boil.

- You want it to gently simmer. Bubbles will rise to the surface and break just below the surface.

- Stir the soup occasionally to keep the solids moving in the liquid; you don't want them to stick to the bottom and burn.

- When the soup really starts to reduce, the chances of it burning increase, so watch it carefully.

Correct Seasonings

- If you've reduced the soup too much, just add more liquid: water or regular-strength broth or stock.

- To correct seasonings, taste the soup. If it needs more salt or other seasonings, add them a little bit at a time.

- If the soup tastes too salty or too intense with one flavor, add more water or regular-strength broth.

- At this point you can add fresh herbs to help punch up the flavor.

THICKENING/STORING

PUREES
Stirring purees into soups thickens and adds body

Purees are the purest method for thickening soups. The only way they affect the flavor is by intensifying it. You don't add any more calories or fat, and the soup retains excellent color and aroma. Choose an ingredient already in the soup to keep the flavor consistent.

Purees are just blended vegetables, peas, or beans that are added to soups to help thicken them. You can make a puree several different ways.

First, just drain a can of beans, peas, vegetables, or fruit and process in a food processor or blender or mash with a potato masher until mostly smooth. Stir this into the soup and simmer until thickened.

You can also remove cooked beans, peas, or vegetables from the almost-finished soup, puree them in a food processor or blender, then return the food to the soup. A few minutes of simmering are all it takes to thicken the soup.

Food Mill

- A food mill is an efficient, old-fashioned way to make smooth purees from vegetables or beans.

- The mill acts as a sieve as well as a masher, so it removes skins and seeds as it reduces the food to a puree.

- Most food mills have a handle that you turn so it processes the food in the bowl.

- They are made of metal or plastic and with proper care can last for years.

How Purees Thicken Soup

- Pureeing breaks open cells in the food.
- This exposes starch to the liquid.
- Starch absorbs some of the liquid.
- Pureeing frees fiber.
- Fiber traps some of the liquid.

Potatoes are often used to thicken soup. Just mash cooked potatoes and add to the soup, or you can grate a raw potato into the soup or use dried potato flakes.

Finally, breadcrumbs, while not technically purees, are a good way to thicken a soup, add fiber, and use up leftover bread. Just stir them in and simmer until dissolved.

· · · · · · · · · · · · GREEN ● LIGHT · · · · · · · · · · · ·

Purees are a great way to use leftover vegetables. Just puree them with a bit of lemon juice to retain their color and freeze in ¼-cup quantities. When you want to thicken a soup, just remove the puree from the freezer, thaw in the microwave, and stir into the soup.

Immersion Blender

- With a handheld immersion blender, you can puree part of the vegetables in the soup without making a mess.

- Just place the blender right on top of the food you want to puree and turn it on for a few seconds.

- Then remove the blender and stir the soup well so the puree incorporates evenly and smoothly.

- Rinse the blender immediately so the food doesn't stick to the blade.

Food Processor

- To use a food processor to make a puree, all you have to do is use a ladle or sieve to remove some of the vegetables.

- Process the food until it's smooth and well blended. Then stir it back into the soup.

- You may want to rinse the food processor bowl with some of the liquid in the soup or with water.

- This will remove all of the puree from the processor bowl so you don't waste anything.

THICKENING/STORING

COOL & FREEZE SOUP

To preserve your soup, learn how to quickly cool it

If you're just chilling a soup to serve the next day, or cooling it down to freeze for longer storage, faster is better.

As soon as the soup is done, or after you've finished serving it, transfer it to a shallow container and place it in the refrigerator. The shallow container helps the soup cool down more quickly, which preserves the flavor, texture, and color.

When the soup is cold, either cover the container it's in or transfer the soup to smaller containers, seal tightly, and re-

frigerate up to three days. Always be sure to cover the soup tightly. One of the dangers of improper packaging is freezer burn, which is dehydration of food in cold temperatures. Freezer burn doesn't affect the quality of the food, but it does affect the texture and flavor. Soups are more forgiving of freezer burn than other foods; if it happens, add more water and reheat slowly.

Always label containers holding your soup with the name

Cool Soup in Fridge

- Cool the soup uncovered so the steam can evaporate. Be sure your fridge is clean.

- If you cover the soup, the steam will condense on the lid and drip back into the soup.

- When the soup has stopped steaming, cover it tightly to avoid transferring flavors to or from the soup.

- When the soup is completely cold, you can transfer it to freezer containers to freeze for later use.

Ice Water Bath

- To cool soup very quickly, place it in an ice water bath. This is an excellent way to chill soups for freezing.

- This cooling method is a good choice if your refrigerator is very full.

- Fill a large container with cold water and add ice. Make sure the ice water doesn't lap over the edges of the soup pot.

- To cool the soup even faster, fill a clean bottle with ice water and use that to stir the soup.

of the soup, reheating instructions, any additions to the soup and garnishes, and the date it was made and frozen. You can freeze soups for up to 6 months. Place the soup in the coldest part of the freezer and check that your freezer is set to 0° Fahrenheit; use a freezer thermometer to be sure.

••••••••••••• RED ● LIGHT •••••••••••••

Don't let soup cool at room temperature. The refrigerator is designed to cool foods quickly. Always refrigerate the soup within 2 hours of its removal from the stove, microwave, slow cooker, or pressure cooker. That time shrinks to 1 hour when the ambient temperature is 80°F.

Hard-Sided Containers

- When you buy freezer containers to hold soup, be sure to read labels.

- Most freezer containers, whether bags or boxes, are made of hard plastic.

- There are disposable containers and containers you can use over and over again. Read the label to see which type you're buying.

Headspace

- When packaging soup for freezing in hard-sided containers, always leave a bit of headspace.

- This only has to be an inch or two of space left between the soup and the lid.

- The soup will expand as it freezes, and that inch of space at the top of the container will accommodate this expansion.

- If you fill the container right to the top, the top will pop off and the soup will develop freezer burn.

THICKENING/STORING

THAW SOUP

Safely thaw your soups to enjoy them months after they are made

You can thaw soup quickly or slowly; the time won't make a difference in the quality of the finished product.

To thaw a frozen soup slowly, place it in the refrigerator for 8 to 24 hours. Not all of the ingredients may be thawed, but they will reheat in the next step. Never thaw soup at room temperature. We need to avoid the danger zone of 40°F to 140°F, which is the range at which bacteria grow. Thawing the soup in the fridge will keep it below 40°F.

To thaw soup quickly, you can microwave it or just place it in a pan on the stovetop. When you microwave a soup to thaw it, you must cook it and serve it immediately. Don't thaw partially in the microwave and then refrigerate for eating later. The microwave creates hot spots that can bring some of the food into the danger zone.

Thawing and heating on the stovetop is the simplest. Just place the frozen block of soup in a saucepan. Add a little wa-

Microwave Soup

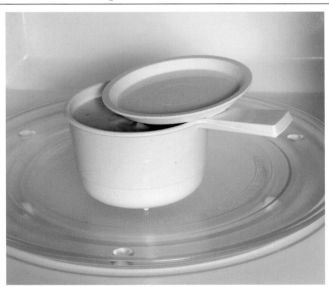

- Place the frozen block of soup in a microwave-safe container.

- Microwave the soup, uncovered, for 4 to 5 minutes on 30 percent power. Remove and see if you can break up the soup.

- Return to the microwave.

- Microwave on 50 percent power for 3 to 4 minutes longer; remove and stir.

- Continue microwaving for 2- to 3-minute intervals. When the soup is thawed, heat until bubbling in the microwave or heat on the stovetop.

Freezer Containers

- Be sure to read directions on the containers you use to freeze soup to see how they can be used.

- Some of these containers shouldn't be heated, so you must transfer the soup to another container before thawing and heating.

- If the container is microwave safe, use that method to thaw the soup.

- Most freezer bags can't be heated, so transfer the soup to a pot or microwave-safe bowl to thaw.

ter or whatever broth you used to make the soup. Heat on low, breaking up the soup as it warms. Then slowly bring the soup to a simmer; simmer until all the ingredients are hot and tender.

· · · · · · · · · · · YELLOW ● LIGHT · · · · · · · · · · ·

When freezing soup, the flavors will concentrate. If you care making soup specifically for freezing, it's a good idea to cut back slightly on the herbs and spices. You can add dried or fresh herbs and ground or freshly grated spices as you re-heat the soup.

Thaw in Fridge

- Never thaw soup on the countertop. Most soups contain meat or dairy products, which can spoil in the danger zone.

- Thawing the soup in the fridge takes longer, but it's safe and you don't have to watch it.

- Just place the soup, in its freezer container, in the refrigerator the night before you want to eat it.

- If the soup hasn't thawed completely, heat it on low until it thaws, then reheat until the soup simmers.

Thaw on Stovetop

- To thaw on the stovetop, just put the soup in a heavy saucepan.

- Run warm water over the outside of the container to easily remove the frozen block of soup. The soup should slip right out.

- Heat the soup over low heat, uncovered. Stir or break up the soup as it starts to thaw.

- Continue to heat the soup, stirring frequently, until it simmers. Taste for seasoning, correct if necessary, and serve.

CHICKEN BROTH

A rich chicken broth is essential to the best soups

Chicken broth is one of the easiest recipes to make, and its quality and flavor are essential to making the best soups.

All you really need for chicken broth is some chicken, filtered water, and a few vegetables. While the broth simmers, the flavor from the chicken and veggies permeates the water, creating a highly seasoned soup base.

Broth can be a soup in itself. Simply heated broth, perhaps sprinkled with a few fresh herbs, is one of the most elegant first course recipes. The best chicken broth is mandatory in several recipes in this book, including Egg Drop Soup and Chicken Noodle Soup. You can get away with canned or boxed soups for other recipes, but for the best flavor, make your own.

Yield: 8 cups

Ingredients

1 1/2 pounds cut-up boneless chicken breasts and thighs

1 onion, chopped

3 cloves garlic

2 carrots, cut into chunks

2 stalks celery, chopped

1/4 cup chopped celery leaves

1 teaspoon salt

1/4 teaspoon pepper

1 bay leaf

1/4 cup chopped parsley

3 lemon slices

10 cups water

Rich Chicken Broth

- Combine all ingredients in a large stockpot. Bring to a boil over medium heat.

- Cover and simmer on low for 2 to 3 hours or until broth tastes rich, occasionally skimming off foam on top.

- Strain broth through a fine sieve, pressing down on the solids to remove as much liquid as possible.

- Refrigerate broth overnight. In the morning remove fat and freeze broth in 1-cup containers up to 6 months.

The foam or scum that forms on broth or stock as it simmers is just protein from the meat and vegetables. It is safe to eat but can make the broth cloudy.

YELLOW ● LIGHT

Once the vegetables have simmered for a long time, they really can't be used for anything else. All of their flavor has been transferred to the broth. So discard the vegetables, or use them in your compost pile. Meats can be used again; cube them and freeze to add to other recipes.

Simmer Broth

- You can reserve the chicken meat from this recipe to use later, but meat simmered this long will usually be tough.

- The flavor of the meat has been transferred to the liquid; taste before you decide to reserve it or not.

- If you do want to reserve the meat, simmer the meat for 20 to 30 minutes, then remove it and reserve for another use.

- The broth will still be well flavored with the essence of the meat and vegetables.

Place in Freezer Containers

- The broth has to be chilled quickly before freezing. Place it in the refrigerator in a shallow pan.

- Or place the pan into a bowl filled with ice water. Stir the soup occasionally so it cools evenly.

- If you want to remove the fat from the broth, let it chill in the refrigerator overnight.

- The fat will solidify, and you can easily remove it. Then ladle the broth into freezer containers, seal, label, and freeze.

CHICKEN STOCK

Chicken stock, made with bones, adds depth of flavor to your soups

Chicken stock is made from the meat, skin, and bones of the bird. Stock is generally richer than broth, since the bones and skin add lots of flavor.

You can use leftover chicken bones for stock. Just freeze them after removing the meat used in other recipes. When you have enough, make stock.

Browning the bones with some of the vegetables adds lots of flavor to the stock and deepens the color. You don't have to brown the bones; just place all the ingredients in a large pot, add the water, and simmer.

If you want to make stock on the stovetop, just place the ingredients in a large pot. Simmer for 3 to 4 hours, skimming the surface occasionally, until the stock tastes rich.

Yield: 8 cups

Ingredients

2 pounds leftover chicken bones

2 carrots, cut into chunks

2 tablespoons olive oil

2 cups chopped leftover cooked chicken, if desired

1 onion

4 whole cloves

4 cloves garlic

1 parsnip, cubed

1 Bouquet Garni

8 cups water

1 teaspoon salt

Chicken Stock

- Place chicken bones in roasting pan; add carrots and drizzle with olive oil. Roast at 400°F for 30 minutes.

- Place bones, carrots, leftover meat, onion studded with cloves, garlic, parsnip, and Bouquet Garni in 4-quart slow cooker.

- Pour 1 cup water into roasting pan to loosen drippings; add with remaining water and salt to slow cooker.

- Cover and cook on low for 7 to 8 hours until stock is rich, occasionally skimming off foam. Strain, chill overnight, then freeze in 1-cup portions.

GREEN ● LIGHT

The size of the container you use to freeze the stock depends on the type of recipes you make most. If you use the stock for sauces, freeze in 1-cup portions. If you use it for soup, chowder, or bisques, freeze in 4-cup portions. Thaw in the refrigerator.

• • • • RECIPE VARIATION • • • •

Bouquet Garni: In cheesecloth or a tea ball, combine 3 stems parsley, 3 sprigs fresh thyme, 10 peppercorns, 1 bay leaf, and 1 sprig fresh rosemary. Tie with kitchen string. Use to flavor broths and soups; discard after use. Use the bouquet garni only once.

Roast Ingredients

- Roast the ingredients until the bones and vegetables start to turn brown.

- The color of the broth will depend on how deeply colored the roasted ingredients are.

- You can roast the ingredients until they are deep brown. This also adds caramelization flavor to the broth.

- To get all of the drippings and brown bits, rinse out the roasting pan with some of the water you'll use for the stock after you put the ingredients in the slow cooker.

Cook in Slow Cooker

- You can cook the stock on high for 3 to 4 hours if you'd like, instead of on low for a longer period of time.

- When you strain the stock, press down on the meat and vegetables to extract as much juice as possible.

- In the slow cooker use less water because there is no evaporation.

- If you want to make this recipe on the stovetop, use 10 cups water. Simmer the stock for 4 to 5 hours, skimming the surface occasionally.

BROTHS & STOCKS

BEEF BROTH

A rich beef broth is easily made and a delicious base for many soups

Beef broth is made from beef meat and lots of vegetables. Onions and garlic add depth of flavor and sweetness to the broth, while carrots and celery add floral notes.

Good broth is made from good quality ingredients. Beef stew meat is used because it is a cut that is full of flavor, but inexpensive.

Broth is made with meat. It's necessary to brown the meat before simmering the broth to add flavor and color to the fin-

ished product. When broth or stock simmers, foam or scum will form on the surface. Skim this off using a large flat spoon and discard.

Use any vegetables or herbs you'd like to flavor your broth, and enjoy the delicious soups you make from it.
Yield: 8 cups

Ingredients

1 pound beef stew meat

2 tablespoons olive oil

1 onion, chopped

3 cloves garlic, minced

3 carrots, cut into chunks

2 stalks celery, chopped

1 (14.5-ounce) can diced tomatoes, undrained

10 cups water

1/4 teaspoon pepper

1 bay leaf

1 1/2 teaspoons salt

1 teaspoon dried marjoram

Beef Broth

- Cut beef into cubes and brown in olive oil in stockpot; add onion and garlic and cook for 5 minutes.

- Add all remaining ingredients and bring to a boil. Reduce heat to low, partially cover pot, and simmer 3 hours, occasionally skimming off foam.

- Strain broth, pressing on solids to remove liquid. Cover and refrigerate overnight.

- In the morning remove fat layer. Strain broth again, if desired, and freeze in 1-cup portions.

······· GREEN ● LIGHT ············
You can make any amount of broth you like, as long as you have a soup or stockpot that's big enough. Keep the proportions roughly the same. Make sure all the ingredients are covered with water, and simmer until done. Don't double the salt or herbs; add them to taste.

· · · · · RECIPE VARIATION · · · ·

Clarified Broth: To clarify any broth or stock, prepare and strain the mixture. Return to a clean stockpot or saucepan. Add ¼ cup cold water and 1 egg white. Bring to a boil, then remove from heat. Let stand 5 minutes; strain the broth through cheesecloth. You can also use crushed eggshells; bring to a boil, let stand, and strain.

Brown Beef

- It takes about 5 to 6 minutes to thoroughly brown cubes of beef.

- You want the beef to turn a rich dark brown color. But don't burn the meat; that would add an acrid note to the entire batch of broth.

- You can brown the onions and garlic, too, or just use them to loosen the drippings from the bottom of the pot.

- For that matter, you could also brown the carrots. Remove the meat, then brown vegetables, stirring occasionally.

Simmer Stock

- For best flavor, simmer the stock, don't boil it. Simmering is defined as just below boiling.

- The bubbles will float gently to the surface and break softly. The food doesn't move much when it is simmering.

- You want the broth to cook slowly to extract all the flavor from the meat and vegetables.

- The broth is done when it tastes done. You may need to correct seasoning at the end, adding more salt, pepper, or herbs.

BROTHS & STOCKS

41

BEEF STOCK
Brown the bones to create a stock that will transform your soups

Beef stock is made from meaty bones, either leftover from another recipe or purchased from your butcher.

The bones add body and richness to the broth that you can't get with just meat. The bones add a bit of gelatin to the stock, making it slightly thicker than broth.

For the best beef stock, you really must brown the bones with some of the vegetables before simmering. Roast them in a hot oven until golden brown. Don't let the bones or vegetables burn, as this will ruin the stock. The stock is done when it tastes rich and beefy.

Use your favorite vegetables, herbs, and spices to make the beef stock your own. And enjoy the delicious soups you can make from this recipe.

Yield: 10 cups

Ingredients

4 pounds beef bones

1 onion, quartered

4 carrots, quartered

2 tomatoes, chopped

2 cloves garlic, minced

12 cups water

1 whole clove

1 teaspoon dried basil

2 teaspoons salt

$1/4$ teaspoon pepper

Beef Stock

- Preheat oven to 425°F. Place bones, onion, and carrots in large roasting pan; roast for 45 to 55 minutes.

- Remove ingredients from pan and place in large stockpot with tomatoes and garlic. Pour off fat.

- Pour water into pan; scrape up pan drippings. Pour into stockpot along with remaining ingredients.

- Bring to a boil, then partially cover, lower heat, and simmer 4 to 5 hours until done. Strain stock, cool, then remove fat and freeze.

• • • • RECIPE VARIATIONS • • • •

Caramelized Onion Beef Stock: Make as directed, except add 2 chopped onions. In the soup pot, heat 2 tablespoons butter. Brown the chopped onions in the butter over low heat, cooking for 20 to 30 minutes until very brown. Add all remaining ingredients; cook as directed.

Root Vegetable Beef Stock: Make recipe as directed, except add 1 cubed potato and 1 cubed peeled parsnip to the stockpot. Add 2 teaspoons dried thyme leaves; omit clove. Clarify the broth after straining by adding 1 egg white; boil, let stand, strain, and freeze.

Brown Bones

- By browning the bones, you are adding wonderful flavor and color to the stock.

- The meat on the bones starts to caramelize, which adds hundreds of flavor compounds to the recipe.

- The vegetables you can roast with the bones include carrots, onions, garlic, celery, mushrooms, and tomatoes.

- Make sure all the ingredients are covered with water in the stockpot before you start cooking. Use filtered water for best results.

Strain Stock

- There are several ways to strain stocks and broth. You can line a colander with cheesecloth and pour the stock through that into a bowl.

- Or you can use a fine mesh strainer and pour the stock through it into a bowl or another pot.

- Press down on the vegetables and meat when you strain the broth.

- This will help remove the last juices full of flavor from the meat and vegetables. Then chill the stock immediately.

SEAFOOD STOCK

Fish trimmings, shrimp shells, and vegetables make a rich and satisfying stock

Seafood or fish stock can be difficult to find in stores, even specialty or gourmet stores. If you make a lot of seafood soups, it's a good idea to make your own and keep it in the freezer.

Shrimp shells, fish bones, and crab shells all have enough flavor to make a rich seafood stock. The best vegetables in-clude onions, garlic, celery, and bell peppers: the same veg-etables used to make gumbos and jambalaya.

If you don't have shrimp shells, just simmer shrimp until they turn pink, shell, freeze the meat, then use the shells for stock. Do the same thing with fish steaks or whole fish.

Yield: 10 cups

Ingredients

½ pound leftover shrimp shells

1 pound leftover fish bones (no heads)

1 onion, chopped

2 cloves garlic, chopped

⅓ cup chopped parsley

1 teaspoon salt

⅛ teaspoon pepper

1 cup dry white wine

10 cups water

1 tablespoon lemon juice

Seafood Stock

- Combine all ingredients except lemon juice in large stockpot and bring to a simmer.

- Partially cover pot and sim-mer 1½ hours or until stock tastes rich.

- Strain stock, pressing on ingredients to remove as much liquid as possible. Stir in lemon juice.

- You can now use the stock, or freeze it in 1-cup por-tions up to 6 months.

Veggie Seafood Stock: Make recipe as directed, except add ½ pound crab shells, 2 carrots cut into chunks, 1 green bell pepper chopped, and 1 red bell pepper chopped to the mixture along with onions and garlic. Simmer soup for 2 to 2½ hours, then strain and freeze.

Fish Stock: Make recipe as directed, but use 2 pounds fish bones and omit the shrimp shells. Add 1 carrot cut into chunks, and omit the parsley. Simmer the stock for 3 to 4 hours until it tastes rich. Strain and freeze as directed.

Ingredients in Pot

Simmer Stock

- Make sure that the fish bones and shrimp shells are fresh or were frozen immediately after cooking.

- For a splurge, use lobster shells in place of or in addition to the shrimp shells.

- For more intense flavor, simmer the shells, bones, onions, and garlic in some butter before adding to the pot.

- Once the bones and shells have been used, they won't have any more flavor, so discard them.

- Taste the stock after it's been simmered and strained. You may want to "correct the seasoning," which means add more salt or pepper if the stock needs it.

- If you add too much salt and pepper, you'll need to add more water and simmer the stock again.

- Keep the stock at a simmer. That means you'll need to control the heat.

- The liquid should form bubbles that burst before they reach the surface.

BROTHS & STOCKS

VEGETABLE BROTH
Knowing the right vegetables to use in a broth makes it classic

Vegetable broth is delicious in everything from consommés to cold pea soup to gazpacho and bean soups. It's also the least expensive broth.

It's called broth because, technically, stock is made from bones, and broth is made without bones.

Root vegetables are most often used to make vegetable broth. Their rich flavor and deep colors help make the broth taste and look rich.

A pressure cooker is a good way to get more flavor out of all of those vegetables and herbs than just simmering, and it's faster, too.

You can save vegetable peelings from other recipes to make broth. Just make sure they're washed, and freeze them as soon as they are made.

Yield: 10 cups

Ingredients

2 onions, quartered

3 carrots, cut into chunks

1 red bell pepper, sliced

2 tablespoons olive oil

2 cloves garlic, minced

12 cups water

1 (14.5-ounce) can diced tomatoes, undrained

1 cup chopped parsnip

1 bay leaf

1 teaspoon dried thyme leaves

1 teaspoon salt

1/4 teaspoon white pepper

Caramelized Vegetable Broth

- Preheat oven to 425°F. In roasting pan, combine onions, carrots, red bell pepper, and olive oil; toss.

- Roast for 45 to 55 minutes until vegetables start to brown. Place in stockpot with garlic.

- Pour 2 cups water into roasting pan; scrape drippings and add to pot along with rest of water and remaining ingredients.

- Bring to a boil, then reduce heat to low, partially cover, and simmer 1 to 2 hours. Strain stock, then freeze or use immediately.

Pressure Cooker Vegetable Broth: Make recipe as directed, except cut vegetables into 1-inch pieces and place into pressure cooker. Cover with water and clamp the lid. Cook at full pressure for 20 minutes, then let the cooker cool on its own, release pressure, and strain broth.

Herbed Vegetable Broth: Make recipe as directed, except add 2 sprigs fresh thyme, 1 sprig fresh rosemary, and ½ cup chopped fresh parsley. Simmer broth for 45 to 55 minutes until the broth tastes rich. Strain, then freeze broth in 1-cup portions.

Prepare Vegetables

- Don't add potatoes when you're making a vegetable broth; they make the soup cloudy. That goes for sweet potatoes, too.

- You don't need to peel the vegetables when making broth. Just rinse them well under cold water.

- Onion skins add flavor and a beautiful color to stock; leave them on.

- You can use any of your favorite vegetables to personalize your vegetable broth.

Brown Vegetables

- You do have to stir the vegetables at least once during the roasting time to make sure they brown evenly.

- You can also brown the vegetables directly in the stockpot. Heat olive oil, then add the vegetables.

- Stir frequently over medium heat until the vegetables are evenly browned.

- Using this method ensures you don't have to deglaze the roasting pan; just scrape the bottom of the pot when you add the water.

CHICKEN NOODLE SOUP
This classic soup is inexpensive and hearty

Everyone's grandma had the best recipe for chicken noodle soup. There are many good reasons it's so popular: It's inexpensive, easy to make, and literally a cure-all for illness.

Research has shown that chicken soup really does make you feel better when you have a cold. The heat, the vitamins and minerals from the stock and vegetables, and the steam are proven remedies.

Homemade stock makes the best chicken noodle soup, but boxed stocks are a good compromise. Onions, garlic, and carrots are de rigueur, but you can add your favorites.

Egg noodles are the classic pasta, but you can use any size or type of pasta. Just cook according to the package directions until al dente.

Yield: Serves 6

Ingredients

4 boneless, skinless chicken breasts, cut into 1-inch cubes

2 tablespoons flour

1 teaspoon salt

1/8 teaspoon pepper

3 tablespoons butter

1 onion, chopped

2 carrots, sliced

1 zucchini, chopped

1 yellow summer squash, chopped

6 cups chicken broth, homemade or store-bought

1 teaspoon dried basil leaves

4 plum tomatoes, peeled and chopped

2 cups egg noodles

1/2 cup grated Romano cheese

1/4 cup chopped parsley

Chicken Vegetable Noodle Soup

- Toss chicken with flour, salt, and pepper. Brown in butter in large pot. Remove chicken as it cooks.

- Add onion and carrots to pot; cook and stir 6 minutes. Add zucchini, summer squash, chicken, broth, basil, and tomatoes.

- Simmer 10 to 12 minutes until vegetables are almost tender. Add noodles to soup; simmer 8 to 10 minutes, until noodles are al dente.

- Serve soup topped with Romano cheese and parsley.

Basic Chicken Noodle Soup: Make recipe as directed, except omit zucchini, squash, carrots, and plum tomatoes. Increase the egg noodles to 3½ cups; simmer just until al dente. Add 2 tablespoons lemon juice and serve topped with chopped parsley.

Grandma's Chicken Noodle Soup: Make recipe as directed, except use a whole frying chicken cut into pieces. Brown the chicken very well, about 10 to 12 minutes, before adding to soup. Simmer the soup for about 2 hours. Remove chicken; remove meat and return to soup. Add noodles and simmer until done.

Brown Chicken

Add Broth

- Browning the chicken is an important first step. It adds a depth of flavor to the soup, and it also thickens the soup.

- The flour used to coat the chicken will thicken the soup, and the drippings left in the pot add rich flavor.

- Let the chicken brown until it releases easily from the pot. If using chicken with skin on it, don't tear the skin or force it.

- You can use boneless, skinless chicken thighs. Simmer 40 to 50 minutes, then shred the chicken and finish the soup.

- To peel tomatoes, drop briefly into boiling water, then into ice water.

- The skins will slip off easily. Their texture can become unpleasant when simmered in liquid.

- When you're ready to serve the soup, taste it. You may want to correct the seasonings.

- Add a pinch more salt or pepper, or some more thyme. Add just a little at a time so you don't over-season the mixture.

CHICKEN & POULTRY

CHICKEN DUMPLING SOUP

Old-fashioned dumplings are perfect and fluffy when cooked correctly

Dumplings are just soft biscuits that are simmered in water or broth. The ultimate comfort food, they can be flavored any way you'd like.

For the best dumplings, follow a few rules. Make sure the liquid is simmering when you drop the dough into it. Cook the dumplings covered; do not peek until the minimum cooking time has passed.

The dumplings will double in size as they cook. They remain soft and tender because they are cooked in a wet environment.

Flavor your dumplings with everything from grated cheese to bits of vegetables and fresh or dried herbs. They are typically served in chicken soup but can be added to any soup.

Yield: Serves 6

Ingredients

4 bone-in, skin-on chicken breasts	8 cups water
1/4 cup flour	1 teaspoon dried thyme leaves
1 teaspoon salt	2 cups frozen baby peas
1/8 teaspoon pepper	1 1/2 cups flour
2 tablespoons butter	1/2 teaspoon salt
2 tablespoons olive oil	1/2 teaspoon baking soda
1 onion, chopped	1/4 cup butter, melted
3 cloves garlic, minced	9 tablespoons buttermilk
4 carrots, sliced	
2 stalks celery, sliced	
2 potatoes, peeled and chopped	

Grandma's Chicken Dumpling Soup

- Coat chicken with flour, 1/2 teaspoon salt, and pepper. Brown chicken in butter and olive oil in large soup pot.

- Cook chicken for 5 to 7 minutes, until you can move it. Turn over and add onion, garlic, carrots, celery, potatoes, water, and thyme.

- Simmer 30 to 40 minutes, until chicken is done. Remove chicken, discard skin and bones, and cube meat; return to soup with peas.

- In a bowl, combine remaining ingredients just until mixed. Drop onto simmering soup; cover and simmer 8 to 10 minutes.

Chicken Cheese Dumpling Soup: Make recipe as directed, except use chicken thighs instead of breasts. Simmer the soup for 50 to 60 minutes, until thighs are done; remove meat and shred. Add ½ cup shredded cheddar cheese to the dumpling dough; simmer as directed.

Easy Chicken Dumpling Soup: Make recipe as directed, except use boneless, skinless chicken breasts. Simmer the soup for 10 to 15 minutes. For dumplings, combine 1½ cups baking mix with the melted butter and buttermilk. Add 2 tablespoons chopped parsley and 1 tablespoon chopped fresh thyme leaves. Simmer dumplings as directed.

Chop Vegetables

- If the skin on the carrots is fine, you don't need to peel them. Just scrub with a kitchen brush and slice the carrots.

- Make sure the vegetables are about the same size so they cook in the same amount of time.

- You can brown the vegetables for more flavor. Just remove the chicken and cook the vegetables until browned.

- Then add the chicken and broth and continue with the recipe as directed.

Add Dumplings

- Stir the dumpling dough as little as possible. Dumplings are quick bread: more mixing just makes them tough.

- Add dried or fresh herbs to the dumplings, or use chicken broth or cream in place of the buttermilk.

- Don't make the dumplings too big; remember they double in size when cooked.

- Drop the dumplings from the side of a spoon. Use your finger or another spoon to push the dough off.

TURKEY BISQUE

Lots of beans are the perfect addition to this rich and creamy bisque

Bisques are usually very elegant soups, pureed and thickened with eggs and cream. But they don't have to be fancy. They can be made with beans and rice and even have chunks of vegetables and meat.

Turkey is a nice substitute for the traditional lobster in bisque. It's inexpensive and flavorful—good for everyday meals.

When adding the milk and egg yolk mixture to the soup,

be sure to stir constantly. You want the soup to be creamy and smooth. The soup has to be heated until it reaches the steaming point, but not the boiling point, or the soup may separate. Serve this soup with scones hot from the oven.

Yield: Serves 4–6

Ingredients

1 (2-pound) turkey tenderloin, cut into 1-inch cubes	4 cups chicken stock, homemade or store-bought
¼ cup flour	2 tablespoons tomato paste
1 teaspoon salt	1 (4-ounce) can diced green chiles, undrained
⅛ teaspoon pepper	
1 teaspoon dried oregano leaves	2 (15-ounce) cans red beans, drained and rinsed
2 tablespoons olive oil	
1 onion, chopped	2 tablespoons cornstarch
2 cloves garlic, minced	
2 green bell peppers, chopped	1 cup milk
	2 egg yolks
3 tomatoes, peeled and chopped	

Chunky Turkey Bean Bisque

- Cut turkey into 1-inch cubes and toss with flour, salt, pepper, and oregano. Brown in olive oil in large pot.

- Add onion and garlic; cook and stir 5 minutes. Add all remaining ingredients except cornstarch, milk, and egg yolks.

- Bring to a boil, then reduce heat to low, cover, and simmer 25 to 35 minutes or until turkey is tender.

- Mix cornstarch, milk, and egg yolks and stir into soup. Heat until steaming, stirring constantly. Top with chopped fresh oregano, if desired.

52

Classic Turkey Bisque: Make recipe as directed, except omit green bell peppers. When the turkey and vegetables are tender, puree the soup using an immersion blender. Then add the milk and egg yolk mixture; heat until steaming.

Onion Cheese Scones: Cook one chopped onion in ½ cup butter until caramelized. In a bowl, combine 1½ cups flour, ½ cup each whole wheat flour and Parmesan cheese, 1 teaspoon each baking powder and baking soda Add onions, butter, ⅓ cup buttermilk, and 1 egg. Shape into 8 biscuits; bake at 400°F 12 to 15 minutes.

Toss Turkey

- Mix the flour, salt, pepper, and oregano before you add the turkey.

- Toss using your fingertips or tongs until the turkey is evenly coated with the flour mixture. If there's any leftover flour mixture, add it to the pot with the turkey.

- Let the turkey cook until it easily releases from the pan; don't tear the meat.

- When adding the liquid, be sure to scrape the bottom of the pan to loosen the flavorful drippings.

Add Slurry

- The slurry helps thicken the soup and adds a velvety texture along with a rich taste.

- Be sure that the egg, milk, and cornstarch are thoroughly mixed and smooth before adding to the soup.

- You want the soup to reach 160°F to cook the egg, but don't let it boil.

- If the soup boils, the eggs may separate and scramble and you won't have a smooth bisque.

CHICKEN & POULTRY

MULLIGATAWNY SOUP

Mulligatawny, which means "pepper water," is a curried chicken soup

Mulligatawny soup is a combination of flavors and ingredients from India via England. When the English occupied India, they were introduced to the recipe. It may be that the soup was invented for the soup course traditionally served in English dinners, which had no place in Indian meals. British employees of the East India Company brought the recipe home to England with them.

The soup was originally made with lots of peppers, but now it's more commonly made with chicken, curry, onion, apples, and rice.

The Indian flavors in this soup are emphasized with the addition of curry powder, ginger, and coconut milk.

Enjoy this creamy and spicy soup with a green salad and some bread sticks.

Yield: Serves 6

Ingredients

- 4 boneless, skinless chicken breasts, cut into 1-inch cubes
- 3 tablespoons flour
- 1 teaspoon salt
- 1/8 teaspoon cayenne pepper
- 1 tablespoon curry powder
- 1/8 teaspoon ground cloves
- 1/4 teaspoon cinnamon
- 2 tablespoons butter
- 1 tablespoon olive oil
- 1 onion, chopped
- 1 tablespoon grated ginger root
- 2 stalks celery, sliced
- 2 carrots, sliced
- 6 cups chicken broth, homemade or store-bought
- 1 Granny Smith apple, peeled and chopped
- 1/2 cup uncooked rice, preferably basmati
- 1 tablespoon lemon juice
- 1/2 cup heavy cream
- 1/2 cup coconut milk

Mulligatawny Soup

- Toss chicken with flour, salt, pepper, curry, cloves, and cinnamon. Brown chicken in butter and olive oil in a pot.

- Remove chicken and set aside. Add onion and ginger to pot; cook and stir 5 minutes.

- Add celery, carrots, chicken, chicken broth, apple, and rice and bring to a simmer. Reduce heat to low and simmer 20 to 25 minutes.

- When rice is tender, add lemon juice, cream, and coconut milk and heat until soup is steaming.

Herbed Bread Sticks: In a bowl, combine ⅓ cup grated Parmesan cheese, 2 tablespoons fresh thyme leaves, 2 teaspoons minced fresh rosemary, and 2 tablespoons ground almonds. Unroll 1 refrigerated breadstick package. Dip bread sticks in cheese mixture to coat. Bake at 350°F 15 to 18 minutes.

Lighter Mulligatawny Soup: Make recipe as directed, except use 8 boneless, skinless chicken thighs instead of breasts. Add 2 green bell peppers chopped and omit the celery. Omit carrots and apple; add another onion and 2 cloves garlic. Simmer as directed and thicken as directed.

Cook Onion and Ginger Root

- To prepare ginger root, first cut off about a 1-inch portion from the larger root.

- Peel it using a swivel-bladed vegetable peeler. Grate on a grater, or use a chef's knife to chop it fine.

- You can cook the onion and ginger just until tender, or let it cook for a longer time to slightly brown the onion.

- Be sure to stir often while these vegetables are cooking so they cook evenly and don't burn.

Add Cream and Coconut Milk

- Coconut milk isn't the liquid found inside a raw coconut. That's called coconut water.

- Coconut milk is made from mixing grated coconut meat with water, then squeezing it through cheesecloth.

- There may be a thicker layer of milk at the top of the can; shake the can before opening to redistribute.

- Don't boil the soup after adding the cream, lemon juice, and coconut milk; just heat it until steaming.

CHICKEN & POULTRY

SPICY CHICKEN CHOWDER
The foods of Tex-Mex add classic spice and flavor to this chowder

Chowders are thicker soups, usually made with cheese and milk added at the end of the cooking time.

You can turn any soup into chowder by adding a slurry and some cheese at the end. True chowders are made from seafood, potatoes, vegetables, milk, and cheese.

The heat of this chowder, or any soup, is well within your control. Chili powder is a more mild addition, while ground chiles or chile paste is potent and should be used with cau-

tion. Cayenne pepper, fresh peppers like jalapeños and serrano peppers, and hot sauce are other ingredients that can increase the heat.

Serve this chowder with a simple fruit salad and some beer or wine for a cooling contrast.

Yield: Serves 6

Ingredients

2 pounds boneless, skinless chicken thighs

1 tablespoon chili powder

3 tablespoons flour

1 teaspoon ground cumin

1 teaspoon salt

$1/8$ teaspoon pepper

$1/8$ teaspoon cayenne pepper

2 tablespoons butter

2 tablespoons olive oil

1 onion, chopped

4 cloves garlic, minced

1 jalapeño pepper, minced

1 red bell pepper, chopped

1 poblano or green bell pepper, chopped

6 cups chicken stock, homemade or store-bought

1 (15-ounce) can chili beans in sauce, undrained

1 (14.5-ounce) can diced tomatoes, undrained

2 cups frozen corn, thawed

$1/2$ cup light cream

Spicy Chicken Chowder

- Cut chicken into cubes. Toss with chili powder, flour, cumin, salt, and peppers.

- Heat butter and olive oil in large pot. Add chicken; brown 4 to 5 minutes; remove. Add onion, garlic, and jalapeño; cook 5 minutes.

- Stir in remaining ingredients except corn and cream; bring to a simmer. Cover, reduce heat to low, and simmer 25 to 35 minutes.

- Uncover and stir in corn and cream; heat through. Serve with shredded cheddar cheese, chopped cilantro and tortilla chips.

Mild Chicken Chowder: Make recipe as directed, except omit cayenne and jalapeño peppers. Add another chopped green bell pepper along with the red bell and poblano peppers. Use boneless, skinless chicken breasts and reduce the cooking time to 15 to 20 minutes.

Curried Chicken Chowder: Make recipe as directed, except omit chili powder and cumin. Use 1 tablespoon curry powder and ⅛ teaspoon allspice to coat the chicken with the flour. And omit the jalapeño pepper. Add 2 stalks chopped celery with the red bell pepper. Stir in ½ cup chutney with the light cream.

Brown Chicken

- When the chicken is coated with flour and spices (before cooking), the flavor is seared into the meat.

- The direct heat also helps develop the flavor of the spices, bringing out their aromatic oils.

- You can substitute 2 pounds boneless, skinless chicken breasts for the thighs in this recipe; reduce cooking time to 15 to 20 minutes.

- The chicken is removed after browning so the vegetables have a chance to brown instead of steam.

Add Corn

- Frozen corn has much less sodium, a sweeter taste, and a firmer texture than canned.

- You could substitute fresh corn cut off the cob for the frozen corn.

- Just stand the cob in the hole of a Bundt pan. Cut down the sides of the cob with a sharp knife, sawing as you go.

- The kernels will fall into the Bundt pan and can be easily added to the soup.

CHICKEN & POULTRY

WATERZOOIE

This Belgian recipe is one of the best chicken soups on the planet

It can be difficult to track down the history of most soups. Waterzooie does not fall into that category. It came from Flanders, Belgium, and is served there today. A combination of white and dark meat chicken, leeks, carrots, celery, and wine are common to all variations of this elegant recipe.

Because this soup is thickened with just egg yolks and cream, it shouldn't be too thick. The defining characteristic of Waterzooie is the intense chicken flavor and velvety texture.

Serve Waterzooie in warmed soup plates, with a thin slice of lemon and some freshly chopped flat-leaf parsley sprinkled on top. A crisp green salad and some Toasted Garlic Cheese Bread are good options; or serve with boiled potatoes and brown bread.

Yield: Serves 6

Ingredients

2 tablespoons butter

1 tablespoon olive oil

1 onion, chopped

1 leek, chopped

3 cloves garlic, minced

2 boneless, skinless chicken breasts

4 boneless, skinless chicken thighs, cut into 1-inch cubes

1/2 teaspoon salt

1/8 teaspoon pepper

3 carrots, sliced

2 stalks celery, sliced

Bouquet Garni

6 cups chicken stock, homemade or store-bought

1 tablespoon lemon juice

1/2 cup dry white wine

3 egg yolks

1/2 cup heavy cream

Waterzooie

- In a pot, melt butter and olive oil. Add onion, leek, and garlic; cook 5 minutes.

- Sprinkle chicken with salt and pepper and add to pot. Add carrots, celery, Bouquet Garni, and stock; simmer 10 to 12 minutes until chicken is done.

- Remove chicken breast and slice. Return to pot with lemon juice and wine; simmer 5 minutes. Remove Garni.

- Whisk egg yolks and cream in small bowl; add ladle of stock to temper. Return to pot; heat 2 to 5 minutes.

Whole Hen Waterzooie: Make recipe as directed, except use a whole stewing hen instead of the chicken breasts and thighs. Brown chicken, then simmer in 8 cups chicken stock until tender, about 1 hour. Remove meat from chicken, strain broth, and proceed with the recipe.

ZOOM

The word *Waterzooie* or *Waterzooi* means "watery mess" in Dutch. It was originally made with fish, until the rivers in the country became too polluted to use the fish. The Belgian people then turned to chicken, and the classic version is made with a whole chicken.

Simmer Soup

- The chicken thighs are cubed, while the chicken breasts are left whole in this recipe.

- The meats cook at different times, so making the thighs smaller allows them to cook through before the chicken breast becomes tough.

- This soup doesn't take long to make; you just have to be sure the chicken doesn't overcook and the vegetables are tender.

- You don't need to add the wine, but it does add a wonderful flavor to the finished soup.

Temper Egg Yolk Mixture

- When you *temper* in cooking it means you regulate the temperature of an ingredient so it blends well with another.

- The egg yolks, in this instance, are tempered by blending in some of the hot liquid.

- When this is thoroughly mixed, the egg yolk mixture is whisked back into the soup.

- This step helps keep the eggs from curdling and ensures a smooth soup. Use a wire whisk for best results.

CHICKEN & POULTRY

BEEF BARLEY SOUP

This simple but delicious soup is the perfect end to a busy day

Barley is a delicious and healthy whole grain that is the perfect addition to soups. Its texture stays chewy and tender no matter how long the cooking time, and it adds a wonderful nutty and meaty flavor.

There are several types of barley available in the supermarket. Unprocessed barley is not eaten; the hull has to be removed so the grain will absorb liquid. This is called "hulled" or "pot" barley. Pearl barley has been polished to remove the bran layer. This makes it a little less nutritious than hulled barley.

Use either variety in this hearty soup. It's perfect for a cold winter night, served with some cornbread hot from the oven.

Yield: Serves 8

Ingredients

2 pounds beef chuck roast

1 teaspoon salt

1/8 teaspoon pepper

1 teaspoon dried marjoram

1 teaspoon dried basil

2 onions, chopped

3 cloves garlic, minced

3 carrots, sliced

1 (8-ounce) package cremini or baby bella mushrooms, sliced

1 cup barley

8 cups beef stock, homemade or store-bought

1 bay leaf

1 (14.5-ounce) can diced tomatoes, undrained

1/4 cup tomato paste

Beef Barley Soup

- Cut the beef into 2-inch pieces and sprinkle with salt, pepper, marjoram, and basil; set aside.

- In a 4- to 5-quart slow cooker, combine onions, garlic, carrots, mushrooms, and barley. Add beef and pour beef stock and bay leaf over all.

- Drain tomatoes, saving the juice; mix the juice with tomato paste; add all to slow cooker.

- Cover and cook on low for 8 to 10 hours until beef and vegetables are tender. Remove bay leaf and serve.

• • • • RECIPE VARIATIONS • • • •

Stovetop Beef Barley Soup: Make soup as directed, except sauté the coated beef in 2 tablespoons olive oil. Add onions and garlic; simmer 5 minutes. Add remaining ingredients and add to the pot. Simmer, covered, 45 to 55 minutes, until barley is tender and meat is cooked.

Caramelized Onion Beef Barley Soup: Make recipe as directed, except brown the coated beef in 2 tablespoons butter; remove to slow cooker. Add onions and garlic; cook and stir 12 to 17 minutes, until the onions turn brown. Combine all ingredients in slow cooker; cook as directed.

Prepare Vegetables

- Before slicing the mushrooms, wipe them with a damp cloth to remove any dirt.

- Trim off the end of the stem, which tends to dry out during storage. Then place the mushrooms, cap side down, on work surface.

- Slice the mushrooms into ⅓-inch slices. Keep the slices even so they cook evenly.

- The carrots should be peeled if the skin is tough; otherwise just scrub with a brush. Cut into ½- to 1-inch pieces; both will cook in the designated time.

Layer Ingredients in Slow Cooker

- The onions, garlic, and carrots have to be placed at the bottom of the slow cooker.

- These ingredients take longer to cook than meats, so they have to be placed nearer to the heat source.

- Make sure the barley is placed low enough in the slow cooker so it is completely covered with liquid.

- Don't lift the lid while the food is cooking. Spin the lid to remove condensation to check on the soup.

VEGETABLE BEEF SOUP
Ground beef adds great flavor and makes this soup inexpensive

Ground beef is an excellent way to get beef flavor and nutrition in a soup for very little cost. The beef has to be browned before you add the rest of the ingredients.

Ground beef is considered "lean" if it has 20 percent or less fat content by weight. That's still a lot of fat, and while that's good in a meatloaf, you don't want that much fat in your soup. So brown the beef and drain it well before continuing with the recipe.

You can use your favorite vegetables in this easy soup recipe. Add some cubed parsnips, potatoes, mushrooms, corn, or more peppers.

Serve with Toasted Garlic Cheese Bread and a fruit salad.
Yield: Serves 4

Ingredients

1 pound lean ground beef	1 teaspoon salt
1 onion, chopped	1/4 teaspoon pepper
3 cloves garlic, minced	1 teaspoon dried marjoram
2 green bell peppers, chopped	1 bay leaf
2 carrots, sliced	2 cups frozen green beans, thawed
2 stalks celery, sliced	1 cup frozen corn
4 cups beef broth, homemade or store-bought	
1 cup water	
4 red tomatoes, peeled, seeded, and chopped	
1/2 cup barbecue sauce	

Vegetable Beef Soup

- In large soup pot, brown ground beef with onion and garlic until beef is browned; drain.

- Add all remaining ingredients except green beans and corn. Bring to a simmer over medium heat.

- Reduce heat to low, cover, and simmer 15 to 20 minutes, until vegetables are tender.

- Add green beans and corn; bring to a simmer. Simmer 5 to 6 minutes, until tender; remove bay leaf and serve.

• • • • RECIPE VARIATION • • • •

Rich Vegetable Beef Soup: Make recipe as directed, except use 1½ pounds top sirloin, cubed, in place of the ground beef. Toss with 2 tablespoons flour, brown in 2 tablespoons butter, then proceed with recipe. Add 1 cup light cream mixed with 1 cup shredded cheese just before serving.

ZOOM

Ground beef comes in several varieties. Ground beef can't have more than 30 percent fat by weight. Hamburger can have beef fat added along with seasonings. Read labels carefully, and abide by expiration dates to the letter.

Brown Beef

- Place the ground beef in a pan and turn the pan to medium.

- Use a fork to break up the beef as it cooks. You'll need to keep breaking up the pieces of meat as they brown.

- When done, the beef will be evenly colored and fine in texture. The onions and garlic will absorb some of the fat.

- For a lower fat version, cook just the beef, drain it and rinse under hot water, and then return to pan.

Prepare Vegetables

- To prepare bell peppers, cut in half and remove the stem by twisting it off.

- Trim off the membranes and remove all the seeds. Place the bell pepper on the work surface, skin side down.

- Cut into strips, then cut those strips into cubes. Repeat with remaining bell peppers.

- Trim off the ends of the celery and carrots and cut into slices ½- to 1-inch thick.

ITALIAN WEDDING SOUP
Traditional Italian soup is hearty and delicious

No, this soup isn't served at Italian weddings. The *wedding* simply means the combination or "marriage" of meatballs and greens in the colorful soup.

The greens can be mustard greens, kale, spinach, or escarole, all of which can be difficult to clean. First remove any dried or wrinkled leaves, then separate them. Chop off the stems and immerse the leaves in a sink full of cold water. Swish them in the water and let the sand and grit fall to the bottom. Then drain and chop the greens.

Because the meatballs cook directly in the soup, you must use lean ground beef—at least 85 percent lean.

Use the best beef broth you can; it's very important to the quality of this soup.

Yield: Serves 6

Ingredients

2 tablespoons butter

1 tablespoon olive oil

2 onions, finely chopped

4 cloves garlic, minced

1/2 cup dried Italian flavored bread crumbs

1 egg

1/2 cup grated Parmesan cheese

1/3 cup minced parsley

1/2 teaspoon salt

1/8 teaspoon pepper

1 pound 90 percent lean ground beef

3 carrots, sliced

3 stalks celery, sliced

8 cups beef broth, homemade or store-bought

1 cup water or dry white wine

1/2 teaspoon salt

1 teaspoon dried oregano leaves

3/4 cup uncooked ditalini pasta

2 cups sliced fresh spinach

Italian Wedding Soup

- In large soup pot, melt butter with olive oil; cook onions and garlic until tender, about 6 minutes. Remove half of mixture to large bowl.

- Add bread crumbs, egg, cheese, parsley, salt, and pepper to onion mixture in bowl; add beef and mix.

- Form meat into 1-inch meatballs; set aside. Add remaining ingredients except pasta and spinach to soup; bring to a simmer.

- Drop in the meatballs. Simmer, uncovered, 45 minutes. Add pasta and spinach; simmer 15 to 20 minutes longer, until tender.

• • • • RECIPE VARIATIONS • • • •

Easy Italian Wedding Soup: Make recipe as directed, except substitute 1 pound frozen fully cooked meatballs for the homemade meatballs. Do not thaw the meatballs before adding to the soup. Make sure the meatballs are hot all the way through before finishing the soup.

Lighter Italian Wedding Soup: Make recipe as directed, except use chicken broth in place of beef broth. Add 2 green bell peppers, chopped. Omit ditalini pasta and add ½ cup orzo pasta; cook until tender. Use 2 cups shredded escarole in place of spinach.

Make Meatballs

- To make the best meatballs, combine all the other ingredients before adding the meat.

- Work the mixture with your hands, mixing it gently but firmly until all the ingredients are evenly combined.

- The secret to the best meatballs is to not overhandle the meat. Roll gently into balls and set aside.

- If you can't find very lean ground beef, bake the meatballs in a 350°F oven 10 minutes to remove some fat before adding to the soup.

Add Pasta and Spinach

- As the pasta cooks in the soup, it will absorb the flavor of the broth and other ingredients, making it more flavorful than pasta cooked in water.

- Cook the pasta according to package directions, but add a few minutes to the stated cooking time.

- The other ingredients in the liquid will slow down the pasta's absorbing water.

- You can use other types of small pasta: Shell pasta, orzo, or even tortellini will work in this recipe.

BEEF BORSCHT

For a cold winter night, this soup is warming and hearty

This isn't the kind of borscht you're used to: It's not pink and not served cold. Beef borscht is simply a hearty beef soup, usually made with a beef shank and beets added along with other vegetables.

The beef bone adds a lot to this soup. It really increases the beefy flavor and adds to the thickness of the soup.

The slow cooker is an ideal way to make this soup. The flavors blend together beautifully, and the meat will cook until it literally falls off the bone. This soup is really nutritious: It's very high in iron, vitamins, and other minerals. You can stir some sour cream mixed with cornstarch into the soup at the end, or top it with sour cream.

Yield: Serves 6-8

Ingredients

2 pounds bone-in beef shank

3 tablespoons flour

1 teaspoon salt

1/4 teaspoon pepper

2 tablespoons olive oil

3 beets, peeled and cubed

1 onion, chopped

4 cloves garlic, minced

3 carrots, sliced

6 cups beef broth, homemade or store-bought

3 red tomatoes, peeled, seeded, and chopped

1 (6-ounce) can tomato paste

1 tablespoon red wine vinegar

1 teaspoon dried dill seed

2 cups chopped red cabbage

2 tablespoons fresh chopped dill

Beef Borscht

- Dredge beef in mixture of flour, salt, and pepper. Brown in oil in a large saucepan. Remove to 5-quart slow cooker with beets.

- Add onions and garlic to pan; cook and stir 4 minutes. Add carrots and 1 cup broth; simmer 5 minutes.

- Pour into slow cooker with remaining ingredients except cabbage and dill. Cover; cook on low 8 to 9 hours.

- Remove beef; cut beef from bone; return to soup with cabbage; cook 30 minutes on high. Garnish with dill.

• • • • RECIPE VARIATIONS • • • •

Russian Borscht: Make recipe as directed, except use 1½ pounds sirloin tip cut into cubes in place of the beef shank. Increase the beets to 4; peel them and slice instead of cutting them into cubes. At the end of cooking time, add 2 tablespoons lemon juice and 1 tablespoon sugar.

Stovetop Borscht: Make recipe as directed, except substitute 2 pounds bottom round steak cut into cubes. Coat with flour as directed; brown in olive oil in a large pot. Add all remaining ingredients except cabbage and dill; simmer 1½ hours. Add cabbage and dill; simmer 20 to 30 minutes until tender.

Brown Beef

- It can be difficult to brown such a large chunk of meat. Use a large pan and take your time.

- Some heavy tongs will help you turn the meat. Be sure you don't move the meat until it releases easily from the pan.

- The onions and garlic are used to add some liquid and help remove the pan drippings.

- Those pan drippings, also called "fond" contain a lot of flavor, and it's important that they are incorporated into the soup.

Add Cabbage

- To prepare the cabbage, first rinse well and then cut in half.

- Remove the core by cutting in a V shape around the core; discard it.

- Place the cabbage cut side down on the work surface. Using a chef's knife, cut across the cabbage at ¼-inch intervals.

- Then cut across the slices until the cabbage falls into small pieces. You don't want big chunks of cabbage in the soup.

MINESTRONE

This hearty Italian soup can be garnished with croutons or cheese

Minestrone is a classic Italian soup that is thick with vegetables and beef. The word comes from the Italian word *minestra*, which means "soup."

This soup can be made in many different incarnations. It can be made without meat at all but thick with beans and vegetables. You can add pasta or rice to help thicken the soup and add character.

Minestrone can be a very inexpensive soup, which is why it is so popular in Italy and around the world. You can make it with just about any vegetable you have in your pantry, refrigerator, or freezer.

Use your favorite vegetables and beans to make this soup your own. Add mushrooms, zucchini, potatoes, or greens or use black, pinto, or navy beans.

Yield: Serves 6

KNACK SOUP CLASSICS

Ingredients

3 slices bacon

1 1/2 pounds beef bottom round, cubed

2 tablespoons flour

1 teaspoon salt

1/8 teaspoon pepper

1 onion, chopped

3 cloves garlic, minced

3 carrots, sliced

3 stalks celery, sliced

3 tomatoes, peeled, seeded, and chopped

1 green bell pepper, chopped

1 red bell pepper, chopped

1 yellow summer squash, chopped

6 cups beef broth, homemade or store-bought

1 (8-ounce) can tomato sauce

1 teaspoon fennel seeds

1 teaspoon dried oregano

2 (15-ounce) cans kidney beans, drained and rinsed

2 cups trimmed green beans

1 cup grated Parmesan cheese

Minestrone

- Cook bacon until crisp in soup pot; drain, crumble, and refrigerate. Toss beef with flour, salt, and pepper; brown in bacon fat.

- Add all remaining ingredients except for bacon, green beans, and cheese. Bring to a simmer, then reduce heat to low.

- Cover and simmer 30 to 40 minutes, until beef is done and vegetables are tender.

- Add bacon and green beans; simmer 5 to 6 minutes longer. Serve with cheese.

68

• • • • RECIPE VARIATIONS • • • •

Vegetarian Minestrone: Make soup as directed, except omit bacon and beef bottom round. Add another onion, 8 ounces sliced mushrooms, and 2 peeled and diced potatoes. Add another can of kidney beans. Simmer the soup 20 to 30 minutes.

Pasta Minestrone: Make recipe as directed, except substitute 3 ounces pancetta for the bacon. Add 1 chopped zucchini and 2 cups shredded cabbage. At the end of cooking time, stir in ½ cup orzo pasta; simmer 10 to 12 minutes, until pasta is al dente.

Brown Beef

- Bacon fat is an excellent flavor enhancer. When you brown meat in the fat, the bacon flavor will permeate the recipe.

- When browning beef, let it stand until it can be easily removed from the pan.

- Don't tear the meat or pull on it to release. You want good caramelization of the flour and beef, which takes time.

- It should take 7 or 8 minutes to thoroughly brown the meat; don't skimp on this step.

Simmer Soup

- It's important that the soup simmer with the cover off so the liquid evaporates and flavor concentrates.

- The soup should not boil vigorously. A simmer is characterized by bubbles rising to the surface.

- The bubbles should break just underneath the surface, barely disturbing the soup. Adjust the heat as necessary to maintain this.

- When you add the beans, the simmering will stop. Let the soup come back to a simmer and start timing.

ALBONDIGAS

This Mexican meatball soup is thick with vegetables

Albondigas is a rich soup from Mexico, made with lots of vegetables and tender meatballs. Classic ingredients used in Albondigas include onion, jalapeño peppers, corn, rice, and lots of tomatoes, along with cilantro and oregano.

A really good beef broth is essential to the success of this soup. Don't substitute beef bouillon cubes and water for a really good homemade or boxed broth.

Traditionally the meatballs aren't browned before they are added to the soup, so you must use a very lean ground beef. Handle the meatball mixture gently for the most tender meatballs.

Serve this rich and spicy soup with a mixed green salad, made with sliced apples and pears, and some warmed flour or corn tortillas.

Yield: Serves 8

Ingredients

1 tablespoon olive oil	1 tablespoon chili powder
1 onion, chopped	
2 jalapeños, minced	1 1/2 pounds 90 percent lean ground beef
3 carrots, sliced	
8 cups beef broth, homemade or store-bought	1 (16-ounce) jar green salsa
	1 (14.5-ounce) can diced tomatoes, undrained
1 egg, beaten	
1/4 cup buttermilk	1 1/2 cups frozen corn
1/3 cup cornmeal	1 teaspoon dried oregano
5 tablespoons dried bread crumbs	1/2 cup uncooked white rice
	1/3 cup chopped cilantro
1/2 teaspoon salt	
1/8 teaspoon cayenne pepper	

Albondigas

- In soup pot, heat olive oil over medium heat. Add onion and jalapeños; cook and stir 4 minutes.

- Add carrots and broth; bring to a simmer. Reduce heat and simmer while preparing meatballs.

- Combine egg, buttermilk, cornmeal, bread crumbs, salt, cayenne pepper, and chili powder; add beef and mix. Form into 3/4-inch meatballs. Drop gently into soup.

- Add remaining ingredients except cilantro and stir gently. Cover and simmer over low heat 1 1/2 hours; sprinkle with cilantro.

•••• RECIPE VARIATIONS ••••

Twenty-Minute Albondigas: Make recipe as directed, except substitute 1 pound frozen precooked Italian seasoned meatballs for the homemade meatballs. Do not thaw meatballs before adding to soup. Simmer 20 to 30 minutes, until meatballs are hot and tender.

Beef and Chorizo Albondigas: Make recipe as directed, except use 1 pound 80 percent lean ground beef. Add ½ pound ground chorizo sausage to the meat mixture. Make meatballs as directed, except bake them at 350°F 15 minutes. Drain and add to soup; simmer as directed.

Make Meatballs

- The cornmeal in these meatballs adds flavor and texture but doesn't offer much structural support.

- That's why you need to use the bread crumbs too. The egg also helps bind the meatball ingredients together.

- Combine all the other ingredients for the meatballs first, then add the meat. Season the meatballs any way you'd like.

- Handle the meatballs gently. You can make them ahead of time and refrigerate until you're ready to make the soup.

Add Meatballs to Soup

- Drop the meatballs gently into the soup. Add them one at a time so they don't stick together.

- All the meatballs need to be added within 2 to 5 minutes so they cook evenly and start to firm up at the same time.

- Don't stir the soup until the meatballs have begun to set, about 20 to 30 minutes.

- Make sure this soup doesn't boil. It should simmer very gently over low or very low heat.

TEX-MEX PORK CHOWDER

This spicy chowder, made with cubes of pork and poblano peppers, is easy and classic

A spicy chowder is just the thing for a cold winter day. These recipes are fun to make because you can add just about any Tex-Mex ingredient you'd like.

Roasted peppers, baby corn, pinto beans, and chopped tomatillos can all be used in this rich and creamy chowder.

You can use pork chops, pork loin, or pork shoulder in this recipe. Don't use pork tenderloin, because it's too low in fat. Trim off excess visible fat and cut the meat into even cubes.

Adjust the heat of the recipe by adding more or less chili powder and cayenne pepper, jalapeño peppers, and salsa. Serve with warmed corn tortillas and a fruit salad.

Yield: Serves 6

Ingredients

2 tablespoons butter

1 pound boneless pork chops, cubed

1 onion, chopped

3 cloves garlic, minced

2 jalapeño peppers, minced

1 poblano or green bell pepper, chopped

1 green bell pepper, chopped

2 tablespoons flour

2 (15-ounce) cans Great Northern beans, drained and rinsed

1 teaspoon salt

1/8 teaspoon cayenne pepper

1 tablespoon chili powder

1 teaspoon ground cumin

1 teaspoon dried oregano leaves

3 cups chicken broth, homemade or store-bought

1 cup light cream

2 tablespoons cornstarch

1/3 cup chopped cilantro

1 cup shredded Pepper Jack cheese

1/3 cup grated Cotija or Parmesan cheese

1/3 cup pine nuts

Tex-Mex Pork Chowder

- In pot, melt butter over medium heat. Brown pork cubes; remove. Add onion, garlic, and peppers; cook 5 minutes.

- Add pork and flour; cook 5 minutes. Add remaining ingredients except cream, cornstarch, cilantro, cheeses, and pine nuts.

- Bring soup to a simmer; reduce heat, cover, and simmer 20 to 30 minutes, until peppers are tender. Combine cornstarch and cream; add to soup and simmer 5 minutes.

- In a small bowl combine cilantro, cheeses, and pine nuts. Sprinkle onto chowder.

Tex-Mex Chicken Chowder: Make recipe as directed, except substitute 1 pound boneless, skinless chicken thighs for the pork chops. Add another onion and another jalapeño to the recipe along with 2 peeled, seeded, and chopped tomatoes. Simmer 25 to 35 minutes before adding cream and cheeses.

Slow Cooker Pork Chowder: Make recipe as directed, except combine all ingredients except cream, cornstarch, cilantro, cheeses, and pine nuts in a 4- to 5-quart slow cooker. Cover and cook on low 7 to 9 hours, until meat is tender. Add remaining ingredients; cover and cook on high 20 to 25 minutes until blended.

Add All Remaining Ingredients

- After the pork is browned, the onions, garlic, and jalapeño peppers help remove the pan drippings.

- Then the flour is added and cooked for a few minutes to remove the raw flour taste and to help the starch cells in the flour swell so they will thicken the liquid.

- You can substitute other beans for the Great Northern Beans or use black-eyed peas.

- The spices used are classic for Tex-Mex cooking, but you can substitute others. Use pure ground chiles or a blend, such as fajita or taco seasoning mix.

Blend Topping

- The topping adds wonderful color, texture, and flavor contrast to the hot and creamy soup.

- Mix it just before serving, because the pine nuts can absorb liquid from the cheese and cilantro and become soggy.

- You can also offer the toppings separately and let each diner select her own. Place each in a small pretty bowl on the table.

- Or offer other toppings, like sour cream, green salsa, or chopped avocado. A cold topping is especially nice on a hot soup.

BEAN & BACON SOUP

Cook this flavorful and filling soup on a cold winter day

If the only bean and bacon soup you've had has been out of a can, you're in for a treat. Real bean and bacon soup, made with dried beans and lots of vegetables, is a very flavorful and inexpensive soup that's simple to make.

Making this soup in two steps ensures that the beans become nice and tender. Beans will not soften properly if they are cooked with salty or acidic ingredients like bacon and tomatoes. So those ingredients are added after the beans are

tender. If you'd like a thicker soup, mash some of the beans using a potato masher or immersion blender before serving.

Serve with a fruit salad and some bakery dinner rolls with a pecan pie for dessert.

Yield: Serves 8

Ingredients

1 pound dried navy beans

1 pound bacon

2 onions, chopped

4 cloves garlic, minced

3 carrots, sliced

2 stalks celery, chopped

7 cups chicken broth, homemade or store-bought

1 potato, peeled and cubed

1 bay leaf

1/2 teaspoon salt

1/8 teaspoon pepper

4 tomatoes, peeled, seeded, and chopped

Bean and Bacon Soup

- Sort over beans and rinse. Place in large pot, cover with water, and let stand overnight.

- In the morning, drain beans. Cook bacon in soup pot until crisp; drain, crumble, and refrigerate. Drain off all but 2 tablespoons drippings.

- Cook onions, garlic, carrots, and celery in drippings 5 minutes. Add beans, broth, potato, and bay leaf; bring to a simmer.

- Cover and simmer 2 to 3 hours, until beans are tender. Add bacon, salt, pepper, and tomato; simmer 1 hour. Remove bay leaf.

There are quite a few varieties of bacon on the market. You can buy plain bacon, thick-cut bacon, smoked bacon, and bacon that has been coated with cracked pepper. Use your favorite type in this easy and inexpensive soup.

• • • • RECIPE VARIATION • • • •

Slow Cooker Bean and Bacon Soup: Make recipe as directed, except after soaking the beans, place them in a large saucepan and cover with water. Simmer 10 minutes, then drain and proceed with the recipe. Cook the soup in a 5-quart slow cooker 6 hours, then add salt, pepper, and tomatoes; cook 2 to 3 hours longer.

Sort Beans

- Dried beans are produce, so, like any vegetable or fruit, you must look them over and wash them before use.

- Sort to remove any shriveled beans, bits of dirt, stones, or twigs. Then rinse the beans well.

- There are a few ways to soften beans. The first is to soak them overnight in cold water.

- Or you can boil the beans 2 minutes, cover, and let stand at room temperature 2 hours; proceed with recipe.

Cook Vegetables in Drippings

- Cooking the vegetables in the bacon drippings allows the bacon flavor to permeate the soup.

- The bacon has to be refrigerated after it's cooked because the beans take so long to soften.

- Remember food safety rules: no perishable food out of refrigeration longer than 2 hours.

- The potato adds some thickness to the soup and helps absorb the bacon fat so the soup is smooth.

SPLIT PEA HAM SOUP
This rich soup simmers all day in your slow cooker

A ham bone is a wonderful thing. It looks raggedy and unappealing, but the flavor it adds to soup is incomparable. Paired with split peas in a classic soup, this inexpensive wonder will help warm you up no matter the weather.

Split peas are dried peas that cook more quickly than dried beans, as they are split by a machine. Because the liquid doesn't have to penetrate through the peas' skin, the peas soften easily, even in the presence of the salty ham.

You can find yellow and green split peas in the supermarket. It doesn't matter which one you choose; they are both delicious and nutritious.

Serve this hearty soup with a spinach salad made with pears and walnuts.

Yield: Serves 6

Ingredients

1 pound split peas

2 onions, chopped

3 cloves garlic, minced

1 meaty ham bone

3 carrots, sliced

2 stalks celery, sliced

2 potatoes, peeled and chopped

2 cups chicken broth, homemade or store-bought

6 cups water

1/8 teaspoon pepper

1 teaspoon dried basil

1 bay leaf

Split Pea Ham Soup

- Sort over peas and rinse. Drain and combine in 5- or 6-quart slow cooker with all remaining ingredients.

- Cover and cook on low 8 to 9 hours or on high 4 to 5 hours.

- When all vegetables and the peas are very tender, remove ham bone. Cut meat off bone; chop and return to slow cooker.

- At this point you can remove bay leaf and puree some of the peas for a thicker soup; otherwise, serve.

Stovetop Split Pea Soup: Make recipe as directed, except cook onions and garlic in 2 tablespoons olive oil in large pot. Add remaining ingredients and bring to a simmer. Cover and simmer soup 1½ to 2 hours, until peas are tender. Remove meat from bone, return to soup, and serve.

Curried Split Pea Soup: Make recipe as directed, except add 1 tablespoon curry powder, ¼ teaspoon ground cloves, and 1 teaspoon dried thyme to the soup. Add 1 chopped green bell pepper along with the vegetables.

Sort Peas

Cut Meat and Return to Soup

- You can't cook regular dried beans or peas with a salty food like a ham hock.

- Because split peas cook easily and don't need a long cooking time, the salty ham bone prevents softening just long enough for the soup to blend.

- Sort over the peas to remove any wrinkled ones and to make sure there are no small stones or dirt hidden among them.

- Then rinse the peas, drain them well, and proceed with the recipe.

- There isn't a lot of meat on a ham bone, but there's more than you think.

- You can usually get 1 to 1½ cups diced meat from the bone after it's cooked.

- The bone adds rich flavor to the soup and also helps to thicken it.

- Cut the meat from the bone after cooking and dice it, then return the meat to the soup. Discard the ham bone after it has been used in the recipe.

MEATBALL CHEESE CHOWDER

For a rich and flavorful chowder, this recipe is perfect

Meatballs made with pork have a slightly lighter texture than meatballs made with beef. They will be spicier if you make them from pork sausage, which is usually heavily seasoned.

Even when baked in the oven, as these meatballs are, they will brown and become slightly crisp on the outside. This caramelization process is very important to the development of the soup's flavor, so don't skip it. It also helps to remove some of the fat.

You can use any combination of cheeses you'd like in this simple chowder. Swiss and cheddar, or cheddar and Havarti, or Asiago and Muenster cheeses would all be delicious.

This soup is a great addition to a thermos tucked into a lunchbox.

Yield: Serves 6

Ingredients

2 tablespoons olive oil

1 onion, finely chopped

3 cloves garlic, minced

1 teaspoon dried tarragon

1/2 teaspoon salt

1/8 teaspoon pepper

1/2 cup buttery round cracker crumbs

1 egg, beaten

1 pound spicy pork sausage

4 slices bacon

1 onion, chopped

3 carrots, sliced

1 green bell pepper, chopped

2 Yukon Gold potatoes, peeled and chopped

4 cups beef stock, home-made or store-bought

1 cup light cream

2 tablespoons cornstarch

1 cup shredded provolone cheese

1/2 cup shredded Cheddar cheese

1/4 cup chopped parsley

Meatball Cheese Chowder

- In a pot cook finely chopped onion and garlic in oil 6 minutes.

- Remove to bowl; add tarragon, salt, pepper, crackers, egg, and sausage; mix. Form into 1-inch meatballs; bake at 350°F 15 minutes; drain.

- Cook bacon until crisp. Drain pot; add onion; cook 5 minutes. Add carrots, pepper, potatoes, and beef stock; simmer 20 minutes.

- Add meatballs; simmer 10 minutes. Add cream mixed with cornstarch and cheeses; heat, but do not boil. Sprinkle with parsley.

RECIPE VARIATION

Beef Meatball Chowder: Make recipe as directed, except use 1 teaspoon marjoram in place of the tarragon. Make meatballs, except use 1 pound 85 percent lean ground beef in place of the pork sausage. Bake meatballs as directed and continue with the recipe.

GREEN●LIGHT

You can bake meatballs or cook them on the stovetop. The baked meatballs will be slightly lower in fat, simply because the fat drips away as the meatballs cook. Use a broiler pan or a pan with a rack to hold the meatballs out of the fat.

Make Meatballs

- You can use sweet Italian sausage, hot sausage, or spicy pork sausage in these meatballs.

- If you can't find bulk sausage, just buy uncooked sausage in casings.

- Remove the meat from the casings by slicing the side. Push the meat out and discard the casings.

- You can make the meatballs ahead of time, but do not bake them until you're ready to make the soup.

Add Cream and Cheese

- The cream mixture will help thicken the soup and bind the fat so it doesn't float on the soup's surface.

- Make this mixture just before adding it to the soup, and mix well to be sure all the cornstarch is dissolved.

- You can add more cheese if you'd like, adding more of each kind or a third type.

- Don't shred the cheese ahead of time; you don't want it to dry out.

SENATE BEAN SOUP

Yes, this soup has been served in the U.S. Senate lunchroom since the early 1900s

Senate Bean Soup is a classic and inexpensive recipe that has been part of American history for a century.

The original recipe included mashed potatoes to help thicken the soup and stretch the ham. The soup currently served in the Senate cafeteria uses just dried beans, ham hocks, onion, butter, salt, and pepper.

There are many versions of this classic bean soup, which is sometimes called Capitol Hill Bean Soup. The basic soup can be dressed up with more vegetables, such as celery, carrots, and bell pepper. Mashing some of the beans and potatoes when they are cooked thickens the soup. Leave some of the beans whole. *Yield: Serves 8*

Ingredients

1 pound navy beans

1 russet potato, peeled and diced

1 pound ham shank

8 cups water

2 onions, chopped

3 cloves garlic, minced

2 tablespoons butter

1 bay leaf

Salt and pepper to taste

½ cup chopped parsley

Senate Bean Soup

- Sort beans and rinse. Place in large pot; add water to cover; soak overnight.

- Drain beans and combine in large pot with potato, ham shank, and water; bring to a simmer.

- In small pan, cook onions and garlic in butter until onions caramelize. Add to soup with bay leaf. Simmer 3 hours.

- When beans are tender, remove ham hock; cut off meat and add to soup. Mash some of the beans and potatoes. Remove bay leaf, heat, and season to taste. Sprinkle with parsley.

Slow Cooker Senate Bean Soup: Make recipe as directed, except combine all ingredients in a 4- to 5-quart slow cooker. Cover and cook on low 8 to 10 hours, until beans are tender. Remove ham shank, cut meat off bone, and return meat to soup; cook 30 minutes longer.

Vegetable Senate Bean Soup: Make recipe as directed, except add 3 carrots, sliced; 3 stalks celery, chopped; and 2 green bell peppers, chopped, along with another potato. Add 1 teaspoon dried basil and 1 teaspoon dried thyme to the soup. Simmer as directed.

Simmer Soup

Remove Meat from Bone

- If you don't want to take the time to soak the beans overnight, you can quick cook them.

- Cover the beans with water, then boil hard for 2 minutes. Cover the pan and remove from heat.

- Let the beans stand, covered, 2 to 3 hours so they start to soften, then proceed with the recipe.

- Simmer the soup, don't boil it, so the ingredients cook gently and don't overcook.

- The soup can be made with a ham bone or ham hocks instead of the shank if they are easier to find.

- The soup wouldn't be Senate Bean Soup without the ham, so use some form, even if it's just cubed ham.

- To remove the meat from the bone, hold it with a large fork as you cut the meat away.

- Discard the bone after it's simmered in the soup; it doesn't have enough flavor for another use.

CREAMY CORN & BACON SOUP

This mild soup is a classic served with muffins or toast

When you want a mild and simple soup that's appealing to any age, choose this one. A bit of bacon adds some salty, smoky flavor to this soup made with lots of cream, corn, and cheese.

This is one of the easiest soups, with ingredients everyone should have on hand. It's delicious served with simple sandwiches or a cold spinach or fruit salad.

You can substitute nonfat light cream, low-fat evaporated milk, or whole milk for the regular light cream if you'd like. This holds true for any soup recipe.

This is an excellent soup to put in a thermos for lunch. Heat the thermos first by rinsing it out with boiling water, then add the soup and seal the thermos immediately to keep the soup hot.

Yield: Serves 4

Ingredients

4 slices bacon

1 tablespoon butter

$^1/_2$ cup minced onion

$^1/_4$ cup chopped celery leaves

3 cups frozen corn

4 cups chicken broth, homemade or store-bought

$^1/_2$ teaspoon dried thyme

$^1/_2$ teaspoon salt

$^1/_8$ teaspoon pepper

1 cup light cream

2 tablespoons cornstarch

Creamy Corn and Bacon Soup

- Cook bacon in soup pot until crisp; remove, drain on paper towels, crumble; set aside.

- To drippings in skillet, add butter and onion; cook and stir until very tender, about 7 minutes. Add celery leaves.

- Add corn, chicken broth, thyme, salt, and pepper; simmer 12 to 15 minutes until corn is tender.

- You can puree some of the corn with an immersion blender at this point. Mix cream with cornstarch and add to soup; simmer 2 minutes. Add bacon and serve.

Popovers: Heat oven to 425°F. Grease 6 preheated popover cups with solid shortening, then spray with nonstick baking spray. Beat 2 eggs, 1 cup flour, 1 cup milk, and ½ teaspoon salt. Fill cups. Bake 20 minutes, then reduce heat to 350°F; bake 25 to 30 minutes longer, until firm.

Corn and Canadian Bacon Soup: Make recipe as directed, except substitute ½ cup diced Canadian bacon for the regular bacon. Add another tablespoon of butter to cook the onions. Add the bacon when you add the chicken broth and simmer it in the soup.

Cook Vegetables

- Cook the vegetables until very tender; the simmering time in this soup isn't enough to soften the vegetables.

- If you'd like even more flavor, let the onions caramelize. This brings out their sugars and adds a depth of flavor to the soup.

- Cook onions 10 to 15 minutes, until they turn brown. Stir frequently and be careful not to let them burn.

- You could add other vegetables to this soup; mushrooms or red bell pepper would be delicious.

Partially Puree Soup

- Use the immersion blender for just a few seconds to puree some of the corn kernels.

- This helps thicken the soup and intensifies the corn flavor. You can completely puree the soup if you'd like.

- This recipe doubles easily to serve more people. Just cook it in a larger pot.

- The soup also freezes well. Cool it in a large shallow container, then ladle into hard-sided freezer containers. Freeze up to 4 months.

PORK & HAM

CREOLE FISH SOUP
Lots of spices and tomatoes make this soup warming

Creole cooking was developed in the Gulf Coast, adapting classic French technique to the food found locally. Creoles were rich plantation owners, as opposed to the Cajuns or Acadians, poor people who used the food because it was available and free.

The food is spicy, with an emphasis on seafood, rice, and hot peppers. Both cuisines are famous for experimentation and adventurous recipes.

Cajun and Creole seasonings blends can be found in the spice aisle and ethnic foods aisle of your supermarket. They are usually a blend of peppers, onion and garlic powder, celery seed, and dried herbs.

Serve this spicy soup with some cold beer and scones warm from the oven for a nice contrast.
Yield: Serves 6

Ingredients

3 tablespoons olive oil

1 onion, chopped

4 cloves garlic, minced

3 carrots, sliced

2 cups sliced cremini mushrooms

2 teaspoons Cajun seasoning blend

1/4 teaspoon cayenne pepper

1 bay leaf

1 teaspoon dried thyme leaves

3 peeled, seeded, and diced tomatoes

5 cups seafood stock, homemade or store-bought

1 cup tomato juice

1/4 teaspoon hot pepper sauce

1 1/2 pounds red snapper fillets, cubed

1 cup sliced okra

2 tablespoons lemon juice

1/3 cup chopped parsley

Creole Fish Soup

- In large pot, heat olive oil over medium heat. Add onion, garlic, carrots, mushrooms, seasoning blend, and cayenne pepper.

- Cook and stir 6 to 7 minutes, until tender. Add bay leaf, thyme, tomatoes, stock, and tomato juice. Simmer 20 minutes, until soup is blended.

- Add hot pepper sauce, fish, okra, and lemon juice; simmer 6 to 8 minutes, until fish is done.

- Remove bay leaf, then sprinkle with parsley and serve immediately.

Cheddar Cream Scones: Preheat oven to 400°F. In bowl, combine 1½ cups flour with 1 tablespoon baking powder, 1 teaspoon soda, ½ teaspoon salt, and 1 teaspoon dried thyme. Add 1 cup heavy whipping cream, 2 tablespoons buttermilk, and 1 cup shredded cheddar. Form into 8 rounds; bake 18 to 20 minutes, until brown.

Cajun Fish Soup: Make recipe as directed, except add 2 minced jalapeño or serrano peppers along with the onions. Omit mushrooms; add 4 peeled, seeded, and chopped tomatoes. Add ½ pound raw small shrimp during the last 10 minutes of cooking time.

Sauté Vegetables

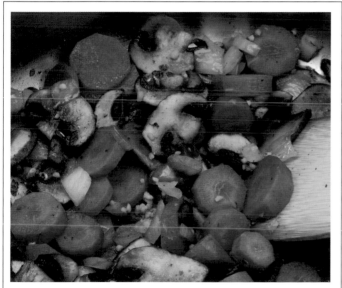

Add Fish

FISH

- For the "holy trinity" of Cajun cooking, use onions, green bell peppers, and celery in place of the carrots and mushrooms.

- The mushrooms will add a lot of liquid to the soup unless they are well browned.

- You can cook the mushrooms just until tender, or cook until browned; it's up to you.

- Other good vegetables to add to this soup include sliced yellow summer squash or zucchini, sliced celery, or a can of tomatoes.

- Typically, fish cooks in 5 minutes per inch of thickness over medium heat.

- Cook the fish until it flakes. When you insert a fork into the fish, it will come apart easily along natural lines.

- As soon as the fish is done, remove the soup from the heat. You don't want the fish to overcook.

- You could also add shrimp, scallops, mussels, clams, or oysters to this dish; cook until the shellfish open. Discard any shellfish that do not open.

SEAFOOD CORN CHOWDER

A hearty chowder uses several types of fish for flavor and interest

Seafood and corn are natural partners. You're used to seeing them together in clam chowder, but this recipe is a bit more complicated.

Using several different types of fish adds a complex flavor and lots of interest to this chowder or any other. All you have to do is time the addition of the seafood so it's all perfectly cooked at the same time.

Cubed fish fillets or steak are usually added first, as they take the longest to cook. Shrimp curls and turns pink in just a few minutes, while clams and oysters, especially if they are chopped or from a can, take even less time.

Enjoy this soup and enjoy making your own variations. *Yield: Serves 6–8*

KNACK SOUP CLASSICS

Ingredients

- 6 slices bacon
- 4 tablespoons butter
- 1 onion, chopped
- 2 shallots, minced
- 2 cloves garlic, minced
- 3 tablespoons flour
- 1/2 teaspoon salt
- 1/8 teaspoon pepper
- 6 cups seafood stock, homemade or store-bought
- 1 teaspoon dried thyme leaves
- 1/2 teaspoon dried basil leaves
- 3 russet potatoes, peeled and diced
- 2 cups frozen corn
- 2 tablespoons lemon juice
- 1 pound haddock fillet, cubed
- 1 pound salmon fillet, cubed
- 1 cup whole milk
- 1 cup light cream
- 1/4 cup minced parsley

Seafood Corn Chowder

- Cook bacon in soup pot until crisp; drain, crumble, and set aside. Drain pot; do not wipe.

- Add butter, onion, shallots, and garlic; cook 5 minutes. Add flour, salt, and pepper; cook 5 minutes. Add stock, thyme, basil, and potatoes.

- Simmer soup 15 to 20 minutes, until potatoes are tender.

- Add corn, lemon juice, and cubed fish. Simmer 6 to 8 minutes until fish flakes. Add milk and cream; heat through. Top with bacon and parsley and serve.

Cheese Flatbread: Preheat oven to 375°F. Open one (10-ounce) tube refrigerated bread stick dough. Remove bread sticks but don't unroll the dough. Combine ¼ cup grated Romano and ¼ cup finely crumbled feta with 1 teaspoon oregano. Press circles into cheese mixture. Bake, cheese side up, 12 to 17 minutes, until browned.

Shrimp Corn Chowder: Make recipe as directed, except add 2 pounds raw medium shrimp, shelled and deveined, in place of the salmon. Add shrimp 2 minutes after you add the corn. Cook the soup 2 to 4 minutes, just until the shrimp curl and turn pink, then serve immediately.

Cook Bacon

Add Milk and Cream

FISH

- When you cook bacon, it leaves behind fat and small bits of bacon, called drippings.

- These bits have a lot of flavor, and you don't want to lose them. So just remove most of the fat but do not wipe the pan.

- You can substitute thick-cut, pepper-coated, smoked bacon, or turkey bacon for the regular product.

- Don't use bacon prepared for the microwave oven in these recipes; it doesn't have enough fat.

- The flour that was used at the beginning of the recipe should thicken the soup to the proper texture.

- If you want a thicker soup, mix a tablespoon or two of cornstarch in with the milk and cream.

- Before you add the fish, you can partially puree or mash the potatoes to make the soup thicker.

- You could also add some shredded cheese, like cheddar or Swiss, coated in a bit of cornstarch; cook just until cheese melts.

MARINER'S SOUP
Fresh herbs add wonderful flavor to this simple soup

Fresh herbs are one of the best additions to fish and seafood. Their delicate flavor complements the mild and sweet flavor of the fish.

White wine is always a good addition to seafood soups. Make sure that you use a wine that you would drink, because the flavor will permeate the soup and concentrate as the liquid evaporates.

Other vegetables would be delicious in this soup: mushrooms, celery, and zucchini. And you can use other types of seafood, too, including shrimp, scallops, mussels, and clams. Cook the mussels and clams just until they open; shrimp and scallops until they turn opaque.

Serve your soup with a chopped fresh fruit salad served on baby spinach leaves.

Yield: Serves 6

Ingredients

1 tablespoon olive oil	1/2 cup orzo pasta
1 onion, chopped	1/2 pound orange roughy, cubed
2 cloves garlic, minced	
1/2 cup dry white wine	1/2 pound halibut fillet, cubed
1 tablespoon fresh thyme leaves	2 tablespoons minced fresh dill
1 teaspoon salt	1/4 cup chopped parsley
1/8 teaspoon pepper	
5 cups seafood stock or clam broth	
4 plum tomatoes, chopped	
1 cup chopped yellow summer squash	

Mariner's Soup

- Heat olive oil in large pot; add onion and garlic and cook 5 minutes.

- Add wine and cook until liquid evaporates. Add thyme, salt, pepper, broth, tomatoes, and squash.

- Simmer, covered, 10 minutes. Uncover and add pasta; simmer 4 minutes.

- Stir in fish and dill; simmer 5 to 6 minutes, until pasta and fish are cooked. Sprinkle with parsley and serve.

Garlic Toast: Broil one side of 8 ½-inch-thick slices French bread until golden. Turn over. In small bowl, combine ½ teaspoon salt with 2 minced garlic cloves; mash until a paste forms. Stir in 2 tablespoons each butter and olive oil and pinch lemon pepper. Spread on toasts and broil until crisp.

Shellfish Mariner's Soup: Make recipe as directed, except add 1 pound raw medium shrimp, 1 pound raw medium scallops, 1 pound mussels, and 1 pound clams instead of orange roughy and halibut. Add clams; cook 1 minute. Add mussels; cook 1 minute. Add scallops; cook 1 minute. Add shrimp; cook 2 to 5 minutes.

Cook Wine

- The wine may evaporate, but the flavor stays behind. The onions and garlic will absorb the wine's flavor.

- Never use cooking wine or cooking sherry in your recipes. They are low quality and can contain a lot of added salt.

- To prepare thyme, hold the sprig and gently run your fingers along the leaves backward; they will fall off.

- You can add the leaves whole, as they are so small, or chop them with a chef's knife.

Cook Pasta

- The pasta will be partially cooked by the time you add the fish. Make sure the fish is cut into 1-inch cubes so it cooks in the specified time.

- The soup will stop simmering when the fish is added because this lowers the temperature.

- Start timing when the soup comes back to a simmer.

- You could use other kinds of pasta: small shells, ditalini, or angel hair. The pasta should cook in 8 to 10 minutes.

FISH

SMOKED SALMON BISQUE

This rich and creamy soup has the most gorgeous color

Smoked salmon is a specialty product found in delicatessens and many large supermarkets. It adds wonderful color and flavor to this rich and creamy bisque.

There are two kinds of smoked salmon: hot smoked and cold smoked. Both types are usually cured first in a mixture of salt, sugar, and water. Hot smoked salmon is fully cooked and becomes firm and stiff. Cold smoked salmon, commonly known as lox, is not really cooked because it only reaches a

temperature of 80°F. You can use hot or cold smoked salmon in this recipe.

For an elegant touch, garnish this special soup with some salmon caviar and chopped fresh dill or parsley.
Yield: Serves 4

Ingredients

3 tablespoons butter

1 onion, chopped

1 tablespoon flour

1 teaspoon salt

1/8 teaspoon white pepper

1/2 teaspoon Old Bay Seasoning

2 tomatoes, peeled, seeded and chopped

1/4 cup dry sherry

2 cups seafood stock, homemade or store-bought

1 cup heavy cream

1 cup light cream

2 egg yolks

1/2 pound smoked salmon, cubed

Smoked Salmon Bisque

- In large pot melt butter; cook onion until tender. Add flour, salt, white pepper, and Old Bay; simmer 5 minutes.

- Add prepared tomatoes, sherry, and stock; simmer 10 minutes.

- Using an immersion blender or food processor, puree the soup.

- In small bowl beat together both creams and egg yolks; add to soup and whisk. Add smoked salmon; heat through, but do not boil. Serve immediately.

YELLOW LIGHT

When you use sherry, it's tempting to reach for the cooking sherry found in most supermarkets. But don't. Cooking sherry is a low-quality product, made with lots of salt added to mask the taste. Use a good dry sherry you'd serve to guests, especially in more expensive soups.

• • • • RECIPE VARIATION • • • •

Scallop Bisque: Make the seafood stock with shrimp shells. Make this recipe as directed, except increase Old Bay Seasoning to 1 teaspoon. Omit the smoked salmon. Simmer 1 pound medium raw scallops in the soup 3 to 4 minutes before adding the cream mixture; continue with recipe.

Blanch Tomatoes

- To peel the tomatoes, first cut a small X in the bottom. Bring a large pot of water to a boil.

- Drop the tomatoes into the boiling water and cook 8 to 10 seconds. Remove the tomatoes and plunge into ice water.

- After a few minutes, remove the tomatoes. The skin should peel off easily; discard the skin.

- Cut the tomatoes in half, gently squeeze out and discard the seeds, and chop the flesh.

Add Cream Mixture

- Beat the heavy cream, light cream, and egg yolks together thoroughly before adding to the soup.

- You can temper the cream mixture if you'd like; just add a spoonful of the hot broth to the cream mixture.

- Stir well with a wire whisk and add to the soup. Stir the soup with a whisk until blended.

- Then add the smoked salmon. Just heat the soup until it steams; don't boil.

SALMON MISO SOUP

In Japan, miso soup is enjoyed any time of the day

This classic Japanese soup is consumed for breakfast, lunch, and dinner. Miso is soybean paste that has been fermented with salt. It adds a rich and salty flavor to the soup.

The soup is made by adding miso to dashi, or Japanese soup stock, made from dried foods like bonito flakes, sardines, kelp, or shiitake mushrooms. Dashi granules are like chicken bouillon cubes, but they have more flavor and higher quality ingredients. You can make dashi from scratch, or just use the granules, which are a perfectly acceptable substitute.

Since this soup is so simple, you can add other vegetables if you'd like. Some sautéed mushrooms or caramelized onions would add a nice depth of flavor.

Yield: Serves 4

Ingredients

1 cup chicken broth, homemade or store-bought

3 cups water

2 teaspoons dashi granules

2 tablespoons miso paste

1 tablespoon grated gingerroot

1/2 cup chopped baby spinach

1 cup drained, diced tofu

2/3 cup cubed smoked salmon

Salmon Miso Soup

- In saucepan combine broth and water along with dashi granules; simmer 5 minutes.

- Add miso paste and ginger root; cook and stir until paste dissolves and soup is smooth.

- Add spinach, tofu, and salmon; cook and stir 4 to 5 minutes, until soup is hot and steaming.

- Serve immediately, garnished with sliced green onion or chopped chives.

Dashi: Place 4 dried shiitake mushrooms and 2 dried morel mushrooms in 5 cups water. Add 1 tablespoon bonito flakes; let soak 15 minutes. Bring to a full boil. Remove from heat, cover, let stand 20 minutes. Strain broth, which is the dashi.

Vegetable Miso Soup: Make soup as directed, except cook 1 chopped onion in 1 tablespoon sesame oil. Combine with 2 cups broth and water; add 1 cup shredded Chinese cabbage; simmer 5 minutes. Add dashi granules and miso paste. Add 1 cup sliced shiitake mushrooms with the tofu and salmon.

Add Miso Paste

Add Spinach, Salmon, and Tofu

FISH

- Miso paste addresses what food scientists call the "fifth taste": umami.

- In addition to salty, sweet, sour, and bitter, umami taste buds detect a meaty taste from glutamates, compounds found in meat and soybeans.

- *Umami* is a Japanese word that means "savory" or "delicious." Soybean paste is an essential ingredient in miso soup.

- Miso paste is inexpensive and a great way to add a rich and meaty flavor to any soup.

- Baby spinach is much more tender than regular spinach and has a delicate flavor.

- To chop it, first rinse in cold water to remove any sand or grit the spinach grows in. Then chop roughly with a chef's knife.

- You can use regular spinach if you'd like a stronger taste.

- Drain the tofu before you dice it and add to the soup so it doesn't add too much liquid to the recipe.

BOURRIDE
This French wonder is served with aioli, or garlic mayonnaise

Bourride is a classic Mediterranean soup from Provence made with fish, garlic, and onions. It's different from bouillabaisse and cioppino because it doesn't use saffron. Instead, you serve it with a garlicky mayonnaise mixture that's heavily seasoned and very pungent, called aioli. The fish commonly used to make this soup include monkfish, white fish, squid, and clams: hearty fish with a firm texture. Use your favorite fish or whatever looks good in the market.

The stew is served over Garlic Toast or Toasted Garlic Cheese Bread placed in the bottom of the bowl. This one-dish meal is delicious served with a baby spinach or mixed green salad with greens like frisee, mesclun, and arugula. Serve extra aioli on the side.

Yield: Serves 6

Ingredients

1 leek, chopped	1 pound orange roughy fillets, cubed
1/2 cup chopped fennel	
3 cloves garlic, minced	1/4 cup chopped parsley
1 teaspoon salt	1/4 cup chopped fennel fronds
1/8 teaspoon pepper	
2 tablespoons olive oil	2 teaspoons grated orange zest
1 tablespoon fresh tarragon leaves	6 pieces Garlic Toast
1/2 cup dry white wine	1/2 cup Aioli
5 cups seafood stock, homemade or store-bought	
1/3 cup orange juice	
1 pound perch fillets, cubed	

Bourride

- In large pot sauté leek, fennel, garlic, salt, and pepper in olive oil 5 minutes.

- Add tarragon and wine; cook and stir until liquid evaporates. Add stock and orange juice; simmer 5 minutes.

- Add cubed fish; simmer 6 to 8 minutes, until fish is done. Combine parsley, fennel fronds, and zest. Place Garlic Toast in bowls.

- Spoon into bowls and top with parsley mixture and aioli.

• • • • RECIPE VARIATIONS • • • •

Aioli: In small saucepan gently cook 4 whole garlic cloves in 2 tablespoons olive oil. In food processor combine ½ cup mayonnaise, ½ teaspoon paprika, 2 tablespoons lemon juice, and the garlic mixture; puree until smooth. Store refrigerated.

Shellfish Bourride: Make recipe as directed, except add 1 pound each raw medium shrimp, scrubbed mussels, and cleaned clams. Add at the very end of cooking time, starting with clams, then adding mussels after 1 minute, and shrimp after 2 minutes; cook 3 to 4 minutes, until done.

Sauté Leek and Fennel

- Leek and fennel need a little bit of special preparation. Both are bulbs grown in sandy soil, so there can be lots of sand in the bulbs.

- Cut the bulbs into ½-inch strips crosswise and immerse in a bowl full of cold water.

- Swish the fennel and leek around so the grit and sand fall to the bottom of the bowl.

- Then remove, shake off excess water, and chop or cube as desired.

Prepare Fish

- If you choose fish fillets from a reliable fishmonger, there shouldn't be any bones in them.

- If you aren't sure, feel the fish with your fingers. If you feel any bones, pull them out gently with tweezers.

- Cube the fish all the same size so they cook evenly.

- Simmer the soup just until the fish is done; it should gently flake when tested with a fork.

MANHATTAN CLAM CHOWDER

This soup calls for tomatoes, which is part of a raging controversy

There really is a raging controversy over what constitutes real clam chowder. Manhattan clam chowder is made with tomatoes, while New England clam chowder is not.

Historians think that tomatoes were added in the 1800s when an influx of Italian immigrants moved into the fishing communities along the East Coast.

If the only clam chowder you've had has been out of a can, you're in for a treat. Even using canned clams, freshly made clam chowder is light-years better than canned.

The other ingredients always used in clam chowder, whether Manhattan or New England, are onions, potatoes, and clam juice. Clam juice is bottled; it's just not made at home. Buy the best you can afford.

Yield: Serves 6

KNACK SOUP CLASSICS

Ingredients

- 6 slices bacon
- 2 tablespoons butter
- 2 onions, chopped
- 3 carrots, sliced
- 3 stalks celery, sliced
- 4 potatoes, peeled and cubed
- 4 tomatoes, chopped
- 1 cup Clamato juice
- 1 teaspoon dried thyme leaves
- 1 teaspoon dried oregano leaves
- 1 teaspoon dried basil leaves
- 1 teaspoon salt
- 1/8 teaspoon pepper
- 3 (6.5-ounce) cans minced clams
- 4 cups bottled clam juice
- 1 tablespoon Worcestershire sauce
- 1/4 cup chopped parsley

Manhattan Clam Chowder

- In large soup pot cook bacon until crisp; drain, crumble, and set aside. Drain all but 1 tablespoon drippings.

- Add butter to drippings; cook onion and carrots 5 to 6 minutes. Add celery, potatoes, tomatoes, Clamato juice, thyme, oregano, basil, salt, and pepper.

- Drain clams; add juice to pot; reserve clams. Add clam juice and Worcestershire sauce; simmer 15 to 20 minutes.

- Add clams and bacon; heat through. Serve topped with parsley.

Cheese Crackers: Beat ½ cup butter with 1 cup each shredded cheddar and shredded Havarti cheese; mix well. Stir in 1 cup flour, ½ cup whole wheat flour, ½ teaspoon salt, and 2 tablespoons minced green onions. Form into long roll 2 inches wide; cut off ¼-inch pieces. Bake at 350°F 14 minutes.

Slow Cooker Manhattan Clam Chowder: Make recipe as directed, except refrigerate bacon. Combine all ingredients except Worcestershire and parsley in a 4- to 5-quart slow cooker. Cover and cook on low 7 to 8 hours, or on high 3½ to 4 hours, until potatoes are tender. Add bacon, Worcestershire, and parsley.

Cook Onions and Carrots

- When you cook the bacon, use a fairly low heat. Don't move the bacon until it releases easily from the pan.

- The bacon drippings have a lot of flavor, so cooking the onion and garlic in them adds flavor to the soup.

- Carrots and onions should be cooked until they are crisp-tender. They will finish cooking in the soup.

- The vegetables add their flavor to the soup and absorb the other flavors as they cook.

Add Clams and Bacon

- You can find both whole and minced clams in the grocery store.

- Most chowders call for minced clams, but you can use whole if you'd like. Or use a combination for more texture.

- The bacon is added toward the end of cooking time so it stays crisp and adds texture to the soup.

- Use smoked bacon, turkey bacon, or peppered bacon for a slightly different flavor.

SHELLFISH

NEW ENGLAND CLAM CHOWDER

This chowder, without tomatoes, is the other side of the controversy

Most clam chowders that you find in a can or even a restaurant aren't very heavy on the clams. Making your own means you can add as many clams as you'd like. Throw in another can or two, or use part diced and part whole clams.

Some people like their clam chowder so thick that a soupspoon can stand up in it. If that's your idea of bliss, add more flour to the sautéed onions and garlic. You can also mash a few of the potatoes to thicken the soup.

Clam chowder is a meal in itself. All you really need is a simple salad and some crackers, either oyster crackers or homemade. For dessert, some brownies would be perfect.
Yield: Serves 6–8

Ingredients

5 slices bacon

2 tablespoons butter

2 onions, chopped

3 cloves garlic, minced

2 tablespoons flour

1 teaspoon salt

1/8 teaspoon pepper

4 (6.5-ounce) cans chopped clams

4 cups bottled clam juice

5 potatoes, peeled and diced

1 cup heavy cream

1/4 cup chopped parsley

New England Clam Chowder

- In large pot cook bacon until crisp. Drain, crumble, and set aside. Drain all but 1 tablespoon drippings from pan.

- Add butter; cook onions and garlic 6 minutes. Add flour, salt, and pepper; cook 5 minutes.

- Drain clams, reserving the juice; set aside. Add juice to pot along with 4 cups bottled clam juice and potatoes. Simmer 25 minutes.

- Add clams, cream, and bacon to soup; simmer 5 to 6 minutes, until hot. Sprinkle with parsley and serve.

Richest New England Clam Chowder: Make recipe as directed, except don't use the clam juice. Increase bacon slices to 8, and add 2 carrots, diced. Add 3 cups light cream to the onion mixture in place of the clam juice. If you can, use freshly shucked clams, cut in half. Add 12 scrubbed Little Neck clams with the bacon.

Fresh Clam Chowder: Make recipe as directed, except omit the canned minced clams. Buy 3 pounds clams in the shell. Scrub them and then steam them in boiling water and wine 4 to 5 minutes. Remove the clams, saving any liquor from them, and dice. Use in recipe, adding at the last minute.

Cook Flour in Onion Mixture

- You're making a roux with the fat and flour. Make sure the flour cooks at least 5 minutes before adding the liquid.

- Use a wire whisk to stir the roux so there won't be any lumps in the chowder.

- If you don't care about the purity of the soup, add some more vegetables.

- Cook some mushrooms with the onions, or add a seeded and chopped green or red bell pepper or two.

Add Clams and Bacon

- Simmer the soup until the potatoes are tender when pierced with a fork.

- You can mash part of the potatoes before adding the clams, cream, and bacon for a thicker soup.

- Either stir the bacon into the chowder or serve it sprinkled on top for more of a color and texture contrast.

- You can use other herbs instead of or in addition to the parsley, like cilantro, fresh thyme, or minced basil.

SHELLFISH

SHRIMP BISQUE
This classic bisque is elegant and flavorful

Shrimp bisque is one of the most elegant and richest soups in any culture. The seafood stock is very important in this recipe. Get the best you can find. Sometimes a fishmonger has the stock; just ask.

You can improve any seafood stock by simmering it a few minutes with reserved shrimp shells. Whenever you have shrimp, just freeze the shells. Add them to the stock and simmer 5 to 10 minutes, then strain.

The vegetables are pureed before you add the cream and shrimp, making a velvety soup.

If you're feeling rich, add more shrimp to this excellent recipe, or garnish with some large cooked shrimp. Serve with a baby spinach salad made with strawberries.

Yield: Serves 6

Ingredients

3 tablespoons butter

1 1/2 pounds medium raw shrimp, peeled

2 tablespoons olive oil

1 onion, chopped

1 leek, chopped

3 cloves garlic, minced

1/4 cup tomato paste

3 tablespoons flour

1 teaspoon salt

1/8 teaspoon pepper

1 teaspoon paprika

1 teaspoon Old Bay Seasoning

4 cups seafood stock, homemade or store-bought

1 1/2 cups heavy cream

1 teaspoon Worcestershire sauce

2 tablespoons sherry

Shrimp Bisque

- In large soup pot melt butter. Add shrimp; cook and stir until shrimp turn pink; remove and refrigerate.

- Add olive oil to pot; cook onion, leek, and garlic until tender, about 7 to 8 minutes. Add tomato paste; cook 2 minutes.

- Add flour, salt, pepper, paprika, and Old Bay; simmer 5 minutes. Add seafood stock; simmer 25 minutes.

- Puree mixture in food processor. Return to pot; add cream, Worcestershire sauce, sherry, and shrimp; heat through.

ZOOM

For the best bisque, if you aren't making your own seafood stock, add some concentrated shrimp base to the canned or boxed stock. It can be found in the seafood aisle of the supermarket; you may have to ask for it. Add a spoonful to the soup when you add the stock.

• • • • RECIPE VARIATION • • • •

Oyster Bisque: Make recipe as directed, except add ¼ teaspoon saffron threads to the seafood stock. Use half seafood stock and half clam juice. Buy 1 pound freshly shucked oysters; chop them coarsely. Add to the soup with the cream, Worcestershire sauce, and sherry; heat 3 to 4 minutes.

Cook Shrimp in Butter

- To peel shrimp, cut along the back and pull off the shell and legs.

- If there's a dark vein running down the back of the shrimp, rinse it out or remove with a sharp knife.

- Do not overcook the shrimp or they will become rubbery and unpleasant in texture.

- Shrimp cook very quickly, so don't leave the stove while they are in the pan. Shrimp are done the second they curl and turn pink.

Puree Soup

- You can puree the soup in a food processor or with an immersion blender.

- For the most elegant soup, puree the mixture until very smooth. You can leave some texture if you'd like.

- You can make this recipe ahead of time. Puree it, then refrigerate. Refrigerate the shrimp and cream, too.

- Reheat gently over low heat until the soup almost comes to a simmer. Add the cream and shrimp; heat through.

SHELLFISH

OYSTER SOUP
You need fresh oysters for the best oyster soup

Oyster soup or stew used to be a classic, traditionally served on Christmas Eve. In the nineteenth century, canned oysters and cream were usually available in the middle of winter, so they were combined to make an elegant soup.

Use canned oysters, smoked oysters, or fresh oysters in this simple soup. For a pure version, omit the vegetables and use oysters, herbs, seafood stock, and heavy cream. The soup can be mild, or you can add some Tabasco sauce or cayenne pepper.

This soup has to be served with oyster crackers, those little round salty bits of crunch. And serve with a fresh spinach salad, made with shredded carrots and some cubed red and yellow tomatoes.

Yield: Serves 6

KNACK SOUP CLASSICS

Ingredients

2 pounds fresh oysters, shucked

1 onion, chopped

1/2 cup chopped celery

1/2 cup chopped mushrooms

2 cloves garlic, minced

3 tablespoons butter

1 teaspoon salt

1/8 teaspoon cayenne pepper

4 cups chicken or seafood stock, homemade or store-bought

1 bay leaf

1 teaspoon dried thyme

1/2 teaspoon dried marjoram

1 cup heavy cream

Oyster Soup

- Make sure that you reserve the liquor when oysters are shucked.

- In large pot cook onion, celery, mushrooms, and garlic in butter 5 minutes; sprinkle with salt and cayenne pepper.

- Add stock and reserved oyster liquor with bay leaf, thyme, and marjoram. Simmer 15 minutes.

- Add oysters and cream; heat until edges of oysters curl; do not boil. Remove bay leaf and serve immediately.

Old Fashioned Oyster Soup: For a classic soup, combine 2 cups milk and 2 cups heavy cream in a saucepan; bring to a simmer. Shuck 1½ pounds fresh oysters, reserving the oyster liquor. Mix 2 tablespoons butter with 2 tablespoons flour and some salt and pepper. Add to soup with oyster liquor and simmer. Add oysters; heat.

Bacon Oyster Soup: Make recipe as directed, except reduce butter to 2 tablespoons. Cook 6 slices bacon until crisp, then drain and crumble. Drain off all but 1 table-spoon drippings. Add butter and proceed with the recipe. Sprinkle the finished soup with the crisp bacon.

Shuck Oysters

- Shucking oysters is a skill that can take years to perfect. You need a large heavy-duty glove and a shucking knife.

- Scrub oysters first. Then hold each one in your glove and work the knife between the shells, near the hinge.

- Twist the knife so the oyster opens. Remove the shell and scrape the meat off.

- Of course you can buy shucked oysters or ask the fishmonger to do it for you. Make sure she saves the oyster liquor.

Add Stock

- The oyster liquor is the liquid that comes out of the oysters when they are shucked.

- Work over a bowl to catch all of that liquid. If you buy shucked oysters, they will be packed in the liquor.

- You can use any type of stock or broth you'd like: seafood, clam, chicken, or vegetable.

- Sprinkle the finished soup with a mixture of chopped flat leaf parsley and fresh herbs used in the recipe.

SHELLFISH

SHRIMP MUSHROOM SOUP
This clear and healthy soup is packed with flavor

Shrimp and mushrooms are natural partners. Supermarkets now carry many varieties of fresh and dried mushrooms. Where once we could only get button mushrooms and, rarely, portobello, now shiitake, cremini, oyster, and dried wild mushrooms like porcini mushrooms and morels are common.

This soup is an excellent first course or starter because it's mildly flavored and won't fill you up. It's a good starter for a meal of Chinese or Japanese food, like a stir-fry or steamed fish.

Serve this elegant soup in flat china soup plates with large soupspoons. You can garnish it with some thinly sliced lemons and chopped green onions in addition to the parsley. *Yield: Serves 6*

Ingredients

1/4 cup butter

1 onion, chopped

1 (8-ounce) package button mushrooms, sliced

1 (8-ounce) package cremini mushrooms, sliced

3 stalks celery, chopped

1 teaspoon salt

1/8 teaspoon pepper

1/2 cup dry white wine

4 peeled, seeded, and diced tomatoes

6 cups seafood stock, homemade or store-bought

1 teaspoon dried basil leaves

2 pounds raw medium shrimp, shelled

1 tablespoon lemon juice

1/3 cup chopped parsley

Shrimp Mushroom Soup

- In large pot melt butter over medium heat. Add onion and mushrooms; cook and stir 6 to 7 minutes.

- Add celery, salt, pepper, and wine; simmer until liquid almost evaporates.

- Add tomatoes, stock, and basil; simmer 10 to 15 minutes, until vegetables are tender.

- Add shrimp and lemon juice; simmer 3 to 4 minutes, until shrimp turn pink. Sprinkle with parsley and serve.

GREEN LIGHT

To reconstitute dried mushrooms, place in a medium bowl and pour boiling water over. Let stand 10 to 15 minutes until the mushrooms soften. Then cut off the mushroom stems, which are usually too tough to eat, and chop or slice the mushrooms. Strain the liquid and add to the soup.

RECIPE VARIATION

Thai Hot and Sour Shrimp Soup: Make recipe as directed, except add 2 tablespoons grated ginger root and 2 minced jalapeño peppers with the onion. Mix 1 teaspoon chile paste with ½ cup stock and add that to the soup. Simmer soup as directed; add ½ cup coconut milk with the shrimp.

Cook Mushroom Mixture

- Cook the onion and mushrooms until the mushrooms turn dark and much of the liquid evaporates.
- Mushrooms have a very high water content. To get the best flavor, you must get rid of that water.
- The concentrated flavor will permeate the soup without diluting it.
- You can add other vegetables to the soup if you'd like. Garlic, carrots, zucchini, or sliced yellow summer squash would all be delicious.

Add Shrimp

- You can prepare the shrimp ahead of time, but not more than 24 hours ahead.
- Store the shrimp, tightly covered, in the coldest part of the refrigerator.
- You can also make the soup ahead of time, up to adding the shrimp and lemon juice.
- Gently reheat over low heat until the soup just barely comes to a simmer. Then add the shrimp and continue with the recipe.

CIOPPINO

This classic Italian dish is gorgeous and delicious

Cioppino is a rich and satisfying fish stew from Italy. Long made from the catch of the day, it can include any combination of fish and shellfish. Serve it with Toasted Garlic Cheese Bread to help soak up the rich broth.

Part of the fun of cioppino is using shellfish like mussels and clams. They are added to the fish whole and cooked just until they open. Cioppino clatters into the bowl when you serve the dish.

The name probably comes from the Italian word *ciuppin*, meaning "chopped." Whether this refers to chopped seafood or chopped vegetables is unknown.

The best cioppino is made with saffron, the world's most expensive legal spice. You can substitute turmeric for almost the same color.

Yield: Serves 6–8

KNACK SOUP CLASSICS

Ingredients

3 tablespoons butter

2 onions, chopped

5 cloves garlic, minced

1 leek, chopped

1 bay leaf

4 peeled, seeded, and diced tomatoes

3 tablespoons tomato paste

8 cups seafood stock, homemade or store-bought

1/4 teaspoon saffron threads or 1 teaspoon turmeric

1/4 cup hot water

1 cup dry white wine

1 bay leaf

1 teaspoon dried basil

1 pound clams, scrubbed

1 pound medium raw shrimp

1 pound mussels, scrubbed

1 1/2 pounds red snapper fillets, cubed

1/2 cup chopped parsley

Cioppino

- In large pot melt butter. Add onions, garlic, and leek; cook and stir 6 to 7 minutes, until almost tender.

- Add bay leaf, tomatoes, tomato paste, and stock. In small bowl combine saffron or turmeric and hot water; let stand 5 minutes and then add to soup.

- Add wine, bay leaf, and basil. Simmer 25 to 35 minutes until soup is blended. Add clams; simmer 5 minutes.

- Add shrimp and mussels; simmer 5 minutes. Add snapper fillets; simmer 4 to 5 minutes longer. Remove bay leaf, top with parsley; serve.

ZOOM

You need to follow special rules when cooking with clams, oysters, and mussels. If these shellfish are open before cooking, discard them. Tap the shells; they may close then. And if they do not open after cooking, discard them. In both cases the shellfish aren't safe to eat.

• • • • RECIPE VARIATION • • • •

Toasted Garlic Cheese Bread: Broil one side of 8½-inch-thick slices French bread until golden. Turn over. In small bowl combine ½ teaspoon salt with 2 minced garlic cloves; mash until a paste forms. Stir in 2 tablespoons each butter and olive oil and ½ cup Parmesan cheese. Spread on toasts and broil until crisp.

Prepare Seafood

Add Saffron

- Most mussels are now farm raised. Because they don't have to attach themselves to rocks, they often don't have beards.

- The beards are those thin threads that protrude from the shell. If they are present, just pull them off and discard.

- Rinse all of the shellfish well before use. Discard any with cracked or broken shells.

- Some recipes call for soaking shellfish in water with salt or cornmeal to get rid of sand; that really isn't necessary.

- Saffron is very expensive, so handle it carefully and don't lose a single thread.

- When dissolved in water and heated, not only does it turn the soup a gorgeous yellow color, it adds an indescribable flavor.

- Turmeric is an inexpensive alternative to saffron. It will add the necessary color to the broth, but it won't add much flavor.

- If you are using turmeric, add another clove or two of garlic for more flavor.

VEGETABLE WILD RICE SOUP
Thick with vegetables and rice, this soup is fun to make

Vegetable soups are inexpensive, healthy, and simple to make. You can use any combination of your favorite vegetables in this recipe. Just be sure to cook the vegetables in stages so they all come out tender and delicious.

For instance, add tender vegetables like zucchini and summer squash toward the end of the cooking time so they retain some character and texture.

You can use any kind of rice in this easy soup; just follow the cooking instructions on the rice package to see how long it must be simmered in the soup. White rice cooks in about 20 minutes, while brown rice can take up to 40 minutes. Basmati or jasmine rice add nice flavor; cook according to package directions.

Yield: Serves 6

Ingredients

4 slices bacon

2 tablespoons olive oil

1 onion, chopped

2 cloves garlic, minced

1 (8-ounce) package mushrooms, sliced

1 cup wild rice

2 carrots, sliced

6 cups chicken stock, homemade or store-bought

1 teaspoon dried thyme leaves

$1/2$ teaspoon dried marjoram leaves

1 zucchini, sliced

1 tablespoon lemon juice

$1/2$ cup shredded Parmesan cheese

Vegetable Wild Rice Soup

- Cook bacon until crisp in large soup pot. Remove, crumble, and refrigerate. Drain pot but don't wipe.

- Add olive oil; cook onion, garlic, and mushrooms 6 to 7 minutes. Add wild rice, carrots, stock, thyme, and marjoram.

- Simmer 25 minutes until rice is almost tender. Add zucchini; simmer 8 minutes. Add bacon and lemon juice; simmer 5 minutes.

- Serve soup topped with shredded cheese and fresh herbs, if desired.

• • • • RECIPE VARIATIONS • • • •

Brown Rice Vegetable Soup: Make recipe as directed, except use 1 cup long-grain brown rice in place of the wild rice. Omit zucchini; add 2 stalks celery, chopped, along with the carrots. Simmer the soup 30 minutes, then add bacon and lemon juice; simmer 5 to 10 minutes, until rice and vegetables are tender.

Greek Vegetable Rice Soup: Make soup as directed, except omit bacon. Use 1 cup long-grain brown rice in place of the wild rice. Omit zucchini; add 2 stalks celery, sliced. Omit thyme and marjoram; add 1 teaspoon dried oregano. Add 1 teaspoon lemon zest and ½ cup olives with the lemon juice; top with feta cheese.

Cook and Crumble Bacon

- To cook bacon, place it in a cold large, shallow pan in a single layer.

- Place the pan over medium heat. Let the bacon cook until it releases easily from the pan.

- Keep turning the bacon until it's brown. You'll know the bacon is done when the hissing and spitting almost stop.

- Drain the bacon on paper towels, then crumble using your fingers to break it apart.

Simmer Soup

- Simmer soups uncovered unless the recipe specifically says to cover.

- If a soup isn't thick enough for your taste when it's done, simmering for a bit longer will help some of the liquid evaporate.

- Simmering is not boiling. It is a much gentler cooking process.

- The bubbles should rise to the surface and break just under the surface, and the food should not move much.

VEGETABLE

CREAM OF ASPARAGUS SOUP
Fresh asparagus makes a deliciously flavored soup

"Cream of" soups are usually found condensed in cans. If that's the only type of cream soups you've ever eaten, this recipe will be a surprise and delight.

The soups are supposed to taste like the essence of the vegetable they feature, so those vegetables must be of the highest quality.

The vegetables are first simmered in some butter, then cooked in broth or water until tender. Puree the mixture un-

til smooth, then stir in some cream for an elegant and easy soup perfect for a first course.

Serve these soups in large, flat soup plates, garnished with a bit of the vegetable that made them.

Yield: Serves 6

Ingredients

1 1/2 pounds fresh asparagus

1 onion, chopped

1 clove garlic, minced

1/2 teaspoon salt

1/8 teaspoon white pepper

2 tablespoons butter

4 cups chicken broth, homemade or store-bought

1 russet potato, peeled and diced

1 tablespoon fresh thyme leaves

1/2 cup light cream

Cream of Asparagus Soup

- Snap off ends of asparagus and set aside. Cut the rest of the stems asparagus into 1½-inch pieces; set aside tips.

- In large pot, cook onion, garlic, salt, and pepper in butter 5 minutes. In another pot combine asparagus ends with broth; simmer 5 minutes.

- Strain broth; add with potato and thyme to onion mixture; simmer 10 minutes. Add asparagus and simmer 5 to 8 minutes until tender.

- Puree the soup. Add cream and asparagus tips; heat through but do not boil.

Cream of Broccoli Soup: Make soup as directed, except use 1½ pounds broccoli, cut into florets, in place of the asparagus. Don't cook the stems with the broth. Omit the potato; add 1 teaspoon dried basil and 1 tablespoon fresh lemon juice when you simmer the broccoli just before pureeing the soup.

Cream of Celery Soup: Make soup as directed, except use 1½ pounds chopped celery in place of the asparagus. Omit the potato; add ⅓ cup chopped celery leaves. After pureeing the soup, strain it. Add 1 cup cream mixed with 2 tablespoons cornstarch.

Snap Asparagus

- When you snap asparagus spears, hold the asparagus spears between your fingers and gently bend.

- The spears will snap where the asparagus becomes tough. The ends are usually discarded, but they add flavor to this soup.

- The ends, even when boiled, will be tough; that's why the broth is strained at this point.

- The tips are not added until the very end. Cook the tender stems in the third step.

Strain Broth

- You can use a large mesh strainer or a colander to strain the broth.

- The asparagus pieces are fairly large, so you don't need to use cheesecloth or a fine mesh strainer.

- You can also puree the soup in a food processor or stand blender; ladle it in batches into the appliance.

- If you'd like, cook the asparagus tips in the soup for a few minutes, then add the cream and heat through.

VEGETABLE

CHILLED BEET BORSCHT
This beautiful soup has the most delightful color and mild flavor

This gorgeous classic recipe for chilled borscht is delicious and fun to eat. The beets make the soup a bright pink color that can be beautifully garnished with everything from fresh herbs to slices of lemon or lime.

Sour cream is blended into the soup after the vegetables are cooked; that changes the deep red of the beets to a beautiful pink. The sour cream also adds a mild flavor and creamy texture to the soup.

Borscht comes from Eastern Europe. Beets were easy to grow and store over the winter, so this soup was a staple among poorer people.

Puree the soup using an immersion blender for the smoothest texture. Serve in chilled soup bowls.

Yield: Serves 6–8

Ingredients

2 pounds small beets, peeled

5 cups chicken broth, homemade or store-bought

1 cup water

1/4 cup lemon juice

3 tablespoons sugar

1/2 teaspoon salt

1/8 teaspoon pepper

2 tablespoons fresh dill weed

1 1/2 cups sour cream, divided

3 tablespoons parsley

1/3 cup chopped green onions

Chilled Beet Borscht

- Cut beets in half and add to large pot along with chicken broth and water.

- Simmer beets 10 to 15 minutes, until very tender. Add lemon juice, sugar, salt, and pepper; heat until sugar dissolves.

- Remove from heat; add dill and 1 cup sour cream; blend soup with immersion blender until smooth. Cover; chill 4 to 6 hours.

- Combine 1/2 cup sour cream, parsley, and green onions. When ready to serve, pour into chilled soup bowls and top with sour cream mixture.

Roasted Beet Borscht: Make recipe as directed, except instead of boiling the beets, place them on a cookie sheet and roast in a 400°F oven 35 minutes until tender. Grate the beets and simmer 10 minutes with 5 cups chicken broth; add remaining ingredients. Puree and chill soup.

Lithuanian Borscht: Make recipe as directed, except simmer the beets in water, remove, and cool. Omit sour cream. Combine beets, chicken broth, and remaining ingredients in food processor. Add 1 peeled, seeded, and chopped cucumber and 2 cups buttermilk. Puree and chill.

Simmer Beets

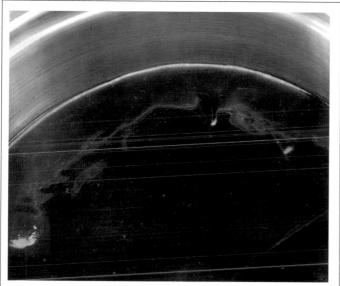

- One complaint many people have about preparing beets is that they stain the hands.

- Beets are used as a dye, so it's no wonder this is a problem. To solve it, just wear thin rubber gloves when preparing the beets.

- Simmer the beets until tender. A knife should slip in and out of the beets with little effort.

- If you can't find small beets, large beets will do. Peel and quarter them before boiling.

Blend Soup

- Using an immersion blender is the easiest method for making the soup.

- You can spoon the soup, a few cups at a time, into a food processor or blender. When blended, pour into a heatproof bowl.

- For a more rustic soup, you can use a potato masher to mash the beets.

- The soup can be served hot; cube the beets before simmering them. Add dill; serve hot, topped with sour cream.

VEGETABLE

SWEET POTATO SOUP
Sweet potatoes turn this soup a gorgeous color

Vegetable soups are so colorful. This beautiful soup has a deep orange yellow color from the sweet potatoes. It's the perfect soup for the holidays.

Sweet potatoes are very good for you. They are full of vitamin A, potassium, and fiber, along with folate and vitamin C. One serving of this soup gives you 50 percent of your daily requirement of vitamin A.

Salty and crisp bacon adds a wonderful contrast to the sweet and creamy soup, but you don't have to use it. Just cook the onions in a couple tablespoons of butter.

Serve this delicious soup with some Garlic Toast and a mixed green salad made with apples and pears.

Yield: Serves 6

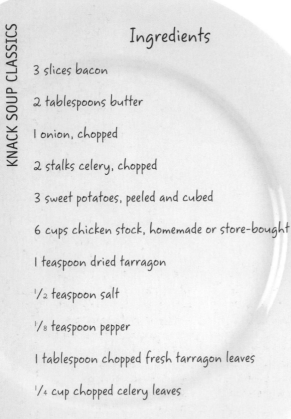

Ingredients

3 slices bacon

2 tablespoons butter

1 onion, chopped

2 stalks celery, chopped

3 sweet potatoes, peeled and cubed

6 cups chicken stock, homemade or store-bought

1 teaspoon dried tarragon

$1/2$ teaspoon salt

$1/8$ teaspoon pepper

1 tablespoon chopped fresh tarragon leaves

$1/4$ cup chopped celery leaves

Sweet Potato Soup

- In large pot cook bacon until crisp; drain, crumble, and set aside. Drain pot; do not wipe out.

- Add butter to pan with onion and celery; cook and stir 4 minutes. Add sweet potatoes; cook 5 minutes longer.

- Add stock, dried tarragon, salt, and pepper; bring to a simmer. Reduce heat and simmer 20 minutes, until potatoes are tender.

- If desired, puree part of the potatoes. In small bowl mix bacon, fresh tarragon, and celery leaves; sprinkle on soup and serve.

Sweet potatoes are not yams, and yams are not sweet potatoes, although the names seem to be interchangeable. Yams are starchy, large root vegetables native to Africa and aren't sweet. Sweet potatoes soften when cooked, have a deep orange color, and taste sweet even without added sugar.

Vegetarian Sweet Potato Soup: Make recipe as directed, except cook onions in 2 tablespoons olive oil. Omit bacon and chicken broth. Use 6 cups vegetable broth. Add 1 teaspoon dried thyme leaves and 2 teaspoons curry powder along with the tarragon. Puree the soup before serving.

Sauté Sweet Potatoes

- You sauté the sweet potatoes before cooking them in the stock to slightly caramelize them.

- This adds wonderful depth of flavor and a smoky sweetness to the soup. You can cook the potatoes longer for more caramelization if you'd like.

- You can use canned, drained sweet potatoes in place of the raw potatoes if you'd like.

- Simmer the soup just 5 to 10 minutes if you use the canned sweet potatoes.

Puree Soup

- This soup can be partially or completely pureed, depending on your mood.

- A totally pureed soup would be delicious as an appetizer or first course, served in tiny white soup bowls or mugs.

- Again, for a more rustic character, puree only part of the soup, leaving some pieces of potato and onion visible.

- This soup can also be served cold. Chill 4 to 6 hours. Stir in some light cream if the cold soup is too thick.

BEER CHEESE VEGETABLE SOUP
Beer adds a great flavor to a cheesy soup full of vegetables

Beer Cheese Vegetable Soup is a hearty and delicious main course soup. Unless served in tiny portions, it can stand as a meal. Don't serve it with anything else!

This is a great soup to serve to a crowd watching the big game, whether in your living room on your flat screen TV or in the stands at a stadium.

The soup has wonderful flavor and texture, and its topping of cheese popcorn makes the soup so fun to eat. Lots of veg-

etables make the soup hearty and nutritious.

You can use nonalcoholic beer to make this soup, or omit it altogether. If you omit it, increase the bacon to six slices to increase the flavor.

Yield: Serves 6

Ingredients

4 slices bacon

1/4 cup butter

1 onion, chopped

2 cloves garlic, minced

3 carrots, sliced

2 stalks celery, sliced

2 cups mushrooms, chopped

1 red bell pepper, chopped

3 tablespoons flour

1 teaspoon salt

1/8 teaspoon pepper

1 (16-ounce) bottle beer

4 cups chicken broth, homemade or store-bought

1 cup light cream

2 cups shredded cheddar cheese

1 cup shredded Colby cheese

6 cups Cheese Popcorn

Beer Cheese Vegetable Soup

- In large pot cook bacon until crisp; drain, crumble, and set aside. Drain pot, then add butter.

- Cook onion, garlic, carrots, celery, mushrooms, and bell pepper 7 to 8 minutes. Add flour, salt, and pepper; cook 5 minutes.

- Add beer and chicken broth; bring to a simmer. Simmer 10 to 12 minutes, until blended.

- Add cream and cheeses; cook and stir until blended, but do not boil. Garnish with bacon and popcorn.

• • • • RECIPE VARIATIONS • • • •

Cheese Popcorn: Pop ¼ cup popcorn kernels in 2 table-spoons butter. Cover pan and shake until popping slows. Place popcorn in bowl, removing unpopped kernels. Sprinkle with ¼ cup grated Parmesan cheese, ¼ cup grated Romano cheese, and 1 teaspoon dried Italian seasoning; toss and serve.

Pure Beer Cheese Soup: Make recipe as directed, except use 8 slices bacon. Use 2 onions and 6 cloves garlic. Omit carrots, celery, mushrooms, and red bell pepper. Increase flour to ¼ cup; add 6 cups stock and 3 cups cheddar cheese. Serve with Cheese Popcorn.

Cook Vegetables

- Don't wash the pot after cooking the bacon; just drain off most of the bacon fat.

- That fat and the drippings from the bacon add intense salty and smoky flavor to the soup.

- Cook the vegetables, stirring frequently, until they are crisp-tender. They'll finish cooking in the liquid.

- Make sure you simmer the flour mixture for at least 3 minutes so the starch molecules absorb the beer and chicken stock.

Simmer Soup

- You can simmer this soup covered or uncovered. The short cooking time means the technique doesn't make much difference.

- Don't boil the soup after the cheese is added. If it does boil, the cheese could separate.

- You could add other vegetables to this soup; sliced zucchini, yellow summer squash, or parsnips would be delicious.

- You can make this soup ahead of time; just don't add the cream and cheese. Refrigerate soup. Heat to a simmer, then proceed.

VEGETABLE

CREAMY FRENCH ONION SOUP

French onion soup gets dressed up for dinner in this easy recipe

French onion soup, whether creamy or classic, is another recipe that should be the main course rather than a first or soup course. This soup is very filling and hearty.

The onions must caramelize for the soup to have its characteristic flavor and color. This takes significant cooking time: 25 to 35 minutes on the stovetop, or almost 3 hours in the oven. Caramelization brings out the sweetness of the onions and adds hundreds of complex flavor compounds.

This soup is the perfect late-night meal after a play or concert. Serve it with some dry white wine and a simple spinach salad, with a lemon pie for dessert.
Yield: Serves 6

Ingredients

1 tablespoon butter	1/2 cup dry red wine
1 tablespoon olive oil	1 cup grated Gouda cheese
3 onions, chopped	
2 cloves garlic, minced	1 tablespoon cornstarch
2 tablespoons flour	1 cup Garlic Croutons
1/2 teaspoon salt	
1/8 teaspoon pepper	
1/2 teaspoon dried oregano	
1/2 teaspoon dried savory	
6 cups beef stock, homemade or store-bought	

Creamy French Onion Soup

- In large saucepan melt butter and olive oil over medium heat. Add onions; cook and stir 25 to 30 minutes, until brown.

- Add garlic; cook and stir 5 to 6 minutes longer. Add flour, salt, pepper, oregano, and savory; cook 5 minutes.

- Add beef stock and wine; simmer 20 minutes. Remove from heat and puree using immersion blender.

- Return to heat. Add cheese tossed with cornstarch; stir until melted. Serve with Garlic Croutons.

Garlic Croutons: Cut 10 1-inch-thick slices French bread into 1-inch cubes. In a small saucepan, combine ⅓ cup olive oil and 4 minced garlic cloves; simmer 5 minutes. Drizzle over bread; toss to coat. Sprinkle with ½ teaspoon salt and ⅛ teaspoon pepper. Bake at 350°F 10 to15 minutes, until brown; remove and cool.

Classic French Onion Soup: Make soup as directed, but roast onions in fat in Dutch oven at 400°F 2½ hours, stirring each hour. Do not puree soup. Use 2 cups cheese. Toast 6 French bread slices. Spoon soup into ovenproof bowls; top with bread and cheese. Broil until cheese browns.

Brown Onions

- Cook the onions slowly over medium or medium-low heat. Don't raise the heat to rush the process.

- As the onions brown, stir and scrape the pot frequently so nothing sticks to the pan and burns.

- If the onions burn, you'll have to throw them out and start over, because that burned flavor will permeate the soup.

- You can brown the onions ahead of time. Caramelized onions also make a nice sandwich spread or soup topping.

Add Cheese

- You can use other types of cheese in this recipe. Shredded Swiss or Gruyère cheese is classic.

- Don't use preshredded cheese; it is coated with ingredients that can prevent smooth melting.

- The cornstarch helps thicken the soup slightly and helps the cheese incorporate with the broth.

- The wine makes the soup slightly acidic so the cheese melts smoothly. If you aren't using wine, add 2 tablespoons lemon juice.

VEGETABLE

CAJUN GUMBO

Gumbo is a blend of cuisines—French, Spanish, African, and American Indian

The Cajun cuisine developed from French-speaking people who were deported from Canada to what is now Louisiana. The British deported the Acadians, who were farmers, to an area not very amenable to farming. The people learned to live off the land and adapted their French recipes.

Gumbo was developed to feed a lot of people using simple ingredients. Seafood, broth, and rice are flavored with lots of peppers and spices to make a hearty and aromatic dish.

All gumbos start with roux, a mixture of flour and fat cooked until brown. This thickens the gumbo and adds incredible flavor that can't be duplicated with anything else.

Yield: Serves 6

Ingredients

3 tablespoons flour

3 tablespoons olive oil

1 onion, chopped

4 cloves garlic, minced

1 jalapeño pepper, minced

5 cups chicken stock, homemade or store-bought

2 stalks celery, sliced

1 pound boneless, skinless chicken thighs, cubed

1 tablespoon Cajun Seasoning

1 green bell pepper, chopped

1 pound andouille sausage, sliced

1 cup sliced okra

½ pound raw medium shrimp

Slow Cooker Cajun Gumbo

- Cook flour in olive oil until light brown; add onion, garlic, and jalapeño pepper; cook 4 minutes.

- Add 1 cup stock; simmer 5 minutes. Add remaining stock and stir well; place in 4-quart slow cooker; add celery.

- Sprinkle chicken with Cajun Seasoning; add to slow cooker with bell pepper and stir well.

- Cook sausage until crisp; add to slow cooker. Cover; cook on low 7 to 8 hours. Add okra and shrimp; cook 35 to 45 minutes; stir and serve.

• • • • RECIPE VARIATIONS • • • •

Cajun Seasoning: Combine 2 tablespoons salt, 1 teaspoon cayenne pepper, ½ teaspoon black pepper, 1 teaspoon paprika, 1 teaspoon chili powder, ¼ teaspoon nutmeg, 1 teaspoon onion salt, ¼ teaspoon garlic powder, 1 teaspoon dried thyme leaves, and 1 teaspoon dried marjoram; store in airtight container.

Creole Gumbo: Make recipe as directed, except add 4 boneless, skinless chicken breasts along with the chicken thighs. Keep breasts whole. Cook as directed, except increase the shrimp amount to 1 pound. Omit okra; add 2 teaspoons filé powder at end.

Make Roux

- The roux is the basis for gumbos. It's made of flour cooked in fat (butter, lard, oil, bacon drippings) until brown.

- This adds flavor and color to the gumbo. It's very important to stir constantly when making a roux.

- The roux will transform from perfect to burned in a matter of seconds, so watch very carefully.

- If the roux burns, even a little bit, you must discard it and start over. The burned flavor will permeate the gumbo.

Place in Slow Cooker

- In a slow cooker you need to place ingredients in a specific order. If you're cooking this in a pot on the stovetop, just combine ingredients.

- While adding the stock to the roux and vegetables, stir with a wire whisk.

- This will help incorporate the stock into the roux so it will evenly thicken the gumbo.

- If the gumbo isn't thick enough for your taste, cook it on high, uncovered, 30 to 40 minutes.

SHRIMP GUMBO

Tender shrimp are paired with the "holy trinity" of onion, celery, and green bell pepper

Shrimp Gumbo is one of the treasures of Cajun cuisine. It can be made with a combination of chicken and shrimp.

This soup, like all gumbos, can be made as mild or spicy as you'd like. You can add everything from jalapeño to chipotle to habañero peppers along with the onions, or keep it mild to let the flavor of the shrimp shine through.

The classic way to serve this gumbo is to cook medium-grain white rice until tender. Spoon the gumbo into a bowl dusted with filé powder, then top with a scoop of rice.

Serve this gumbo with some ice-cold beer and a fresh fruit salad piled onto chilled plates.

Yield: Serves 6

Ingredients

3 tablespoons vegetable oil

3 tablespoons flour

1 onion, chopped

3 cloves garlic, minced

2 stalks celery, sliced

1 green bell pepper, chopped

6 cups seafood stock, homemade or store-bought

2 tomatoes, peeled, seeded, and chopped

3 tablespoons tomato paste

1 teaspoon salt

1/8 teaspoon cayenne pepper

1 bay leaf

2 pounds medium raw shrimp

1 teaspoon dried thyme

2 teaspoons filé powder, if desired

Shrimp Gumbo

- In heavy pot combine vegetable oil and flour. Cook over low heat until brown.

- Add onion, garlic, celery, and green bell pepper; cook 4 minutes. Add stock, tomatoes, tomato paste, salt, cayenne pepper, and bay leaf.

- Simmer 25 minutes. Add shrimp and thyme; simmer 5 to 6 minutes, until shrimp curl and turn pink.

- Remove bay leaf. Remove pot from heat and stir in file powder with a whisk. Cover and let stand 10 minutes, then serve.

ZOOM

Filé powder, the classic thickener for gumbo, is made from sassafras leaves. The roots and bark of the plant contain a carcinogenic ingredient called Saffrole. Older copies of *The Joy of Cooking* claim filé powder should not be used. But the leaves, when harvested very young, do not contain Saffrole, so are safe.

• • • • RECIPE VARIATION • • • •

Chicken and Shrimp Gumbo: Make recipe as directed, except start with ¼ pound andouille sausage. Remove sausage, add oil, and brown 6 chicken thighs. Remove, then make roux. Add 2 minced jalapeño peppers with onions. Add sausage and chicken with stock; simmer until done, then continue with recipe.

Add Vegetables to Roux

- Be careful when adding the vegetables to the dark roux; the water in the vegetables spatters easily.

- You can use any vegetables you'd like in this easy recipe. More peppers add color and flavor.

- Use red, yellow, and orange bell peppers, or try poblano or Anaheim peppers for a bit more kick.

- Mushrooms or zucchini would also be good additions. Cut the vegetables to the same size so they cook evenly.

Add Filé Powder

- Filé powder should not be cooked, so it is added last, and the soup is removed from the heat first.

- You must stir as you add the filé powder, as it starts to thicken when heated.

- Sprinkle the powder evenly over the gumbo and stir constantly to prevent lumps.

- You can also dust the soup bowls with filé powder and then add the gumbo; it will thicken as you eat.

CHICKEN GUMBO

Chicken makes a flavorful gumbo that is quite inexpensive and delicious

Gumbo made from chicken is easy and inexpensive. This recipe can be loaded up with all the vegetables you'd like.

Using chicken thighs makes a richer dish that's less expensive than one made with chicken breasts. The thighs also stay truer to the original purpose of gumbo, which was to feed a crowd for very little money.

The roux in this recipe is made with oil and bacon drippings for more flavor. Choose smoked bacon or thick-cut bacon to add more emphasis to this ingredient.

Serve the gumbo in warmed soup plates, with a scoop of hot cooked rice mixed with fresh chopped thyme and parsley.
Yield: Serves 6

Ingredients

5 slices bacon

1 tablespoon vegetable oil

1/4 cup flour

1 onion, chopped

3 cloves garlic, minced

2 stalks celery, chopped

1 red bell pepper, chopped

2 pounds boneless skinless chicken thighs, cubed

2 teaspoons Creole seasoning

1/8 teaspoon cayenne pepper

4 tomatoes, peeled, seeded, and chopped

5 cups chicken stock, homemade or store-bought

1 cup tomato juice

1 bay leaf

1 teaspoon Worcestershire sauce

1 teaspoon dried thyme leaves

1 1/2 teaspoons filé powder

Chicken Gumbo

- In large pot, cook bacon until crisp; drain, crumble, and set aside. Add oil to drippings; add flour and cook until brown.

- Add onion, garlic, celery, and bell pepper; cook 5 minutes. Sprinkle chicken with Creole seasoning and cayenne pepper and add.

- Add remaining ingredients except filé powder; simmer 30 to 40 minutes, until chicken is tender.

- Remove bay leaf. Let gumbo stand, covered, 10 minutes, then stir and serve in bowls dusted with filé powder.

····· RECIPE VARIATIONS ·····

Lighter Chicken Gumbo: Make recipe as directed, except use 4 slices turkey bacon. Use 2 pounds boneless, skinless chicken breasts, but do not cube them. Simmer the mixture 12 to 18 minutes, until the chicken is tender; remove chicken and shred. Return chicken to gumbo and let stand, covered, 10 minutes before serving.

Chicken and Sausage Gumbo: Make recipe as directed, except use 1 pound andouille sausage in place of the bacon. Slice and brown the sausage. Do not drain; add the oil and make a dark roux. Continue with the recipe, adding the sausage with the chicken thighs.

Add Vegetables to Roux

- The "holy trinity" of celery, onion, and red bell pepper are used in this classic gumbo recipe. Add them carefully; they'll spatter in the hot roux.

- You could add mushrooms or other types of bell pepper to increase the vegetable amount.

- Cook the vegetables until tender, stirring frequently so the roux doesn't burn.

- Creole seasoning can be found in the spice aisle or the international foods aisle of any supermarket.

Add Stock

- You can use chicken stock or broth for the liquid in this gumbo recipe. Just make sure it's good quality.

- Simmer the gumbo until the chicken is tender. If you use whole chicken thighs, this will take longer than cubes.

- This gumbo can be made a day ahead of time. Just make it completely, chill it, then reheat to a simmer.

- Don't add the filé powder until you're ready to serve the dish.

SAUSAGE GUMBO

Several kinds of sausage add fabulous flavor to this easy gumbo

The sausages used in gumbo include andouille, boudin, and Polish sausage. All three are combined in this rich gumbo that serves a crowd.

Andouille sausage is a spicy coarse sausage made of smoked meat, onions, and wine. Boudin is a soft sausage that comes in white and dark hues. Boudin usually has rice added to the meat before it's stuffed.

The amounts of vegetables used in this recipe can vary. Add more if you like more, use less if you want the gumbo to be heavy on sausage.

This recipe is high in fat and calories, so make it only on special occasions. You can use any types of sausage you'd like. *Yield: Serves 8*

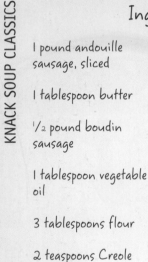

Ingredients

1 pound andouille sausage, sliced	3 cloves garlic, minced
1 tablespoon butter	1/2 pound Polish sausage, sliced
1/2 pound boudin sausage	5 cups chicken stock, homemade or store-bought
1 tablespoon vegetable oil	3 tomatoes, peeled, seeded, and chopped
3 tablespoons flour	1 cup chopped okra
2 teaspoons Creole seasoning	
1 onion, chopped	
1 yellow bell pepper, chopped	
2 stalks celery, sliced	
2 carrots, sliced	

Sausage Gumbo

- Cook andouille in butter until fat renders; remove. Add boudin, cook gently until firm, remove; slice both.

- Drain all but 3 tablespoons fat; add oil and flour; cook until brown.

- Add Creole seasoning, onion, bell pepper, celery, carrots, and garlic; cook 5 minutes. Add Polish sausage, stock, and tomatoes.

- Bring to a simmer; simmer 10 minutes. Add andouille, boudin, any juices from sausages, and okra; simmer 15 minutes.

126

ZOOM

The word *gumbo* may have come from the word *okra* in African dialects. Okra is an inexpensive and common vegetable in the South and adds a thickening quality to gumbo. Gumbo often contains a dark roux along with the "holy trinity" of onion, celery, and green bell pepper.

• • • • RECIPE VARIATION • • • •

Slow Cooker Sausage Gumbo: Make recipe as directed, except after adding vegetables to the roux, cook just 2 minutes. Place all ingredients except sausages and okra in 4- to 5-quart slow cooker. Refrigerate sausages while gumbo cooks. Cover and cook on low 7 hours. Add sausage and okra; cook 1 to 2 hours longer.

Cook Sausages

- Andouille is a smoked sausage, which means it's firmer and doesn't have to be handled carefully.

- You can slice the andouille sausage before you cook it to release more of the fat and juices.

- Boudin is a fragile sausage and has to be cooked carefully or it will burst.

- Prick the boudin sausage several times with the tines of a fork to help release juices as it cooks. Cook the boudin until it is firm.

Add Sausages and Okra

- Choose a Polish sausage that is fully cooked, so it doesn't have to be cooked separately before adding to the gumbo.

- You don't want to simmer the okra for a long time or the gumbo will get too sticky.

- To prepare fresh okra, rinse the pods and cut off the stems. Slice the okra into ¼-inch slices.

- You can use frozen okra, thawed according to the package directions, instead of fresh if you'd like.

127

GUMBO Z'HERBS

This gumbo features lots of greens and vegetables for a wonderful variation

Ham, sausages, lots of greens, and herbs make this wonderful gumbo a symphony of flavors, textures, and colors.

This gumbo is the most complicated of all the gumbo recipes. It can use up to nine types of greens and five or six different meats. Use your favorites to create your own recipe.

The "herbs" in the title doesn't refer to actual herbs, like thyme or basil, but to the deep greens used in the recipe and the green color of the finished dish.

Use any combination of dark greens to make this unique recipe. Serve it with a scoop of hot cooked medium-grain rice mixed with chopped parsley and basil.

Yield: Serves 8–10

Ingredients

1 pound collard greens	1 meaty ham bone
1/2 pound mustard greens	7 cups beef stock, homemade or store-bought
1/2 pound spinach leaves	2 bay leaves
1 bunch watercress	1/2 teaspoon pepper
1/2 head green cabbage	1/4 teaspoon cayenne pepper
4 slices bacon	1 teaspoon dried thyme leaves
2 onions, chopped	
6 cloves garlic, minced	1/2 teaspoon ground allspice
3 stalks celery, chopped	2 teaspoons filé powder, if desired
2 green bell peppers, chopped	
1 pound smoked fully cooked sausage links	

Gumbo Z'Herbs

- Sort greens, immerse in sink full of cold water, change water, then soak 5 minutes. Drain, shaking off water.

- Chop greens; place in pot. Cook bacon in skillet, crumble, and refrigerate.

- Add onions and garlic to skillet; cook 5 minutes. Add to pot with greens, celery, bell peppers, sausage, ham bone, stock, bay leaves, peppers, thyme, and allspice.

- Simmer 2 hours; remove meat and bay leaves. Puree soup, chop meat, return to pot with bacon; simmer 20 minutes. Add filé powder, if using, and serve.

128

• • • • RECIPE VARIATIONS • • • •

Vegetarian Gumbo Z'Herbs: Make recipe as directed, except add ½ pound baby beet greens and turnip greens with the rest of the greens. Omit the bacon; use 3 table-spoons olive oil to cook the onion and garlic. Increase onions to 3 and garlic to 8 cloves. Omit sausage and ham; use vegetable broth.

Meaty Gumbo Z'Herbs: Make recipe as directed, except add romaine lettuce and chicory to the greens. Add 1 pound beef stew meat and 4 boneless, skinless chicken thighs along with the sausage and ham bone. Add ¼ tea-spoon ground cloves and ½ teaspoon Tabasco sauce.

Clean Greens

- Greens have to be washed thoroughly, usually immersed in several changes of water.

- They are grown in sandy soil and can accumulate a lot of grit between their leaves, which has to be removed.

- Remove the stems from the greens after washing and before you chop them.

- Coarsely chop the greens using a chef's knife. You want fairly large pieces so they give texture to the gumbo.

Remove Meat from Bone

- Remove all the meat you can from the ham bone and cut it into fairly small pieces.

- Since the greens are pureed, the ham and bacon are the only discrete pieces in the gumbo, besides the rice.

- You don't have to puree the greens if you'd like a gumbo with more rustic character.

- An old saying about Gumbo Z'Herbs is: The more greens you add to the pot, the more friends you will have.

VEGETARIAN GUMBO
Gumbo doesn't have to be made with meat or seafood

Lots of vegetables, spices, and herbs make this vegetarian gumbo dish as rich as the meaty varieties.

It's very important that the roux in this vegetarian gumbo be cooked until nice and dark to give lots of flavor and body to the finished dish. Watch the roux carefully; don't leave the stove while it's cooking. If you're unsure about your cooking skills, make the roux in the oven.

Many vegetarians crave spicy food. You can increase the spices in this recipe, add hot chile peppers, or pass a bottle of hot sauce at the table.

Serve this gumbo with hot cooked rice, a salad made of arugula and mesclun, and some Garlic Toast.
Yield: Serves 6

Ingredients

3 tablespoons vegetable oil

3 tablespoons flour

2 onions, chopped

4 cloves garlic, minced

3 stalks celery, chopped

1 red bell pepper, chopped

1 yellow bell pepper, chopped

2 carrots, sliced

4 red tomatoes, peeled, seeded, and chopped

2 yellow tomatoes, peeled, seeded, and chopped

1/2 teaspoon salt

1/4 teaspoon cayenne pepper

1 bay leaf

1 teaspoon dried thyme

1 teaspoon dried oregano

7 cups vegetable stock, homemade or store-bought

1 tablespoon filé powder

Vegetarian Gumbo

- In large pot combine oil and flour; cook and stir until browned, about 20 minutes.

- Add onion, garlic, celery, and bell peppers; cook 5 minutes. Add carrots and tomatoes.

- Sprinkle with salt, cayenne pepper, bay leaf, thyme, and oregano and stir. Add stock.

- Bring to a simmer; simmer 20 to 25 minutes, until gumbo is blended. Turn off heat, stir in filé powder, and let stand 10 minutes before serving.

• • • • RECIPE VARIATIONS • • • •

Oven Roux: Mix 2 cups flour and 1¼ cups canola or peanut oil. Place in a heavy pan and bake at 350°F 1½ to 2 hours, stirring every 30 minutes, until the mixture is deep golden brown. Refrigerate or freeze; thaw and simmer before continuing with the recipe.

Spicy Vegetarian Gumbo: Make recipe as directed, except use 3 onions and 8 garlic cloves. Increase the cayenne pepper to ½ teaspoon and add ½ teaspoon Tabasco sauce. Add 2 minced jalapeño and 1 minced habañero peppers along with the onions and garlic.

Cook Vegetables in Roux

- The vegetables are cooked in the roux to add liquid to the roux and to begin softening the vegetables.

- You can add other vegetables to the recipe if you'd like. Mushrooms and more bell peppers are good choices.

- Since this gumbo is made quickly, it isn't a good choice for cooking ahead of time.

- Add other spices and herbs to the gumbo, like basil, marjoram, allspice, and cloves.

Add Filé Powder

- Only add filé powder after removing the gumbo from the heat.

- If you don't want to add filé powder, the gumbo will be less thick; that's okay.

- For a smokier gumbo, you can add ¼ to ½ teaspoon liquid smoke. This is a safe product that is made by pushing smoke through water.

- This gumbo recipe is fairly mild; add dried or hot minced chile peppers to taste.

GAZPACHO

Gazpacho is the perfect soup to serve on a summer day

Gazpacho is a Spanish soup, traditionally made with stale bread, olive oil, garlic, and vinegar. Tomatoes and other vegetables were added later in the soup's history.

If you look at farmers' markets and large grocery stores, you'll find lots of what are called "heirloom" tomatoes. These tomatoes are made from seeds harvested from nonhybrid plants. The seeds are usually from plants at least fifty years old, before growers started to hybridize the fruit.

You can, of course, make gazpacho from just ripe red tomatoes, but try colored tomatoes for a really beautiful dish.

Serve your gazpacho in chilled glass bowls with a sprinkling of fresh herbs and some cooked shrimp or crab.

Yield: Serves 6

Ingredients

- I shallot, minced
- I red onion, chopped
- I cucumber, peeled, seeded, and chopped
- I red bell pepper, chopped
- 4 plum tomatoes, skinned and chopped
- I beefsteak tomato, skinned, seeded, and chopped
- 2 yellow tomatoes peeled, seeded, and chopped
- 2 tablespoons olive oil
- 2 tablespoons lemon juice
- I tablespoon lime juice
- $1/2$ teaspoon salt
- $1/8$ teaspoon pepper
- I teaspoon dried basil
- 2 cups chicken or vegetable broth, homemade or store-bought
- 2 cups tomato juice
- I cup small cooked shrimp
- $1/4$ cup grated Romano cheese
- $1/4$ cup minced parsley

Gazpacho

- Prepare shallot, red onion, cucumber, bell pepper, all the tomatoes and combine in large food processor.

- Process until finely chopped. Remove to large bowl and add olive oil, lemon juice, lime juice, salt, pepper, and basil.

- Add broth and tomato juice and mix gently. Cover and chill 4 to 6 hours.

- When ready to serve, toss shrimp with cheese and parsley; use to top soup.

132

••••• RECIPE VARIATION •••••

Traditional Gazpacho: Make recipe as directed, except omit cucumber and red bell pepper. Add another chopped beefsteak tomato. Place Gazpacho in a food processor with 2 cups cubed rustic Italian bread; process until smooth. Refrigerate 6 hours before serving. Omit shrimp, parsley, and cheese.

ZOOM

Heirloom tomatoes come in amazing varieties of colors, shapes, flavors, and textures. Some of the most common names include the flavorful Brandywine, Green Zebra, Cherokee Purple, and Mortgage Lifter, which is a pink and juicy tomato. Buy them from farmers or grow in your garden.

Blanch Tomatoes

- You don't have to remove the tomato skins for a more rustic soup. In that case, don't puree the soup; just mash slightly.

- To peel the tomatoes easily, first cut a small X in the bottom. Drop tomatoes into boiling water for just a few seconds.

- Then put the tomatoes in ice water 1 to 2 minutes. The peel should slip off easily.

- Cut the tomatoes in half and squeeze to remove seeds; coarsely chop flesh.

Process Soup

- To prepare cucumber, peel, cut in half, and remove seeds with a spoon, then slice or chop the cucumber.

- You can process this soup until totally pureed or just evenly chopped.

- Traditional gazpacho is usually made in a mortar and pestle to a very smooth consistency.

- Garnish the soup with everything from fresh herbs to Garlic Croutons to freshly cooked seafood.

133

BLOODY MARY SOUP
Like the drink, this soup is spicy and hot

A Bloody Mary is a cocktail made with tomato juice, vodka, and spices like Tabasco and Worcestershire sauce. It's seasoned with celery salt, pepper, and lemon juice.

This drink is easily transformed into a simple soup perfect as an appetizer or first course. Ladle it into small glass bowls or even shot glasses, garnished with a small piece of celery from the celery heart with the leaves still attached.

The soup can be served hot or cold. If you choose to serve it cold, make sure to season the soup well, since the cold blunts the taste.

The soup can be made with or without vodka. The vodka adds a sharp note and makes the soup more authentic, but it's delicious without.

Yield: Serves 6

Ingredients

2 tablespoons butter

1 onion, chopped

2 red tomatoes, diced

1 yellow tomato, diced

3 tablespoons tomato paste

2 teaspoons Worcestershire sauce

1/2 teaspoon salt

1/8 teaspoon pepper

3 cups chicken broth, homemade or store-bought

1 tablespoon orange juice

1/4 cup vodka, if desired

1/4 teaspoon hot sauce

1 celery stalk, chopped

2 tablespoons chopped fresh parsley

1/4 cup grated Romano cheese

1 tablespoon prepared horseradish

Bloody Mary Soup

- Melt butter in large saucepan. Add onion; cook and stir 5 minutes, until tender.

- Add tomatoes, tomato paste, Worcestershire, salt, pepper, and chicken broth; stir well and simmer 15 minutes.

- Remove from heat and puree the soup using an immersion blender. Stir in orange juice, vodka, and hot sauce.

- In small bowl combine celery, parsley, cheese, and horseradish. Serve soup hot or cold, topped with celery mixture.

Vegetarian Bloody Mary Soup: Make recipe as directed, except use 2 tablespoons olive oil instead of butter, omit the Worcestershire sauce, and use 3 cups vegetable broth in place of the chicken broth. Omit Romano cheese; use 2 tablespoons horseradish. Serve the soup cold with Herbed Oyster Crackers.

Herbed Oyster Crackers: In bowl, combine 2 tablespoons dried parsley, ¼ cup instant minced onion, 1 teaspoon garlic salt, 1 teaspoon onion salt, 1 teaspoon dried dill, and ⅛ teaspoon pepper with ½ cup oil. Mix and drizzle over 4 cups oyster crackers. Bake at 275°F 20 minutes, until browned.

Prepare Vegetables

- The soup can be served unpureed, partially pureed, or completely pureed, depending on your taste.

- If you just chop all the vegetables finely, you don't need to process or puree them at all.

- Add other vegetables if you'd like; sauté sliced mushrooms or red or yellow bell peppers with the onions.

- You can use plain or flavored vodka in this recipe. Orange vodka or spiced vodka would be nice in this soup.

Mix Topping

- Make the celery mixture ahead of time and store it, covered, in the refrigerator.

- This soup can be served with other toppings, like pesto or a combination of fresh herbs.

- Since Bloody Marys are traditionally served with

- a celery stick, some type of celery garnish is appropriate.

- This soup would also be delicious topped with guacamole or chopped avocados, or a mixture of avocados, tiny grape tomatoes, and shredded cheese.

SUN-DRIED TOMATO CHOWDER
Two kinds of sun-dried tomatoes add richness to this chowder

Sun-dried tomatoes have been literally dried in the sun—also in food dehydrators and ovens. They come in two varieties: dried and packed in oil.

The dried tomatoes are hard and leathery, and have to be reconstituted in liquid before they're ready to eat. The tomatoes packed in oil can be eaten immediately. Their flavor is quite intense, so they are usually minced or chopped before being used in recipes.

The oil that the tomatoes are packed in is very flavorful and a good way to start this soup. It can be used in any recipe where you want an intense tomato flavor.

Enjoy this delicious soup with its beautiful color and flavor. *Yield: Serves 6*

Ingredients

½ cup dry sun-dried tomatoes

1 cup hot water

1 tablespoon butter

1 tablespoon oil from tomatoes

1 onion, chopped

3 cloves garlic, minced

¼ cup sun-dried tomatoes in oil, drained and chopped

2 stalks celery, sliced

2 red tomatoes, peeled, seeded, and chopped

2 cups frozen corn

4 cups chicken broth, homemade or store-bought

1 teaspoon salt

1 teaspoon dried marjoram leaves

⅛ teaspoon pepper

⅛ teaspoon cloves

1 cup light cream

1 tablespoon cornstarch

Sun-Dried Tomato Chowder

- In small bowl soak dried tomatoes in hot water for 25 minutes. Drain, reserving water; chop tomatoes.

- In large pot heat butter and oil over medium heat. Add onion and garlic; cook and stir 5 minutes. Add sun-dried tomatoes, celery, red tomatoes, and corn.

- Add broth, reserved soaking liquid, salt, marjoram, pepper, and cloves; bring to a simmer. Simmer 10 to 15 minutes until blended.

- Mix cream and cornstarch in small bowl; add to soup. Cook and stir until soup is thickened.

Homemade Sun-Dried Tomatoes: Cut ripe tomatoes in half and remove seeds. Arrange on a food dehydrator; dry 6 to 7 hours, until the tomatoes feel like raisins. Or, bake the tomatoes at 150°F 12 to 20 hours, turning the tomatoes occasionally, until dried. Vacuum seal the tomatoes or freeze up to 3 months.

Slow Cooker Tomato Chowder: Make recipe as directed, except after onions and garlic are sautéed, combine them with the tomatoes and all other ingredients except cream and cornstarch in 3- to 4-quart slow cooker. Cover and cook on low 7 to 8 hours. Add cream and cornstarch; cook on high 10 to 15 minutes.

Soak Tomatoes

- Using two kinds of sun-dried tomatoes in this recipe offers a contrast in texture and enhances the flavor.

- The air-dried tomatoes should be rehydrated before use. Just soak them in warm water 20 to 30 minutes.

- The soaking water has flavor, so use it in the soup, too.

- The tomatoes packed in oil are tender and ready to eat. Drain and chop or mince, then use in the recipe.

Add Broth and Spices

- You can use vegetable broth if you'd like for a vegetarian version of this easy soup.

- The cloves bring out the flavor of the tomatoes and add a hint of spice. You could use allspice or nutmeg instead.

- Use fresh minced marjoram if you'd like; a tablespoon of fresh is equal to a teaspoon of dried.

- Make this soup ahead of time, but don't add the cream slurry. Refrigerate; then heat it, add the slurry, and simmer until thickened.

ROASTED TOMATO SOUP

When roasted, tomatoes take on a sweetness and depth of flavor

Roasting tomatoes concentrates their flavor and color and intensifies their sweetness. All you do is cut the tomatoes into pieces; toss them with onions, garlic, and olive oil; and roast them in the oven until they are shriveled.

These shriveled tomatoes, while not beautiful, are packed with flavor. They can be seasoned before or after roasting. Seasoning them before they roast helps bring out the flavor of the tomatoes and the seasonings.

Using three kinds of tomatoes adds to the depth of flavor of the recipe. Any combination of tomatoes would work well; think about trying some heirloom varieties for more interest.

Enjoy this soup with some hearty sandwiches for an elegant lunch on the porch.

Yield: Serves 6

Ingredients

4 red tomatoes, quartered

3 yellow tomatoes, quartered

1 cup grape tomatoes

2 onions, chopped

3 cloves garlic, chopped

3 tablespoons olive oil

$1/2$ teaspoon salt

$1/8$ teaspoon pepper

4 cups vegetable broth, homemade or store-bought

1 teaspoon dried basil

$1/2$ cup julienned fresh basil leaves

$1/4$ cup freshly grated Parmesan cheese

Roasted Tomato Soup

- Line 2 jelly roll pans with parchment paper and place red and yellow tomatoes, cut side up, on one pan.

- Place grape tomatoes, onions, and garlic on the other.

- Drizzle all with olive oil and sprinkle with salt and pepper. Roast at 375°F; large

tomatoes 35 to 40 minutes, grape tomatoes 15 to 20 minutes, until tomatoes darken.

- Remove all to large pot with broth and dried basil; simmer 15 minutes. Partially puree with immersion blender; top with fresh basil and cheese.

Fresh Tomato Soup: Make recipe as directed, except don't roast the tomatoes. Heat olive oil in large pot; sauté onions and garlic 5 minutes. Add all tomatoes, broth, and seasonings; simmer 15 to 20 minutes. Mash tomatoes or puree soup; top with basil and cheese.

Curried Roasted Tomato Soup: Make recipe as directed, except sprinkle the red and yellow tomatoes with 1 tablespoon curry powder. Continue with soup, but omit dried and fresh basil. Add 1 teaspoon dried thyme leaves and garnish with 1 tablespoon chopped fresh thyme.

TOMATO

Roasted Vegetables

Puree Soup

- You can peel the tomatoes before or after roasting, if you'd like. The skins will slip off easily after roasting.

- The roasted and dried tomatoes you buy in the store usually have the skins still attached.

- You can roast the vegetables ahead of time. Just cover and let stand at room temperature 4 to 6 hours.

- Then combine the vegetables with the broth and basil; simmer as directed and continue with the recipe.

- This soup can be pureed in a stand blender, in a food processor, or with a handheld immersion blender.

- Completely puree the soup for a more elegant soup; leave some chunks of tomato and onion for a rustic look.

- You can serve this soup hot or cold. To serve cold, cover and chill 4 to 5 hours.

- You may want to stir in some more broth if the soup becomes thick when chilled. Garnish only when serving the soup, not before.

TOMATO BISQUE

This creamy and smooth soup tastes like the essence of tomatoes

Several different forms of tomato cooked until tender, then combined with cream, makes an elegant soup that's delicious for a formal dinner starter.

Experiment with heirloom tomatoes in any tomato soup. The color and flavor will be different each time, but that's part of the fun.

This soup can be served hot or cold. With any soup that can be served at these temperature extremes, you may have to thin the soup to the desired consistency. Use the same liquids you use to make the soup so as not to dilute the flavor.

This soup should be made in the summer, when tomatoes are at their peak. Either pick the tomatoes from your backyard or browse through a farmers' market.

Yield: Serves 4–6

Ingredients

- 1 onion, chopped
- 3 cloves garlic, minced
- 2 tablespoons butter
- 2 tablespoons flour
- 1/2 cup chopped oil-packed sun-dried tomatoes
- 5 red tomatoes, peeled, seeded, and chopped
- 2 yellow tomatoes, peeled, seeded, and chopped
- 1 bay leaf
- 1 teaspoon salt
- 1/8 teaspoon pepper
- 1 teaspoon dried thyme leaves
- 4 cups chicken broth, homemade or store-bought
- 1 cup water
- 1 cup heavy cream
- 1/3 cup minced oil-packed sun-dried tomatoes
- 1 tablespoon fresh thyme leaves

Tomato Bisque

- In large pot cook onion and garlic in butter. Add flour; cook and stir 5 minutes. Add sun-dried tomatoes and red and yellow tomatoes.

- Cook 5 minutes, then add bay leaf, salt, pepper, dried thyme, broth, and water. Simmer 30 minutes.

- Remove bay leaf, puree soup using immersion blender. Then strain soup through a fine strainer; return to clean pot.

- Add cream to soup; heat through, do not boil. Garnish soup with minced tomatoes and fresh thyme.

.... RED●LIGHT ....

You can't make sun-dried tomatoes packed in oil at home. Any homemade flavored oil can be contaminated with botulism. This dangerous bacterium grows in an anaerobic environment. The spores can live on produce and will start growing in oil. Only use commercial varieties of foods packed in oil.

· · · · RECIPE VARIATION · · · ·

Roasted Tomato Bisque: Make recipe as directed, except mix onions and garlic with red and yellow tomatoes on cookie sheet. Drizzle with 2 tablespoons olive oil; roast at 400°F 30 to 40 minutes. Simmer with thyme, broth, and water; continue with recipe. Don't strain soup.

Cook Tomatoes

- Use your favorite combination of tomatoes in this luscious soup.

- You could also change the herbs. Oregano, basil, and marjoram, or a combination of them, would be delicious.

- Or you could add more vegetables, like chopped celery, sliced mushrooms, or a chopped green or red bell pepper.

- If the soup is a bit acidic when you taste it, add a teaspoon or two of sugar.

Strain Soup

- For formal occasions, strain the soup before you add the cream. This makes a very smooth mixture.

- For less work and a more rustic look and texture, don't strain the soup. Just puree the mixture and add the cream.

- The material left in the strainer when the soup is strained can be saved for making broth; freeze it.

- Or you can add that food to your compost pile in your backyard.

THREE TOMATO PASTA SOUP
Tiny pasta adds texture and interest to this classic soup

When pasta cooks in a flavored liquid, you won't believe the difference in taste. Pasta absorbs flavors as it cooks, which is why you must always season pasta cooking water.

When cooked in soup, pasta also has a slightly different texture. The acid in the tomatoes keeps the pasta from becoming very soft. It has a wonderful al dente texture, with a slight bite in the center.

This soup is a variation on the classic tomato rice soup found in cans that we all loved as children. Made with fresh tomatoes, the soup has a wonderful fresh and sweet flavor.

Serve this soup in mugs with large soupspoons and lots of napkins.

Yield: Serves 6

Ingredients

2 tablespoons butter

1 tablespoon olive oil

1 red onion, chopped

2 cloves garlic, minced

3 red tomatoes, peeled, seeded, and diced

2 yellow tomatoes, peeled, seeded, and diced

2 cups cherry tomatoes, diced

1 teaspoon salt

$1/8$ teaspoon pepper

2 cups tomato juice

3 cups vegetable stock, homemade or store-bought

$1/2$ cup chopped fresh basil leaves

$1/2$ cup ditalini pasta

$1/2$ cup grated Parmesan cheese

Three Tomato Pasta Soup

- In large pot heat butter and olive oil over medium heat. Add onion and garlic; cook and stir 5 minutes.

- Add all of the tomatoes; cook and stir 8 to 9 minutes, until liquid evaporates.

- Add salt, pepper, juice, and stock; simmer 20 minutes. Puree the soup using an immersion blender.

- Add basil and pasta; simmer 8 to 9 minutes, until pasta is tender. Stir in cheese and serve.

Garlic Tomato Pasta Soup: Make recipe as directed, except use a yellow onion in place of the red onion. Add 4 or 5 cloves of garlic when you cook the onions in the butter and olive oil. Use 6 red ripe tomatoes. Use orzo pasta or small shell pasta; cook according to package directions.

Canned Tomato Pasta Soup: Make recipe as directed, except use 2 14-ounce cans diced tomatoes, and 1 16-ounce can stewed tomatoes, all undrained, in place of the red and yellow tomatoes. Use the cherry tomatoes. Use chicken broth; proceed with recipe.

TOMATO

Cook Tomatoes

- For a more rustic soup, don't peel the tomatoes. Just cut them in half, squeeze out the seeds, and chop.

- Many of the vitamins and minerals and much of the fiber of tomatoes is in the skin.

- The tomatoes can burn easily because they are high in sugar, so watch them carefully while cooking.

- You want the liquid from the tomatoes to evaporate to concentrate the flavor and color.

Add Pasta

- When you cook pasta in liquids other than water, the cooking time changes.

- The acids and salts in this soup slow down the cooking time by a few minutes.

- Make sure you adjust the cooking time for each type of pasta you use.

- Add about 2 to 3 minutes to the cooking time on the box, and keep checking until the pasta is al dente.

BACON POTATO CHOWDER
This thick chowder has the rich flavors of bacon and cream

Now we're getting into soups that are decadent and very filling! Potatoes have formed the backbone of soups for generations. They cook up rich and creamy and have the best nutty, earthy taste.

And because potatoes are so inexpensive and keep so well, these soups really give you a lot of value for your money.

Traditionally, low-starch potatoes like Red Bliss and Superior are used when potatoes are cooked in water. They become creamy because they are waxy and low in starch. But you can use any potato in a soup.

Yukon Gold potatoes add a buttery taste and gold color, while purple potatoes make soup purple! Perhaps that's too strange. Russets and Yukon Golds thicken potato soups best. *Yield: Serves 6–8*

Ingredients

10 slices thick cut bacon

2 tablespoons butter

2 onions, chopped

4 cloves garlic, minced

2 tablespoons flour

1/2 teaspoon salt

1/8 teaspoon pepper

1 teaspoon dried basil leaves

6 cups vegetable broth, homemade or store-bought

3 carrots, sliced

6 russet potatoes, peeled and diced

1 1/2 cups shredded cheddar cheese

1 tablespoon cornstarch

1 cup light cream

1 cup milk

Bacon Potato Chowder

- Cook bacon until crisp in large pot; drain, crumble, and set aside. Drain all but 2 tablespoons drippings; add butter.

- Cook onions and garlic 6 minutes; add flour, salt, pepper, and basil; cook 5 minutes.

- Add broth; bring to a simmer. Add carrots and potatoes; bring to a simmer again; cook 20 minutes.

- Mash some of the potatoes in the pot. Stir in bacon, cheese tossed with cornstarch, cream, and milk; heat through, but do not boil.

144

Thick-Cut Bacon: Thick-cut bacon is much sturdier than regular bacon, so it stands up to the long cooking time in the moist environment. This type of bacon has to be cooked slowly, over medium-low heat, so it cooks through and becomes very crisp. Don't turn the bacon until it releases easily from the pan.

• • • • RECIPE VARIATION • • • •

Ham Potato Chowder: Make recipe as directed, except use 1½ pounds ham, cubed, in place of the bacon. Cook the onion and garlic in 2 tablespoons butter and 2 tablespoons olive oil. Add the ham to the soup along with the stock. Add 1 teaspoon dried thyme along with the basil.

Cook Bacon

- Thick-cut bacon is actually deep-fried; it cooks in the large amount of fat it releases.

- You can reduce the fat content by removing some of the fat as it is rendered.

- When the bacon is an even brown color and the sound has really reduced, remove to a stack of paper towels.

- Let the bacon stand for a few minutes, then cut it with a knife into small pieces.

Simmer Soup

- For a richer, deeper soup, use beef broth in place of the vegetable broth.

- To test the potatoes for doneness, slide a sharp knife into one. It should go in easily with little effort and come back out easily.

- Use a potato masher, a large fork, or an immersion blender to mash some of the potatoes.

- Leave some potatoes whole to add to the character and texture of the soup.

TWO POTATO CHOWDER
Russet and Yukon Gold potatoes add color and flavor to this soup

Russet potatoes and Yukon Gold potatoes are the two used in this easy soup. But you can use a combination of any two varieties. Russet potatoes and sweet potatoes would be delicious, or red potatoes and Yukon Gold potatoes.

Rosemary and thyme are a nice combination with potatoes. The earthiness and strong flavor of rosemary, combined with the lemony, minty flavor of thyme, add a great dimension to the soup.

Mustard is a great addition to potato soups. It adds a tangy, spicy note. You can use plain yellow mustard, Dijon mustard, honey mustard, or coarse-grained mustard.

Serve this soup with a green salad made with mixed greens, croutons, and blue cheese and a glass of nice dry white wine.

Yield: Serves 6–8

Ingredients

2 tablespoons butter

1 tablespoon olive oil

1 onion, chopped

3 shallots, minced

3 tablespoons flour

1 teaspoon salt

¼ teaspoon white pepper

6 cups chicken broth, homemade or store-bought

3 russet potatoes, peeled and cubed

3 Yukon Gold potatoes, peeled and cubed

2 cups frozen corn

1 teaspoon minced fresh rosemary leaves

2 teaspoons minced fresh thyme leaves

1 cup light cream

2 tablespoons Dijon mustard

Two Potato Chowder

- Heat butter and olive oil in large pot over medium heat. Add onion and shallots; cook and stir 5 minutes.

- Add flour, salt, and pepper; cook and stir 5 minutes. Add broth; bring to a simmer, stirring with wire whisk.

- Add potatoes, corn, rosemary, and thyme. Bring to a simmer; simmer 15 to 20 minutes, until potatoes are tender.

- Partially puree soup. In bowl, combine cream and mustard; stir into soup; heat through.

146

Grilled Bread Sticks: Cut an Italian bread loaf in half crosswise, then cut each piece lengthwise into 8 bread sticks. Mix ½ cup melted butter, ¼ cup olive oil, 2 teaspoons dried Italian seasoning, and 1 teaspoon each garlic and onion powder. Dip bread sticks in this mixture, then grill over low heat 5 to 8 minutes.

Sweet Potato Chowder: Make recipe as directed, except use 3 russet potatoes and 2 large sweet potatoes, both peeled and cubed. Add the sweet potatoes to the broth first; simmer 10 minutes, then add russet potatoes; simmer until tender. Proceed with soup.

Cook Flour

- You're making a white roux in this recipe, since the flour is cooked only 5 minutes.

- For a toasty flavor you can cook the flour with the onions and shallots 10 to 15 minutes, until it begins to turn color.

- The flour will still have its thickening properties, but will add a complex flavor to the soup.

- A wire whisk is essential for creating a smooth roux and therefore a smooth and creamy soup.

Add Cream and Mustard

- Light cream enhances the flavors of the potatoes and creates a velvety texture.

- For a richer soup, you can use heavy cream, and for a lighter soup, use fat-free half-and-half or evaporated milk.

- Take some time to browse through your grocery store's condiment aisle to see all the different kinds of mustard available.

- Mix the cream with the mustard and stir with a wire whisk so the mustard dissolves evenly in the soup.

POTATO

VICHYSSOISE
Potatoes and leeks make an elegant soup perfect for a first course

This soup with the fancy name is just cold potato soup. But it's much more than that. Onion, leeks, and garlic cooked in butter make a flavorful base for this elegant soup.

The origins of this soup are murky; it may have been invented in New York City or in France in the 1800s.

When the soup is well seasoned and served with a sprinkling of chives, it's fit for the fanciest party. It's also an excellent soup to serve on a hot summer day. The soup is very inexpensive, especially if you omit the leeks and use another onion and another clove of garlic.

For a change of pace, make the soup with Yukon Gold or sweet potatoes.

Yield: Serves 6

Ingredients

2 tablespoons butter

1 onion, chopped

2 leeks, chopped

2 cloves garlic, minced

5 potatoes, peeled and chopped

1 teaspoon salt

1/8 teaspoon white pepper

1 bay leaf

2 sprigs thyme

6 cups chicken broth, homemade or store-bought

1/2 cup light cream

1/4 cup sour cream

1 tablespoon chopped chives

Vichyssoise

- Melt butter in large saucepan. Add onion and leeks; cook and stir 5 minutes.

- Add garlic, potatoes, salt, pepper, bay leaf, and thyme; cook and stir 4 minutes.

- Add chicken broth; bring to a boil. Cover pan, reduce heat to low, and simmer 20 to 30 minutes, until potatoes are tender.

- Remove from heat and puree. Remove bay leaf and thyme stems and chill. Stir in cream and sour cream before serving; top with chives.

Bacon Chive Muffins: Mix 2 cups flour, 2 tablespoons sugar, 1 teaspoon each baking soda and baking powder, 2 tablespoons minced chives. Mix 2 eggs, ¾ cup buttermilk, and ⅓ cup oil; add to dry ingredients. Add 1 cup shredded cheddar and ½ cup crisp bacon bits. Spoon into twelve muffin cups. Bake at 400°F 20 to 25 minutes. Yield: 12 muffins.

Sweet Potato Vichyssoise: Make recipe as directed, except add another garlic clove and use 3 sweet potatoes, peeled and chopped, in place of the regular potatoes. Simmer soup 30 to 40 minutes, until potatoes are tender. Add 1 teaspoon dried thyme leaves, and garnish the soup with chives and grated Parmesan cheese.

Prepare Vegetables

Add Cream

POTATO

- Be sure to thoroughly rinse the leek after cutting it apart to remove grit and sand that is trapped when the leek grows.

- The leek and onion will soften at about the same rate, but the garlic is added later so it doesn't burn.

- Be sure to cook the potatoes until they are very tender for the smoothest and creamiest soup.

- An immersion blender and a food processor work equally well to puree the soup.

- Use a whisk to add the cream and sour cream; stir until the soup is smooth.

- The soup should chill 4 to 6 hours. Stir once or twice during the chilling time.

- When you are ready to serve the soup, you may need to add some more cream or milk if it's too thick.

- Correct the seasoning, if necessary, by adding more salt and pepper. Serve the soup in chilled bowls so it stays cold longer.

CREAM OF POTATO SOUP
The classic recipe is satisfying and easy to make

Cream of potato soup is one of the simplest soups to make, but one of the most difficult to make well. The soup has to contain lots of spices and be well seasoned, or it will just be bland and boring.

Herbs and spices that complement potatoes include celery, thyme, mustard, dill, and pepper. Use variations of these ingredients, like dry mustard powder and celery seeds, to add flavor and character to this soup.

This soup can be used as a base for lots of variations, too. Add some shrimp or other seafood, add a cup or two of chopped ham, or add sautéed mushrooms and bell peppers to make a potato vegetable soup.

Yield: Serves 6–8

Ingredients

1/4 cup butter

1 leek, chopped

4 cloves garlic, minced

3 tablespoons flour

5 cups chicken stock, homemade or store-bought

1 teaspoon salt

1/8 teaspoon pepper

1/2 teaspoon dried dill weed

1/2 teaspoon celery seed

1 teaspoon dried thyme

1/2 teaspoon mustard powder

6 russet potatoes, peeled and diced

1/2 cup finely shredded carrots

2 stalks celery, diced

2 cups light cream

Cream of Potato Soup

- In large pot melt butter over medium heat. Add leek and garlic; cook and stir 6 minutes.

- Sprinkle with flour; cook and stir 5 minutes. Add stock, salt, pepper, dill, celery seed, thyme, and mustard powder; bring to a simmer.

- Add potatoes, carrots, and celery; stir well, then simmer 15 to 20 minutes, until potatoes are very tender.

- Partially puree soup using immersion blender. Stir in cream; heat through, but do not boil.

ZOOM

The secret to potato soup is to use enough salt. The potatoes absorb salt like sponges. When the soup is almost done, taste it and keep adding salt. When the soup suddenly tastes alive and rich, you've added the right amount.

• • • • RECIPE VARIATION • • • •

Cream of Potato Vegetable Soup: Make recipe as directed, except add an 8-ounce package sliced cremini mushrooms and cook in the butter with leek and garlic. After the mixture has been partially pureed, add 1 cup frozen corn and ¼ cup dry white wine and simmer until done.

Cook Leek and Garlic

- You can substitute one chopped onion for the leek if you'd like, or use a minced shallot in place of the garlic.

- You can add other vegetables at this point, including chopped mushrooms or green onions.

- Cook the vegetables gently in the butter. You don't want them to brown; just soften.

- When you add the stock and seasonings, stir well with a wire whisk so the soup will be smooth.

Rustic Soup

- The soup should simmer gently, not boil, until the vegetables are very tender. Test using a sharp knife.

- For a rustic soup, you can use a potato masher to mash some of the potatoes, leaving others whole.

- Garnish the soup with some chopped chives or sliced green onions.

- A sprinkle of thyme or some thyme sprigs is another good garnish, giving your guests a hint of what's to come.

LOADED BAKED POTATO SOUP
Just like a loaded baked potato, this soup has it all

Think of your favorite toppings for a baked potato: bacon, sour cream, shredded cheese, sautéed onions, garlic. Now think of all of those ingredients combined in a rich and thick soup.

This is a soup to enjoy and have fun making. It's a delicious soup to serve after a sledding party or after a cold afternoon at a football game.

Because the potatoes are baked before simmering in the soup, its texture is a bit different from Cream of Potato Soup. The potatoes will be a bit softer and creamier.

You can add anything you'd like to this soup to make it your own. Add some salsa for a Tex-Mex flair, or cook some curry powder with the onions and butter.
Yield: Serves 6–8

Ingredients

5 russet potatoes

6 slices bacon

3 tablespoons butter

1 onion, chopped

2 cloves garlic, minced

1 cup grated carrot

1 cup sliced mushrooms

3 tablespoons flour

1 teaspoon salt

1/4 teaspoon white pepper

Pinch nutmeg

3 cups chicken broth, homemade or store-bought

3 cups milk

1 cup shredded cheddar cheese

1/2 cup sour cream

1 tablespoon cornstarch

1/3 cup basil pesto

Loaded Baked Potato Soup

- Prick potatoes; bake at 400°F 50 to 60 minutes, until tender. Let cool 30 minutes; remove flesh.

- Cook bacon in pot until crisp. Drain, crumble, and set aside. Drain pot.

- Add butter, onion, garlic, carrot, and mushrooms; cook 6 minutes. Add flour, salt, pepper, and nutmeg; cook 5 minutes.

- Add broth and potato flesh; simmer 15 minutes. Add milk, cheese, and sour cream mixed with corn-starch; heat through. Puree soup and garnish with bacon and pesto.

Baked Sweet Potato Soup: Make recipe as directed, except use 4 sweet potatoes, baked, instead of the russet potatoes. Add 1 tablespoon curry powder with the onion and garlic. When you add the potato flesh to the soup, add 1 minced green bell pepper. Use Havarti cheese.

Potato Skins: Mix 3 tablespoons oil, 3 tablespoons Romano cheese, ½ teaspoon salt, ½ teaspoon paprika, and 1 teaspoon chili powder; brush on reserved potato skins. Bake at 425°F 15 minutes, turning once. Top with 1 cup shredded cheddar cheese; 4 slices bacon, crumbled; and ½ cup sour cream.

Remove Potatoes from Skins

- If you're planning to make potato skins, be careful when removing the flesh from the skin.

- Use a spoon and cradle the potato in your hand. Leave about ¼ inch potato flesh in the skins to hold them together.

- You can break the potato flesh up with a spoon before adding it to the soup.

- You can freeze the potato skins, well wrapped, up to 2 months. Thaw in the refrigerator overnight.

Puree Soup

- For a chunkier soup, just partially puree the mixture. If you like it really rustic, add the potato skins, too!

- If you are going to puree the soup in a food processor, do it in two or three batches.

- Any more soup at once and it may overflow the food processor and make a mess, or hurt you.

- You can stir the bacon and pesto into the soup or use it as a garnish.

POTATO

SWEET POTATO BISQUE

Sweet potatoes, so rich in vitamin A, are transformed into an elegant soup

Sweet potatoes were made for this recipe. The root vegetables are already rich and smooth, with a wonderful sweet taste. Combine that with cream and spices in a soup, and you've taken the vegetable to a new level.

This soup is a great idea for the holidays. It's a new way to serve sweet potatoes, and gets you away from those casse-roles topped with mini-marshmallows.

The apple adds a lighter accent to the soup, but you can leave it out for a more intense flavor. Orange is another fruit that will accent sweet potatoes, either the juice or the zest.

Yield: Serves 6

Ingredients

2 tablespoons butter	1 teaspoon salt
1 Granny Smith apple, peeled and chopped	$1/8$ teaspoon pepper
1 onion, chopped	$1/4$ teaspoon cinnamon
3 cloves garlic, minced	Pinch nutmeg
1 tablespoon grated ginger root	Pinch allspice
3 sweet potatoes, peeled and cubed	1 cup light cream
1 carrot, peeled and sliced	2 tablespoons cornstarch
6 cups chicken stock, homemade or store-bought	

Sweet Potato Bisque

- In large pot melt butter; add apple, onion, and garlic; cook and stir 5 minutes.

- Add ginger root, sweet potatoes, and carrot; cook 5 minutes. Add broth, salt, and pepper; bring to a simmer.

- Simmer 15 to 25 minutes, until vegetables are tender. Add cinnamon, nutmeg, and allspice.

- Puree soup using immersion blender. Combine cream and cornstarch; add to soup and heat through.

• • • • RECIPE VARIATIONS • • • •

Spicy Sweet Potato Bisque: Make recipe as directed, except add 1 minced habañero pepper and 1 chopped poblano pepper to the soup with the sweet potatoes. Omit cinnamon, nutmeg, and allspice; add 2 tablespoons adobo sauce and 1 tablespoon chili powder. Garnish with roasted pumpkin or sunflower seeds.

Sweet Potato Mushroom Bisque: Make recipe as directed, except add 2 cups sliced button or cremini mushrooms. Omit apple, cinnamon, nutmeg, and allspice. Add 1 teaspoon each dried thyme and dried marjoram with the salt and pepper. Garnish with crumbled bacon and some chopped chives.

Cook Sweet Potatoes

- To grate the ginger root, cut off a piece, peel it, and grate on a microplane grater.

- Cut the sweet potatoes into even cubes about ½-inch square so they cook evenly and are done at the same time.

- You don't want to cook the sweet potatoes until they're crisp; they should just soften.

- This step also lets the sweet potatoes absorb some of the flavor from the onion, garlic, and ginger root.

Simmer Soup

- You can use vegetable broth instead of chicken broth for a vegetarian version.

- You can use leftover cooked sweet potatoes or drained canned potatoes in this soup.

- If you do, add the carrots, simmer 10 minutes, then add the potatoes. Simmer another 5 to 10 minutes to blend soup; proceed with recipe.

- Garnish soup with chopped fresh apple and grated cinnamon or with sour cream and candied ginger root.

POTATO

CREAMY LENTIL BISQUE
The humble lentil becomes a fancy soup with just a few ingredients

Lentils are one of the most inexpensive foods in the world, as well as the most nutritious. They are fat free and contain lots of fiber and the vitamin B complex. They are also high in iron and protein.

Lentils are a healthy food for other reasons, too. They help lower cholesterol and regulate blood sugar levels, all for about 200 calories a cup.

Lentils are very quick cooking compared to other dried beans and peas. You don't need to soak them or even use the quicker boil-and-soak method.

Even though lentils are so inexpensive and easy to find, they can be made into an elegant soup with little effort. This is a soup to make often.

Yield: Serves 6

Ingredients

1 tablespoon olive oil

1 onion, chopped

3 cloves garlic, minced

1 teaspoon salt

$1/8$ teaspoon pepper

3 carrots, sliced

2 stalks celery, sliced

2 cups red lentils, rinsed

2 tablespoons tomato paste

1 teaspoon dried basil leaves

5 cups chicken broth, homemade or store-bought

1 cup water

1 cup light cream

1 tablespoon cornstarch

Creamy Lentil Bisque

- In large pot heat olive oil; add onion, garlic, salt, and pepper; cook 5 minutes.

- Add carrots and celery; cook 4 minutes. Then add lentils, tomato paste, basil, and 1 cup chicken broth; stir until blended.

- Add rest of chicken broth and water; simmer 40 to 50 minutes, until lentils are tender.

- Puree the soup in a food processor or with immersion blender. Combine cream with cornstarch; add to soup and cook 10 minutes.

Gougere: Mix 1 cup milk, ¼ cup butter, ½ teaspoon salt, and ½ teaspoon thyme in pan; bring to rolling boil. Add 1 cup flour; stir until ball forms. Remove from heat; add 4 eggs, then 1 cup shredded Gruyère. Drop by teaspoons onto greased cookie sheet; bake at 375°F 12 to 17 minutes, until puffed and golden brown.

Curried Lentil Bisque: Make recipe as directed, except add 1 tablespoon curry powder when you cook the onions and garlic. Omit tomato paste and basil; add ½ cup chutney blended with the cream and cornstarch. Garnish with chopped pistachios.

Sort Lentils

- Like all produce lentils must be sorted and rinsed before using in soups or any other recipe.

- When lentils are harvested, twigs, small pebbles, leaves, stems, and dirt can be mixed with them.

- Spread the lentils on a plate or countertop and look through them. Discard shriveled lentils as well as any extraneous material.

- Then rinse the lentils with cool running water and drain. They're now ready to use.

Add Lentils

- Lentils need at least 30 minutes of cooking to become tender.

- You can cook lentils al dente or until they fall apart and practically dissolve in the soup; it's up to you.

- You can use both of these characteristics in your soup to add texture and interest.

- Cook lentils for a long time, until they fall apart, then add more 30 minutes before the soup is done so some remain discrete.

LENTIL

LENTIL & POTATO SOUP
Potatoes and lentils are an odd, but sublime, combination

Lentils and potatoes are a delicious combination that makes a hearty soup for pennies per serving. This soup is very filling and satisfying and can be flavored many different ways.

Instead of using warm spices like curry or cumin, add herbs like basil and thyme for a bright taste. Or add hot chile peppers and cumin to make the soup spicy and hot.

As long as the potatoes are cut into a size smaller than a ½-inch cube, they will cook in the same time frame as the lentils, so the soup is easy to make.

Any combination of vegetables can be used in this soup. Use exotic mushrooms, or add a chopped green, yellow, or red bell pepper.

Yield: Serves 6

Ingredients

3 tablespoons butter

1 onion, chopped

4 cloves garlic, minced

2 carrots, sliced

2 russet potatoes, peeled and cubed

2 cups sliced mushrooms

1 stalk celery, with leaves, chopped

1 teaspoon salt

⅛ teaspoon pepper

1 teaspoon curry powder

1 teaspoon cumin

⅛ teaspoon cardamom

⅛ teaspoon nutmeg

2 cups green lentils

6 cups vegetable broth, homemade or store-bought

2 cups baby spinach

Lentil and Potato Soup

- In large pot melt butter; add onion and garlic. Cook and stir 5 minutes.

- Add carrots, potatoes, mushrooms, celery, salt, pepper, and curry powder; cook and stir 5 minutes.

- Add cumin, cardamom, nutmeg, lentils, and broth; bring to a simmer. Simmer 30 to 40 minutes, until lentils are tender.

- Partially puree soup, if desired. Add spinach; simmer 5 to 6 minutes, until soup is steaming.

Spicy Lentil Potato Soup: Make recipe as directed, except add 2 minced jalapeño or serrano peppers with the onions and garlic. Omit curry, cumin, cardamom, and nutmeg; add 1 tablespoon chili powder and 1 teaspoon cumin. Omit 1 cup water; add 1 cup salsa; simmer until lentils and potatoes are tender.

Lentil Sweet Potato Soup: Make recipe as directed, except substitute 1 sweet potato, peeled and cubed, in place of the russet potatoes. Increase curry powder to 2 teaspoons. Omit spinach; add ½ cup heavy cream and heat until steaming. Garnish with sunflower seeds and chopped celery leaves.

Cook Vegetables

Add Lentils and Broth

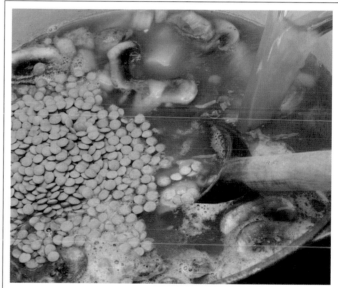

- You can substitute olive oil, vegetable oil, or bacon fat for the butter if you'd like.

- Or for a very low-fat soup, simmer the onions and garlic in about ¼ cup vegetable broth.

- This is a trick you can use with any soup if you're interested in very low-fat foods.

- This technique will also work with chicken and beef broth. The flavor of the onions and garlic won't be as intense.

- Lentils are one of the oldest foods known to humans. They are delicious in soups or salads.

- You can keep dried lentils in the pantry for a long time—up to two years. Decant into plastic or glass jars for best results.

- In fact, different lentils arrayed in glass jars make a pretty and useful kitchen decoration.

- Interestingly, lentils are never available fresh, only dried. You can use a combination in this recipe if you'd like.

LENTIL

LENTIL SCOTCH BROTH
Barley is usually used in Scotch broth; lentils are a nice change

Scotch broth is a rich soup made from lamb or beef bones, along with root vegetables like carrots, turnips, and onions.

Barley is the grain usually used in Scotch broth, but lentils are a good and almost authentic substitute. They make the soup slightly more cloudy than barley but are still very delicious.

Use more unfamiliar root vegetables, like parsnips, turnips, and swedes, also known as rutabagas, in this soup. These knobbly roots are peeled and diced. They add a sweet and earthy taste to the soup.

Serve this broth with some biscuits or crackers hot from the oven, along with a winter fruit salad of apples and pears in a sweet, tart dressing.

Yield: Serves 6–8

KNACK SOUP CLASSICS

Ingredients

2 pounds lamb shanks

1 teaspoon salt

1/8 teaspoon pepper

2 tablespoons olive oil

1 onion, chopped

2 carrots, sliced

1 parsnip, cubed

1 teaspoon salt

1/4 teaspoon pepper

8 cups water

2 cups green lentils

2 cups baby spinach

1 tablespoon lemon juice

Lentil Scotch Broth

- Sprinkle lamb shanks with salt and pepper. Brown in olive oil over medium heat.

- Add onion; cook and stir 5 minutes. Add carrots, parsnip, salt, pepper, and water.

- Bring to a simmer; cover and simmer 2 hours. Remove lamb shanks; cut off meat and return to soup. Simmer soup, uncovered, 40 minutes to reduce.

- Add lentils to soup; simmer 40 to 50 minutes, until tender. Add spinach and lemon juice; heat through, until spinach wilts.

Cheese Biscuits: Mix 2 cups flour, 1 teaspoon each baking powder and baking soda, ½ teaspoon garlic salt. Cut in ⅓ cup butter until particles are fine. Add ½ cup buttermilk, 1 cup shredded cheddar, and ¼ cup grated Parmesan. Drop onto greased cookie sheets; bake at 400° 12 to 15 minutes.

ZOOM

Lentils come in several colors and types. Green or brown lentils are the most common, along with black, or beluga, lentils and red lentils. French lentils, also known as Puy, are a dark blue green color. Don't cook lentils in a pressure cooker, as they can clog the valve.

Brown Lamb Shanks

Add Water

- Because this soup is supposed to be brothy instead of creamy, the lamb shanks aren't coated in flour.

- Just sprinkle them with salt and pepper and cook until nicely browned.

- Don't move the shanks until they release easily from the pan. Pull on them gently; if they won't move, leave them alone.

- When you add the onion, stir well to remove all the browned bits from the bottom of the pan.

- Since you're using lamb shanks in this recipe, water is the preferred liquid.

- Using beef or even chicken broth would make the flavor of the soup too intense.

- This soup can be made in a slow cooker. Just cook, without the lentils, on low 7 to 8 hours.

- Remove the meat from the shanks, return to soup with the lentils, and cook on high 50 to 60 minutes, until the lentils are tender.

LENTIL

LENTIL SOUP

Lentils are the perfect soup ingredient: tender, nutty, and delicious

Different colored lentils cook to different textures. French and Puy lentils remain the firmest, even after longer cooking times. Green lentils become more tender, but don't disintegrate and retain their shape.

Brown lentils, which are the most common, become quite soft when cooked. For a lentil soup with several textures, cook for a long period using brown lentils, then add Puy or green lentils during the last 45 minutes of cooking time.

The key to a good lentil soup is layering the flavors with several types of vegetables, spices, and herbs—although you can make lentil soup with just water, lentils, and an onion or two. Enjoy these easy soups.

Yield: Serves 6

KNACK SOUP CLASSICS

Ingredients

1 tablespoon olive oil

1 tablespoon butter

1 onion, chopped

1 leek, chopped

2 cups sliced mushrooms

3 carrots, sliced

1 teaspoon salt

1/4 teaspoon pepper

1 teaspoon cumin

1/2 teaspoon ground coriander

2 cups Puy lentils

5 cups chicken or vegetable broth, homemade or store-bought

1 cup water

2 tablespoons lemon juice

Lentil Soup

- In large pot heat olive oil and butter over medium heat. Add onion and leek; cook and stir 5 minutes.

- Add mushrooms, carrots, salt, and pepper; cook 4 minutes longer. Add cumin, coriander, and lentils.

- Pour in broth and water; bring to a simmer. Simmer 30 to 40 minutes, until lentils and vegetables are tender.

- You can puree the soup at this point or leave it alone. Stir in the lemon juice just before serving.

Mini-Focaccia: Open 1 can refrigerated breadstick dough; don't unroll. Separate into 8 rounds. Mix ⅓ cup grated Romano cheese, 2 cloves minced garlic, and 2 teaspoons minced fresh rosemary. Press on dough to make 6-inch circles. Brush with 2 tablespoons olive oil; sprinkle with cheese mixture. Bake at 375°F 10 to 15 minutes.

Simplest Lentil Soup: Make recipe as directed, except add 3 cloves minced garlic. Omit leek, mushrooms, and carrots. You can use some of these vegetables if you'd like. When onions and garlic are tender, add the spices and lentils with the broth. Simmer until lentils are tender.

Cook Onion and Leek

- For a more complex flavor without adding any more ingredients, caramelize the onion and leek.

- Just keep on cooking them, stirring frequently, until the onions and leek are brown.

- The deeper the color, the sweeter and more intense the flavor. Just don't let them burn.

- For more flavor and a stronger soup, you could also cook the mushrooms until deep brown.

Add Lentils

- You can add as much as 8 cups broth or as little as 4, depending on how thick you want the soup to be.

- Other spices and herbs would be good in this recipe; try dried basil and thyme, or curry powder and cinnamon.

- Red, green, or black lentils can be used instead of the Puy lentils if you'd like.

- Puree or partially puree the mixture, or mash with a potato masher, for a different texture.

LENTIL

LENTIL CHICKPEA SOUP

Aromatic spices add a warm flavor to this easy soup

Chickpeas and lentils are natural partners. And this soup, made with vegetables, ginger root, and warm spices, is evocative of Morocco and the Middle East.

Chickpeas are also known as garbanzo beans. These legumes are nutty with a smooth texture. They take a long time to cook, so using canned chickpeas is an excellent alternative. Just drain and rinse them before use.

The combination of lentils and chickpeas doesn't provide complete proteins. You need to combine legumes with wheat, rice, or corn to make the full complement of amino acids your body needs.

Serve this lovely soup with some chewy and well-seasoned Herbed Bread Sticks and a mixed green salad with some chopped green and yellow bell peppers.

Yield: Serves 6

Ingredients

2 tablespoons olive oil

1 onion, chopped

3 cloves garlic, minced

3 carrots, sliced

2 cups sliced cremini mushrooms

1 tablespoon grated ginger root

1 teaspoon salt

1/8 teaspoon pepper

1/2 teaspoon cinnamon

1/2 teaspoon paprika

2 tomatoes, peeled, seeded, and chopped

1 1/2 cups black lentils

4 cups vegetable broth, homemade or store-bought

3 cups water

1 (15-ounce) can chickpeas, drained and rinsed

Lentil Chickpea Soup

- In large pot heat olive oil over medium heat. Add onion, garlic, and carrots; cook and stir 5 minutes.

- Add mushrooms, ginger root, salt, and pepper; simmer 5 minutes, stirring frequently.

- Add cinnamon, paprika, tomatoes, lentils, broth, and water; bring to a simmer.

- Simmer soup 30 to 40 minutes, until lentils are very tender. Add chickpeas; simmer 5 minutes longer.

Herbed Lentil Chickpea Soup: Make recipe as directed, except add 1 teaspoon dried thyme leaves and 1 teaspoon dried marjoram leaves along with the salt and pepper. Omit ginger root, cinnamon, and paprika. When the soup is done, add 2 tablespoons minced fresh basil leaves. Garnish soup with fresh thyme sprigs.

Cheesy Yeast Rolls: In saucepan melt 2 tablespoons butter in ¾ cup buttermilk. Pour into bowl; add 1 package yeast and 1 egg; beat. Add 2 cups flour, 1 tablespoon sugar, 1 teaspoon thyme, ¼ teaspoon salt, ¾ cup Parmesan cheese; beat well. Divide among 12 greased muffin cups; let rise 30 minutes. Bake at 375°F 18 to 23 minutes.

Prepare Vegetables

- Cremini mushrooms are baby portobellos. They are light brown and have a nutty, rich flavor.

- To prepare, just wipe with a damp cloth and trim off the bottom of the stems. Slice and add to soup.

- If you want to use dried mushrooms, soak ½ cup in 1 cup boiling water until soft.

- Trim off stems and discard; chop tops. Strain the soaking liquid and add to soup.

Add Lentils and Broth

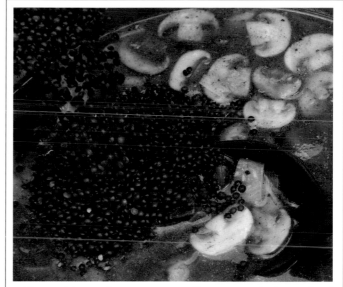

- You could use other types of lentils if you'd like. Green and Puy lentils keep their shape best in soup.

- For a thicker soup, use red or brown lentils. They will almost dissolve into the broth, thickening the soup.

- You can use chicken or beef broth in this recipe for a heartier flavor, or just use water.

- For added flavor, grate some fresh cinnamon and nutmeg over the soup just before you serve it.

LENTIL

BARLEY LENTIL BEEF SOUP
There aren't many soups heartier or easier than this

For one of the richest, heartiest, and most filling soups on the planet, turn to this one. The beef becomes meltingly tender, the barley adds a slightly chewy nuttiness, and the lentils provide a wonderful color, flavor, and texture contrast.

This is the soup to make on a cold and snowy day when the schools are closed and everyone is cozy at home.

The Puy lentils will retain their shape and texture in this soup, round and shiny dark green nuggets against the white barley and dark brown meat.

This soup doesn't need much to be a complete meal. Serve it with some hot scones or Cheese Muffins hot from the oven and a chocolate layer cake for dessert. Yum.

Yield: Serves 6

Ingredients

2 pounds beef bottom round

2 tablespoons flour

1 teaspoon salt

1/4 teaspoon pepper

1 teaspoon dried marjoram leaves

1 teaspoon dried oregano leaves

2 tablespoons butter

2 onions, chopped

3 cloves garlic, minced

3 carrots, sliced

2 stalks celery, sliced

1/2 cup barley

1/2 cup Puy lentils

4 tomatoes, peeled, seeded, and diced

6 cups beef stock, homemade or store-bought

2 cups water

1/2 cup red wine

1 bay leaf

Barley Lentil Beef Soup

- Cut beef into 1½-inch cubes; sprinkle with flour, salt, pepper, marjoram, and oregano.

- Brown beef in butter in large saucepan, about 4 to 5 minutes. Remove from pan. Add onions and garlic to pan; cook and stir 4 minutes.

- Place carrots, celery, barley, lentils, and tomatoes in 4- to 5-quart slow cooker. Add onion mixture; top with beef.

- Add stock, water, wine, and bay leaf. Cover and cook on low 8 to 9 hours, until blended. Remove bay leaf; serve.

166

Quinoa Lentil Soup: Make recipe as directed, except use ½ cup quinoa instead of barley. Rinse the quinoa well before adding it to the soup. Add 1 cup chopped mushrooms along with the carrots and celery. Omit oregano; add 1 teaspoon dried thyme leaves.

Barley Lentil Chicken Soup: Make recipe as directed, except substitute 2 pounds boneless, skinless chicken breasts, cut into strips, for the beef bottom round. Use chicken broth in place of the beef broth. Omit marjoram and oregano; use 1 teaspoon each thyme and basil leaves, and use white wine in place of the red.

Brown Beef

Layer Ingredients

LENTIL

- Browning the beef makes the soup taste richer because it caramelizes. The sugars and proteins in the meat break down and recombine.

- Flour also browns during this step, which adds a nutty flavor to the soup

- and helps in the thickening process.

- Don't skip this browning step, especially for slow cooker soups.

- Since no browning takes place in the slow cooker, you must do it manually.

- If you'd prefer to cook this soup on the stovetop, brown the beef and add onions and garlic.

- Then just add the remaining ingredients and simmer 2 to 3 hours until beef, barley, and lentils are tender.

- The onions and garlic are cooked in the pan drippings so they help release the drippings from the pan.

- You can add a bit of stock to the pan, too, to make sure all the flavorful drippings are included in the soup.

MUSHROOM EGG DROP SOUP
This simple soup is quick to make and satisfying

Egg drop soup is a classic Chinese recipe. This delicate soup is made even more delicious by the addition of several different types of mushrooms.

In a soup as simple as this one, the quality of the broth is very important. If you haven't made broth from scratch before, this soup is the time to try it. The mushrooms will add flavor to the soup, but the broth has to be very flavorful to begin with.

The second secret is to stir the soup in one direction while you add the egg. A squeeze bottle makes perfect strands of tender egg. Enjoy this easy soup.

Yield: Serves 6

Ingredients

1 cup sliced button mushrooms

1 cup chopped portobello mushrooms

1 cup enoki or shiitake mushrooms, trimmed

3 tablespoons butter

4 cups chicken broth, homemade or store-bought

$1/8$ teaspoon ground ginger

2 teaspoons cornstarch

2 eggs

$1/4$ cup slivered fresh basil leaves

$1/4$ cup minced green onion

Mushroom Egg Drop Soup

- In saucepan cook mushrooms in butter 6 minutes. Add chicken broth, ginger, and cornstarch; let simmer over low heat while you prepare the eggs.

- Beat eggs and pour into a small clean squeeze bottle with a small tip.

- Turn off the heat and slowly add the egg, squeezing the bottle gently, while constantly stirring the soup in one direction only.

- When the egg has formed cooked strands, stir in basil and garnish with green onion; serve immediately.

Classic Egg Drop Soup: Make recipe as directed, except add 1 minced onion and cook it in the butter; omit all the mushrooms. Add a pinch of grated nutmeg to the egg mixture. Add eggs as directed; garnish with parsley instead of onion.

Shrimp Toast: Remove crusts from 4 slices white bread and cut each into 4 triangles; lightly toast. Chop ⅓ pound raw shrimp with 1 tablespoon butter, 1 teaspoon grated ginger root, 2 tablespoons minced onion, and 1 egg. Spread over toast. Fry in peanut oil, turning once, 1½ to 2 minutes, until golden brown.

Egg in Squeeze Bottle

Stir Soup

- For the purest flavor, use a brand new squeeze bottle. You can find them in any supermarket in the baking aisle.

- Other squeeze bottles that contained other ingredients may retain aroma or flavor.

- Don't beat the eggs until you're ready to add the egg to the soup. Work quickly but carefully.

- You can flavor the egg if you'd like; add salt and pepper, ground ginger, or herbs or spices like thyme or five spice powder.

- The heat has to be off when you add the egg so it doesn't overcook and stays silky.

- The strands of egg should be very tender, so make sure they don't overcook.

- You want the eggs to be as evenly shaped as possible. The stirring motion helps the eggs stretch out as they cook.

- With practice you'll be able to make egg drop soup that looks like that of your favorite Chinese restaurant.

MUSHROOM

169

CREAM OF MUSHROOM SOUP

Just the pure essence of mushrooms in a creamy and velvety soup

Cream of mushroom soup doesn't have a very good reputation, because the only type most people have had is the canned condensed version.

While that may make recipe shortcuts and acceptable soup, there's nothing like the real thing, made with fresh and dried mushrooms.

Dried mushrooms are made from less common varieties, like morel or porcini. They have a woodsy, earthy taste that

adds a wonderful depth of flavor to the soup.

This soup is so special that it deserves its own course. Serve it, along with some simple water crackers, as part of an elegant meal.

Garnish the soup with some fresh chopped tarragon and thyme leaves and a slice of mushroom.

Yield: Serves 6

Ingredients

¹/₂ cup dried wild mushrooms

1 cup water

3 tablespoons butter

1 onion, chopped

2 cups sliced button mushrooms

2 cups sliced cremini mushrooms

1 teaspoon salt

¹/₈ teaspoon white pepper

¹/₂ teaspoon dried tarragon

4 cups chicken or vegetable broth, homemade or store-bought

1 teaspoon dried thyme leaves

1 cup light cream

2 tablespoons cornstarch

1 tablespoon sherry

Cream of Mushroom Soup

- Soak dried mushrooms in water 30 minutes. Drain, reserving liquid; strain liquid. Cut off mushroom ends and chop.

- Melt butter in pot; add onion and button and cremini mushrooms. Cook and stir 10 minutes to brown mushrooms.

- Add salt, white pepper, tarragon, wild mushrooms, reserved liquid, broth, and thyme; bring to a simmer.

- Simmer soup 15 to 20 minutes, until mushrooms are tender. Combine cream and cornstarch; add to soup with sherry; heat until thickened.

Cream of Wild Mushroom Soup: Make recipe as directed, except use three varieties of dried wild mushrooms, about ¾ cup each before reconstituting. Strain the liquid very well through cheesecloth; substitute it for part of the chicken stock. Discard mushroom stems; chop the rest, then sauté; continue with the recipe.

ZOOM

Dried mushrooms include porcini, morels, shiitake, oyster, truffle, boletes, and black trumpet. They store very well, as long as they are kept in an airtight container. The liquid you use to reconstitute them is very flavorful, as long as it is well strained after the mushrooms are soft.

Prepare Wild Mushrooms

- The dried mushrooms are usually reconstituted in twice as much water as mushrooms.

- The water has to be boiling hot to force the liquid into the cells of the mushrooms.

- Dried mushrooms are very low in calories, have no fat or sodium, and are very high in fiber. They are also a good source of vitamin D.

- You have to discard the stems; they just don't become soft enough to be edible.

Add Seasonings and Broth

- Salt is essential to the taste of this soup. When you add the cream and cornstarch, taste the soup.

- Add salt a pinch at a time, tasting the soup after each. When the flavor suddenly blooms, you've added the perfect amount.

- This is another soup where a very good quality broth or stock is essential.

- You can substitute low-fat evaporated milk, nonfat half-and-half, or even heavy cream for the light cream.

MUSHROOM

PUMPKIN MUSHROOM BISQUE
This fall soup has the most gorgeous color, flavor, and texture

When the leaves turn color and the weather starts to feel cooler, that's the time to make this soup. It's full of the earthy flavors and rich colors of fall.

Solid pack canned pumpkin, not pumpkin puree, is the ingredient to use in this soup. The puree has added ingredients that will change the flavor and texture of the soup.

You can use any type of mushroom you can find in the su-permarket or farmers' market. Just wipe them with a damp cloth, trim the ends of the stems, and add to the pot.

This soup is perfect to serve as the centerpiece for a fall luncheon. Offer some Onion Cheese Scones and a salad made with baby spinach, apples, and bacon.

Yield: Serves 6

Ingredients

3 tablespoons butter

1 onion, chopped

1 tablespoon minced ginger root

2 cups sliced cremini mushrooms

1/2 teaspoon salt

1/8 teaspoon pepper

1/2 teaspoon curry powder

1/2 teaspoon pumpkin pie spice

2 tablespoons brown sugar

1 (15-ounce) can solid pack pumpkin

3 cups chicken stock, homemade or store-bought

1 cup water

2 egg yolks

1 cup light cream

1 tablespoon cornstarch

Curried Croutons

Pumpkin Mushroom Bisque

- In large pot melt butter over medium heat. Add onion, ginger root, and mushrooms; cook 10 minutes.

- Add salt, pepper, curry powder, pie spice, brown sugar, and pumpkin; cook and stir 5 minutes.

- Gradually add stock and water, stirring constantly until blended. Simmer 15 minutes.

- In bowl beat egg yolks, cream, and cornstarch; slowly add to soup. Heat through but do not boil. Serve with Curried Croutons.

Mushroom Bisque: Make recipe as directed, except add 2 more cups of sliced mushrooms, any variety. Omit the ginger root, curry powder, pumpkin pie spice, brown sugar, and canned pumpkin. Add 2 cloves minced garlic and 1 teaspoon each dried thyme and marjoram. Finish soup as directed.

Curried Croutons: Cut 3 slices oatmeal bread into cubes. Melt ¼ cup butter and add 2 teaspoons curry powder; drizzle over bread cubes and toss to coat. Sprinkle bread with mixture of 2 tablespoons brown sugar and 2 tablespoons sugar. Bake at 400°F 8 to 10 minutes, until crisp.

Simmer Mushrooms and Onions

- You can cook the onions and mushroom until they are just tender, or until they become a deeper brown.

- The soup will be delicious either way; it just depends on if you want a soup with a lighter flavor or a deep flavor.

- You can add other vegetables to the soup, like garlic or red or yellow bell peppers. Add with the broth.

- Substitute a minced leek and shallots for the chopped onion. You can also add more mushrooms.

Add Pumpkin

- To easily remove the pumpkin, open both ends with a can opener.

- Remove one end and use the other end to push the puree from the can. Add to soup in small spoonfuls.

- Stir the mixture well so the pumpkin cooks and caramelizes a little bit.

- You also want the pumpkin to blend with the vegetables so the broth can blend with it for the smoothest soup.

MUSHROOM

MUSHROOM WILD RICE CHOWDER

Wild rice adds nutty flavor and chewy texture to this thick chowder

Chowder made with mushrooms, chicken, vegetables, and wild rice has the most wonderful rich and earthy flavor.

This soup, like most chowder, shouldn't be served as a course or part of a dinner. It is hearty enough to serve as the centerpiece of the meal.

Variations are easy. Use chicken thighs instead of breasts; use thyme, oregano, or marjoram instead of basil. Vary the mushrooms—use button or dried mushrooms, or use brown rice in place of the wild rice.

You can also add ethnic flavors to the soup—curry powder for Indian, spicy chile peppers and salsa for Tex-Mex, or oregano and olives for a Greek touch. Enjoy this hearty soup with some hot scones or biscuits.

Yield: Serves 6

Ingredients

2 tablespoons butter

2 chicken breasts, cubed

2 tablespoons flour

1 teaspoon salt

1/8 teaspoon pepper

1 teaspoon dried basil leaves

1 onion, chopped

2 cloves garlic, minced

2 cups sliced cremini mushrooms

1 cup sliced shiitake mushrooms

1 cup wild rice

6 cups chicken stock, homemade or store-bought

1 cup water

2 carrots, sliced

1 cup frozen corn

1/2 cup heavy cream

1 cup shredded Swiss cheese

1 tablespoon cornstarch

Mushroom Wild Rice Chowder

- Melt butter in large pot. Sprinkle chicken with flour, salt, and pepper; cook in butter until done, about 9 to 11 minutes. Remove.

- Add basil, onion, garlic, and mushrooms to pot; cook and stir to loosen drippings, about 10 minutes.

- Add wild rice, stock, and water; bring to a simmer. Cover and simmer 30 minutes.

- Add carrot and corn; simmer 20 minutes. Add chicken and cream, then cheese tossed with cornstarch; heat through until thickened.

• • • • RECIPE VARIATIONS • • • •

Vegetarian Mushroom Chowder: Make recipe as directed, except add another 2 cups sliced button or ½ cup dried wild mushrooms. Omit the chicken breasts. Use vegetable stock in place of chicken broth. You can use soy milk and soy cheese if you'd like for a vegan soup.

Mushroom Ham Chowder: Make recipe as directed, except add 1½ cups cubed ham in place of chicken breasts. You can still use chicken broth, but vegetable broth would work well, too. Add 1 teaspoon dried thyme to the soup; finish as directed.

Cook Chicken

- Cut chicken into 1-inch pieces and toss with flour, salt, and pepper.

- After the chicken is cooked in the first step, you should refrigerate it if your kitchen is warm.

- If you use chicken thighs in place of breasts, cook them 10 minutes to start the recipe.

- Then add with the carrots and corn; simmer 20 to 30 minutes, until chicken is thoroughly cooked.

Cook Mushrooms and Onion

- The mushrooms and onion can be cooked just until crisp-tender, or until brown and all the liquid evaporates.

- If you decide to cook the vegetables until brown, be sure to keep an eye on them.

- The vegetables can turn from brown to burned in a matter of seconds.

- Other vegetables that would be good in this soup include artichoke hearts, diced potatoes, or chopped red bell peppers.

MUSHROOM

CURRIED MUSHROOM BISQUE

A creamy bisque is the perfect first course for a formal dinner

Mushrooms are generally very mild. The differences in their taste are subtle, so they combine well in soups.

Classic bisques are made with ground seafood shells to make a very concentrated stock. But the definition has expanded to include any creamy soup that is thickened with milk or cream and sometimes eggs.

If you love curry powder, you can use 3 or 4 teaspoons instead of just 2. Use a good variety of curry powder for best results.

Serve this soup in white stoneware or ceramic bowls or bisque china. It's a great starter for a dinner of roast chicken, scalloped potatoes, and greens and fruit salad.

Yield: Serves 6

Ingredients

$1/2$ cup dried morel mushrooms

1 cup water

1 onion, chopped

4 cloves garlic, minced

2 teaspoons curry powder

2 tablespoons butter

1 cup sliced button mushrooms

2 cups sliced shiitake mushrooms

$1/2$ teaspoon salt

$1/8$ teaspoon pepper

$1/2$ teaspoon dried marjoram leaves

3 cups chicken broth, homemade or store-bought

1 cup light cream

1 tablespoon cornstarch

Curried Mushroom Bisque

- In microwave-safe glass cup, place morel mushrooms; add water. Microwave on high 1 minute.

- In large saucepan cook onion, garlic, and curry powder in butter 4 minutes. Add button and shiitake mushrooms; cook 4 minutes.

- Drain morel mushrooms, reserving liquid; strain liquid. Trim and add to pot; cook 2 minutes. Sprinkle with salt, pepper, and marjoram.

- Add broth and strained soaking liquid, simmer 15 minutes; puree. Stir in cream and cornstarch until soup is thick and smooth.

Cheese Focaccia: Unroll 1 can refrigerated pizza dough; press on cookie sheet. Make indentations with fingers. Cook 4 cloves garlic in 2 tablespoons olive oil; drizzle over dough. Add 1 tablespoon each fresh thyme and marjoram, 1 cup shredded provolone, and ½ cup Parmesan. Bake at 400°F 12 to 17 minutes.

Herbed Mushroom Bisque: Make recipe as directed, except add 2 teaspoons each fresh thyme, basil, marjoram, and oregano. Omit curry powder. Beat 2 egg yolks with the cream and cornstarch; add and heat until soup is steaming.

Prepare Mushrooms

Add Slurry

- Wild mushrooms always have to be trimmed before use. If the stem isn't as tender as the rest of the mushroom, cut it off and discard.

- If the stems are tender, just trim off the bottom of the stem and discard. Add the mushrooms whole or sliced.

- You can slice or chop the mushrooms. This doesn't really matter since the soup is pureed.

- Use an immersion blender or transfer the soup, in batches, to a food processor.

- Use a wire whisk to mix the cream and cornstarch slurry and to mix it into the hot soup.

- For an even more elegant soup, you can strain it after it's pureed, before adding the cream and cornstarch.

- Press on the solids in the strainer to get every drop of flavorful liquid.

- Garnish with some sliced mushrooms sautéed until brown in a bit of butter, along with tiny croutons.

MUSHROOM

MUSHROOM BARLEY SOUP

Mushrooms and barley make a thick soup perfect for a cold night

For a soup that will warm you up on the coldest day, this is the recipe to try. Mushrooms and barley are natural partners. The tender mushrooms and slightly chewy barley, cooked in a rich beef broth, complement each other very well.

This soup is so thick, it is almost a stew. If you prefer a thinner soup, add more broth or water or reduce the barley to ½ cup.

Other vegetables would also be delicious in this soup, like chopped celery, bell peppers, or zucchini. Or add root vegetables like sliced carrots, diced peeled russet potatoes, or sweet potatoes.

Serve this soup in stoneware bowls or heavy mugs with some Garlic Toast.

Yield: Serves 6

Ingredients

2 tablespoons olive oil

1 tablespoon butter

1 onion, chopped

2 cloves garlic, minced

2 cups sliced button mushrooms

1 cup sliced cremini mushrooms

1 cup chopped portobello mushrooms

¾ cup barley

6 cups beef broth, homemade or store-bought

½ teaspoon salt

⅛ teaspoon pepper

1 teaspoon dried thyme leaves

Pinch nutmeg

Mushroom Barley Soup

- Heat olive oil and butter in large pot. Add onion, garlic, and all the mushrooms; cook and stir 10 minutes.

- Add barley, broth, salt, pepper, thyme, and nutmeg; bring to a simmer.

- Partially cover pot and simmer soup 35 to 45 minutes, until barley and mushrooms are tender.

- Serve soup with Garlic Croutons and a dollop of sour cream.

Beef and Mushroom Barley Soup: Make recipe as directed, except add 1½ pounds beef sirloin tip, cut into 1-inch cubes. Cook in olive oil and butter before you add the onion. Add 1 cup water with the beef broth. Simmer soup 50 to 60 minutes, until the beef and barley are tender.

Vegetarian Mushroom Barley Soup: Make soup as directed, except add 2 cups sliced carrots and 3 stalks sliced celery along with the barley. Use vegetable broth in place of beef broth. And add 1 teaspoon dried marjoram with the thyme and nutmeg.

Prepare Mushrooms

Add Barley and Broth

- Other mushroom combinations that would be good in this soup include shiitake and button mushrooms.

- Or think about using oyster, shiitake, and portobello mushrooms, all thinly sliced.

- Packaged mushrooms will last only two to three days in your refrigerator.

- The mushrooms can be sliced or chopped in this recipe. If they are very small, just trim the stems and add whole.

- You can use hulled, or pot, barley in this soup, or use pearl barley.

- Pearl barley is just hulled barley that has been more polished so it cooks a bit more quickly.

- For a lighter soup, use vegetable or chicken broth or stock. If you choose this option, add more herbs like basil or oregano.

- Taste the soup just before you serve it to see if it needs more salt, pepper, or other herbs.

MUSHROOM

VEGETABLE BEAN SOUP

Beans and vegetables cook to perfection in this hearty soup

Dried beans are some of the most inexpensive and nutritious foods in the supermarket. There are dozens of varieties, all delicious in soups. Dried beans and peas come in all the colors of the rainbow. In fact, you can make very beautiful soups just by varying the types of dried beans and peas you use.

Dried beans will triple in volume when cooked. So if you start with 1 cup dried beans, you'll end up with 3 cups cooked.

Canned beans can be substituted for dried. These only need to be reheated, as they are ready to eat right out of the can.

Enjoy this delicious and hearty soup with some crisp bread sticks and a green salad.

Yield: Serves 6–8

Ingredients

I pound dried navy beans, sorted

2 tablespoons olive oil

2 onions, chopped

3 cloves garlic, minced

3 carrots, sliced

2 russet potatoes, peeled and cubed

I teaspoon dried oregano

I teaspoon dried thyme

6 cups vegetable broth, homemade or store-bought

I teaspoon salt

1/8 teaspoon pepper

Vegetable Bean Soup

- Rinse beans and drain. Place in large pot, cover with cold water, and let soak overnight. In the morning, rinse and drain beans.

- In soup pot heat olive oil and cook onions and garlic 5 minutes.

- Add carrots, potatoes, seasonings, broth, salt, pepper, and beans.

- Bring to a simmer; reduce heat, cover, and simmer 2 to 3 hours, until beans are tender.

····· RECIPE VARIATIONS ·····

Pressure Cooker Bean Soup: In pressure cooker, heat olive oil; add onion and garlic. Cook and stir 5 minutes. Add carrots, potatoes, oregano, thyme, beans, and stock. Cover and bring to high pressure. Cook soup 15 minutes. Release pressure and test beans; if not soft, cook 5 minutes longer. Add salt and pepper.

Beef Vegetable Bean Soup: Make recipe as directed, except add 1½ pounds beef sirloin tip, but cut into 2-inch pieces. Brown it in the olive oil, remove, then add the onions and garlic and cook, stirring to remove pan drippings. Add remaining ingredients and simmer soup as directed until beans and beef are tender.

Sort Beans

- Even with the excellent processing facilities packers use now, some extraneous material will escape scrutiny.

- You must always sort beans before cooking them. One tiny pebble can ruin your whole recipe.

- Soaking beans not only reduces the cooking time, but helps get rid of gas-producing sugars.

- Large beans need to soak longer than small ones. And the more you soak the beans, the shorter the total cooking time.

Add Beans

- If you want to make this soup but don't have time to soak the beans overnight, use the quick-soak method.

- Sort beans, place in large pan, and cover with water. Bring to a boil; boil 2 minutes.

- Remove beans from heat, cover, and let stand 2 hours. Drain beans, rinse if desired, and continue with the recipe.

- Garnish the soup with a mixture of grated Parmesan cheese and more dried or fresh herbs.

PASTA E FAGIOLI

This classic Italian soup is full of vegetables, beans, and pasta

Pasta e Fagioli, which many people pronounce "Pasta Fazool," is a thick and rich soup that is hearty and so good for you.

The name literally means "pasta and beans," and the soup was originally peasant food. It's made from inexpensive and readily available ingredients.

You can make this soup with any bean, pasta, and vegetable combination. Leave out the ham bone, add some cubed round or sirloin steak, use chicken thighs, or omit the meat altogether. This is a very versatile recipe.

For a thicker soup, add more pasta; for a thinner soup, use less. Serve the soup with some hot Garlic Toast, a mixed green salad with a Parmesan dressing, and red wine.

Yield: Serves 6

Ingredients

1 pound dried navy beans

2 tablespoons olive oil

1 onion, chopped

3 cloves garlic, minced

2 stalks celery with leaves, chopped

2 carrots, sliced

1 ham bone

4 cups chicken broth, homemade or store-bought

4 cups water

1 teaspoon dried basil

1 bay leaf

1 teaspoon sugar

1/4 teaspoon pepper

1 cup orzo pasta

1/2 cup Pesto

Pasta e Fagioli

- Sort beans and rinse; cover with cold water and soak overnight. Drain in the morning.

- In large pot heat olive oil; cook onion and garlic 5 minutes. Add celery, carrots, and ham bone.

- Pour in broth, water, basil, bay leaf, sugar, and pepper. Simmer 2 to 3 hours, until beans are tender.

- Remove meat from ham bone; return meat to soup with pasta. Simmer 10 to 12 minutes, until tender. Serve with Pesto.

• • • • RECIPE VARIATIONS • • • •

Pesto: In food processor, combine 2 cups fresh basil leaves, ½ cup shredded Parmesan cheese, ½ cup toasted pine nuts, 2 cloves garlic; process until finely chopped. Add ⅓ cup extra virgin olive oil and 2 to 3 tablespoons water; process. Store in refrigerator.

Red Bean Fazool: Make recipe as directed, except use 1 pound dried red beans in place of the navy beans. Omit ham bone; add ⅓ pound diced prosciutto. Add 1 teaspoon oregano to the soup along with the dried basil. Simmer soup as directed, but add 1½ cups ditalini pasta in place of the orzo.

Add Ham Bone

- You may have to ask for the ham bone at the butcher shop or supermarket. Also ask at the deli.

- The butcher may give you a good price on it, if she has one that was left over after making sliced ham.

- Most people throw celery leaves away, but they add lots of flavor to the soup.

- Rinse the leaves well and chop finely. Their flavor is fresher than celery and a little bit lemony.

Add Meat and Pasta

- The bone adds rich flavor to the soup. You should be able to get one to two cups of meat off the bone.

- Remove bone from soup with tongs and place on a large plate.

- Hold the bone with the tongs or with a fork and cut the meat from the bone. You can then chop the meat.

- Cook pasta until just al dente.

BLACK BEAN SOUP
Black beans have the best smooth texture and nutty flavor

Black beans are also called turtle beans, because they look like a turtle's back. They are black on the outside but usually a red or creamy white on the inside.

Black beans are one of the healthiest foods you can eat. They are full of fiber, protein, and B vitamins like folate and thiamin. They are fat free and delicious, with a rich and nutty flavor.

To help reduce sodium, look for low-sodium canned beans.

By rinsing, draining, then rinsing the beans again, you can reduce the sodium content somewhat.

Season the soup with warm spices or fresh or dried herbs. Use any of your favorite vegetables and any meat from chicken to ham—or no meat at all.

Yield: Serves 6

Ingredients

2 tablespoons olive oil

1 onion, chopped

4 cloves garlic, minced

2 carrots, chopped

1 red bell pepper, chopped

2 (15-ounce) cans black beans, drained and rinsed

5 cups beef broth, homemade or store-bought

1/8 teaspoon pepper

1 teaspoon cumin

1/3 cup chopped cilantro

Black Bean Soup

- In large pot heat olive oil. Add onion and garlic; cook and stir 6 minutes.

- Add carrots, bell pepper, black beans, broth, pepper, and cumin.

- Bring to a simmer; simmer 15 minutes, until vegetables are tender.

- Scoop out 1 cup beans. Puree remaining soup. Return whole beans to soup and heat through; top with cilantro.

• • • • RECIPE VARIATIONS • • • •

Caramelized Onion Scones: Cook 1 chopped onion in ½ cup butter 20 minutes. Mix 1½ cups flour, ½ cup whole wheat flour, 1 tablespoon sugar, 2 teaspoons baking powder, and ½ teaspoon salt. Add onions, ¼ cup heavy cream, and 1 egg. Form into circle; cut into 8 wedges. Bake at 400°F 14 to 17 minutes.

Dried Black Bean Soup: Sort 1 pound dried black beans, rinse, cover with cold water, and boil 2 minutes. Remove from heat, cover, and let stand 2 hours. Drain beans, cover with water, and simmer 2 hours until tender. Continue with recipe as directed, using the cooked beans in place of the canned.

Cook Onion and Garlic

- When you cook onions and garlic in olive oil to start a soup, the oil carries the flavors throughout the whole recipe.

- In any soup recipe, the onions can be cooked until crisp-tender, tender, or caramelized.

- It's important to remove the thick and sweet liquid the beans are packed in by rinsing with cool water.

- This liquid is too sweet and heavy for the soup, and it is very high in salt.

Remove Beans to Keep Whole

- You don't need to puree this soup; it can be served as is, topped with some sour cream and cilantro.

- Or remove one cup of the beans and mash those; return to the soup and heat through.

- You can also partially mash some of the beans and vegetables right in the pot with a potato masher or immersion blender.

- Garnish the soup with some sour cream mixed with Parmesan cheese and lemon juice.

HAM WHITE BEAN CHOWDER

Bacon and ham add great flavor to this thick and hearty chowder

Bean chowders are easy to make, filling, and inexpensive. The addition of potatoes helps thicken the chowder and adds characteristic flavor and texture.

Because the ham and bacon are quite salty, it's easier to use canned beans in this recipe. Dried beans have to be cooked without much salt or they won't soften properly.

Any type of cheese would be delicious in this chowder. Swiss cheese is the inexpensive cousin of Gruyère, or try cheddar, Havarti, or Gouda. Shred the cheese using the large hole on a box grater. Shred the cheese right before you add it to the chowder.

Serve this soup with hot Cornbread fresh from the oven, slathered with butter.

Yield: Serves 6

Ingredients

6 slices thick-cut bacon

1 tablespoon olive oil

2 onions, chopped

4 cloves garlic, minced

4 carrots, sliced

2 cups cubed ham

2 russet potatoes, peeled and diced

2 (15-ounce) cans cannellini beans, drained and rinsed

1 teaspoon dried marjoram leaves

1/2 teaspoon salt

1/8 teaspoon pepper

1 bay leaf

6 cups chicken stock, homemade or store-bought

2 cups frozen corn

1 cup shredded Gruyère cheese

1 cup light cream

1 tablespoon cornstarch

Ham White Bean Chowder

- In soup pot cook bacon until crisp; drain, crumble, and refrigerate. Drain pan; do not wipe.

- Add olive oil; cook onions, garlic, and carrots 5 to 6 minutes. Add ham, potatoes, cannellini beans, marjoram, salt, pepper, bay leaf, stock, and corn.

- Bring to a simmer; cover and simmer on low heat 20 to 25 minutes, until vegetables are tender. Remove bay leaf.

- Add bacon, cheese, and cream mixed with cornstarch; heat until thickened, about 5 to 6 minutes, but do not boil.

186

• • • • RECIPE VARIATIONS • • • •

Chicken White Bean Chowder: Make recipe as directed, except use 1½ pounds boneless, skinless chicken thighs in place of the cubed ham. Cube the chicken and brown in the olive oil before adding the onions and garlic. Continue making the soup as directed, except use dried basil in place of the marjoram.

Cornbread: Mix ¾ cup flour, ¼ cup whole wheat flour, 1 cup yellow cornmeal, ½ cup sugar, ½ teaspoon salt, 2 teaspoons baking powder, and 1 teaspoon baking soda. Add ½ cup each buttermilk and heavy cream, 1 egg, and ⅓ cup melted butter. Bake in greased 9-inch pan at 400°F 20 to 30 minutes.

Cook Vegetables

- Thick-cut bacon keeps its texture in this soup, while regular bacon would fall apart and be lost among the other ingredients.

- The vegetables will absorb some of the bacon flavor from the drippings as they cook.

- You could substitute sweet potatoes or Yukon Gold for the russet potatoes if you'd like.

- Peel the potatoes for more thickening power; leave the peels on for a more rustic look.

Add Cheese and Cream

- You can use other types of canned beans: navy beans, red kidney beans, or pinto beans.

- The cream mixed with cornstarch will help thicken the chowder to the proper consistency; add more cornstarch for a thicker chowder.

- If you'd like thicker chowder, you can mash some of the beans and the potatoes with a potato masher or immersion blender.

- Then add the bacon, cheese, and cream mixed with cornstarch to finish the soup; serve piping hot.

BLACK-EYED PEA SOUP

Black-eyed peas are eaten on New Year's Day in the South for good luck

Black-eyed peas are white dried beans with a small black dot centered with a white spot near the middle of the pea.

Black-eyed peas are often used in Southern cooking and soul food. They pair well with bacon, ham, and greens and are an inexpensive source of protein, B vitamins, and calcium.

You can use the "holy trinity" of onion, celery, and green bell peppers in this soup as the base, or add mushrooms, artichoke hearts, or tomatoes.

Serve this soup steaming hot with hot Cornbread dripping with melted butter for New Year's Day or anytime during the winter for a warming and lucky meal.

Yield: Serves 6

Ingredients

3 cups dried black-eyed peas, sorted

3 slices bacon

2 onions, chopped

3 cloves garlic, minced

2 carrots, sliced

1 ham hock

7 cups water

1/4 teaspoon pepper

1 bay leaf

1 cup basmati rice

2 cups baby spinach leaves

1 tablespoon lemon juice

Black-Eyed Pea Soup

- Sort peas and rinse; drain and cover with cold water. Soak overnight, then drain.

- In large pot cook bacon until crisp; drain, crumble, and set aside. Drain pot; do not wipe.

- Add onion, garlic, and carrots; cook 5 minutes. Add peas, ham hock, water, pepper, and bay leaf; simmer 2 to 3 hours, until peas are tender.

- Remove ham hock; cut off meat and return to pot with rice. Cook 20 to 25 minutes, then add spinach and lemon juice. Simmer 4 to 5 minutes.

ZOOM

The tradition of eating black-eyed peas for good luck dates back to the Civil War. Northern troops considered black-eyed peas and corn to be unsuitable for human consumption, so left them in the fields for the Southerners to eat. The combination of peas and corn makes complete protein.

• • • • RECIPE VARIATION • • • •

Slow Cooker Black-Eyed Pea Soup: Make recipe as directed, except combine soaked and drained peas, onions, garlic, and carrots sautéed in bacon fat, ham hock, water, pepper, and bay leaf in 5-quart slow cooker. Cover and cook on low 9 to 10 hours. Add rice; cook 30 minutes on high. Add spinach and lemon juice; serve.

Add Peas and Ham Hock

Add Spinach

- You can use 1 to 2 cups diced cubed ham instead of the ham hock if you'd like.

- Be sure the ham hock is covered in water, and that the beans are covered too, so they cook evenly.

- Simmer the soup covered so the water doesn't cook away.

- You can use 2 15-ounce cans black-eyed peas, rinsed and drained, in place of the dried. Use half chicken broth and simmer 1 hour until the broth tastes rich.

- Other dark greens work well in this soup. Think about using chopped kale, mustard greens, or watercress.

- The heavier greens need to be cooked longer than the baby spinach; simmer them 15 to 20 minutes.

- The lemon juice adds a touch of brightness to the soup at the end of the cooking time.

- For a creamy soup, omit the lemon juice and add ½ cup light or heavy cream.

189

TUNISIAN CHICKPEA SOUP
This simple and spicy soup is for garlic lovers

Chickpeas, also known as garbanzo beans, are a wonderful meat substitute. The peas have a very rich meaty flavor and nutty texture that satisfy even the most ardent meat-lover.

This soup uses spices and ingredients from Africa and the Mediterranean, including cumin, garlic, and lemon juice. The recipe is simple, which means the broth has to be well seasoned and full of flavor.

You can make this soup as mild or spicy as you'd like. Traditionally it's meant to be spicy and warming.

Serve the soup in flat warmed soup plates drizzled with a bit of best-quality extra-virgin olive oil and accompanied with some crisp hot Garlic Toast or garlic bread.
Yield: Serves 6

Ingredients

2 tablespoons olive oil

1 teaspoon cumin seeds

1 onion, chopped

5 cloves garlic, minced

1 red bell pepper, chopped

2 (15-ounce) cans garbanzo beans, drained and rinsed

4 cups chicken or vegetable broth, homemade or store-bought

2 teaspoons harissa or 1 teaspoon red chile paste

1/4 teaspoon pepper

2 tablespoons lemon juice

6 pieces Garlic Toast

3 tablespoons extra-virgin olive oil

Tunisian Chickpea Soup

- In large pot heat 2 tablespoons olive oil over low heat. Add cumin seeds; cook and stir until fragrant.

- Add onion, garlic, and red bell pepper; cook and stir 6 minutes.

- Add beans, broth, *harissa*, and pepper; bring to a simmer. Simmer 15 to 20 minutes, until blended; stir in lemon juice.

- Place Garlic Toasts in six soup bowls and spoon soup over. Drizzle with extra-virgin olive oil and serve.

ZOOM

Harissa is a hot paste made from dried red chile peppers used in North African cooking. You can find it in the international foods aisle of most supermarkets, or make it yourself. Soak dried red chile peppers in water, drain, then process with garlic, salt, olive oil, and cumin.

• • • • RECIPE VARIATION • • • •

Slow Cooker Tunisian Chickpea Soup: Make recipe as directed, except use 1 pound dried chickpeas for the canned. Soak them overnight, then rinse, drain, and boil 1 hour. Combine all ingredients in 4-quart slow cooker; cover and cook on low 8 to 9 hours.

Sauté Cumin Seeds

- Cumin seeds are toasted to help bring out their flavor and release essential oils.

- Add the seeds to the hot oil and cook just a few seconds until fragrant. The seeds may also make a popping sound.

- Don't let the seeds burn. If they do, you have to wash the pan and start all over again.

- Be careful when you add the onion, garlic, and bell pepper to the cumin seeds and oil; it can spatter.

Add Beans and Harissa

- If you can't find *harissa* and don't want to make it yourself, you can substitute red chile paste.

- In addition to the paste, add a pinch of ground coriander and caraway, ingredients commonly used in *harissa*.

- You can use other beans in place of or in addition to the chickpeas, including black beans and pinto beans.

- For a richer soup, use beef broth or stock in place of the chicken or vegetable broth.

VEGETARIAN MINESTRONE
Minestrone is a heavy and healthy vegetable soup

The most important ingredient in any vegetarian soup is the broth. A vegetarian broth is easily made using inexpensive ingredients and will pay you back many times over. If you don't have the time to make a vegetable broth from scratch, add some onions, celery, and carrots to a boxed or canned broth and simmer 5 to 10 minutes to make it rich and add more depth of flavor.

Minestrone is a highly seasoned soup. You can use fresh or dried herbs. If you choose to use fresh herbs, add three times the amount of dried called for in the recipe.

Serve this soup with freshly grated Parmesan cheese and some Toasted Garlic Cheese Bread, along with some red wine.

Yield: Serves 6

Ingredients

2 tablespoons olive oil

1 onion, chopped

3 cloves garlic, minced

2 carrots, sliced

1/2 teaspoon salt

1/8 teaspoon pepper

1 teaspoon dried oregano

4 tomatoes, peeled, seeded, and chopped

2 (15-ounce) cans cannellini beans, drained

6 cups vegetable broth, homemade or store-bought

1/2 cup orzo pasta

1 yellow summer squash, diced

1 red bell pepper, chopped

3 dashes Tabasco sauce

Vegetarian Minestrone

- In large pot cook onion and garlic in olive oil 5 minutes. Add carrots, salt, pepper, and oregano; cook and stir another 5 minutes.

- Add tomatoes, beans, and broth; bring to a simmer. Simmer 15 to 20 minutes, until carrots are tender.

- Add pasta; simmer 5 minutes. Then add squash, red bell pepper, and Tabasco.

- Simmer another 4 to 8 minutes, until pasta is tender and squash and bell pepper are crisp-tender.

Slow Cooker Minestrone: Make recipe as directed, except after cooking the onion and garlic in olive oil, combine all ingredients except pasta, squash, bell pepper, and Tabasco sauce in 4-quart slow cooker. Cover and cook on low 7 to 8 hours. Add remaining ingredients; cover and cook on high 20 minutes.

Pressure Cooker Minestrone: Cook onion and garlic in olive oil; add carrots, salt, pepper, and oregano; cook 3 minutes. Add remaining ingredients except beans and pasta. Bring to high pressure; cook 10 minutes. Release pressure. Cook pasta separately and add to soup with beans.

Add Beans and Tomatoes

- Other canned beans will work well in this recipe. Try red kidney beans, Great Northern beans, or garbanzo beans.

- You can substitute one or two 14.5-ounce cans of diced tomatoes, undrained, for the fresh tomatoes.

- Or look for seasoned diced tomatoes. They can be seasoned with chiles or with onion and garlic.

- Sun-dried tomatoes, finely minced, would be a good addition to this soup. Use dried or those packed in oil.

Add Squash and Bell Pepper

- Tender vegetables are added at the end of cooking time so they stay crisp-tender and don't get too soft.

- Other vegetables that would be delicious in this soup include artichoke hearts and chopped or sliced zucchini.

- You can use different types of pasta in this soup, too. Try a large shape like penne or gemelli, or filled tortellini.

- Cook the soup longer until the pasta is tender, about 5 to 6 minutes. Keep tasting the pasta until it's al dente.

BROCCOLI BISQUE
This soup is so delicious it will tempt even broccoli haters

Broccoli is a strongly flavored vegetable that can be bitter when cooked in a small amount of liquid. Broccoli cooked in soup becomes tender, nutty, and slightly sweet.

This bright green soup retains its color because of the acidity of the lemon juice. Cream is added because it is a bisque, but you don't have to use it for a truly vegetarian soup.

Broccoli is a very healthy vegetable. It's part of the crucifer-ous family, with lots of anti-cancer properties, including fiber, beta carotene, and vitamin C. It also has phytochemicals called indoles, which help prevent cancer.

This soup can be served hot or cold. Garnish with some chopped nuts and serve with warm muffins.
Yield: Serves 6

Ingredients

2 tablespoons butter or olive oil

1 onion, chopped

2 cloves garlic, minced

1 1/2 pounds broccoli, trimmed

1/2 teaspoon salt

1/8 teaspoon pepper

1 teaspoon dried basil

4 cups vegetable broth, homemade or store-bought

1/2 teaspoon curry powder

1 tablespoon lemon juice

1 cup light cream or soy milk

1/3 cup sour cream

Broccoli Bisque

- In large pot cook onion and garlic; cook and stir 5 minutes.

- Cut off broccoli florets; set aside ½ cup; blanch reserved florets. Peel stems and chop. Add chopped broccoli to pot with salt, pepper, basil, broth, and curry powder.

- Bring soup to a simmer; simmer 8 to 10 minutes, until broccoli is tender. Add lemon juice.

- Puree soup using immersion blender or food processor. Stir in light cream or soy milk and sour cream; heat through. Garnish with reserved florets.

• • • • RECIPE VARIATIONS • • • •

Herbed Broccoli Bisque: Make recipe as directed, except add ½ teaspoon dried marjoram and 1 teaspoon dried thyme. Omit curry powder. Add 3 cloves garlic with the onions and add 1 russet potato, peeled and diced, with the broccoli stems. Garnish soup with fresh thyme sprigs.

Cheese Pull-Apart Bread: Open a 10-ounce can refrigerated soft bread stick dough; do not unroll. Place rolls, overlapping, in two rows of four biscuits on cookie sheet. Brush with 2 tablespoons olive oil. Sprinkle with 1 cup shredded cheddar, ¼ cup grated Romano cheese, and 1 teaspoon dried basil. Bake at 350°F 15 to 20 minutes, until brown.

Prepare Broccoli

- To prepare the broccoli, first rinse it thoroughly and then strip off any leaves.

- Trim the bottom of the bunch and cut off the florets. Peel the stems and cut into small pieces.

- The florets are used as a garnish for the soup. You can cook them and puree along with the stems if you'd like.

- You can substitute a 16-ounce package of frozen broccoli for the fresh if you'd like. Just thaw, drain, and add to the soup.

Add Cream to Soup

- The light cream adds a velvety smoothness, and the sour cream makes the soup a bit thicker.

- You can use all light cream or all sour cream, for that matter. Stir the soup with a wire whisk to thoroughly blend it.

- For a completely vegan soup, you can omit the cream or use soy milk or a vegan sour cream.

- If you're not vegan, garnish the soup with some crumbled blue cheese and chopped walnuts.

ROASTED RED PEPPER SOUP

Roasted peppers become intensely flavored in this simple soup

Red bell peppers are sweet, tender, and delicious added to any soup. But a soup featuring these vegetables is very special.

Roasting peppers concentrates the flavor and adds a smoky taste to the sweet vegetable. When roasted, the skins come off easily, making the soup velvety smooth.

Adding roasted tomatoes to the mix increases the soup's depth of flavor and boosts the vitamin A and C content.

This is another soup that can be served hot or cold. If you are going to serve it cold, garnish with just the fresh basil; omit the cheese.

Enjoy this simple soup as the starter for a multi-course meal, or eat it with some muffins for lunch on the porch.

Yield: Serves 6

Ingredients

4 red bell peppers, cut in half

2 tomatoes, cut in half

1 onion, chopped

2 cloves garlic, minced

2 tablespoons butter

1 tablespoon olive oil

$1/2$ teaspoon salt

$1/8$ teaspoon pepper

4 cups vegetable broth, homemade or store-bought

1 teaspoon dried basil

2 tablespoons lemon juice

$1/3$ cup chopped fresh basil

$1/3$ cup grated Romano cheese or soy cheese

Roasted Red Pepper Soup

- Place peppers and to-matoes, skin side up, on broiling rack. Broil 6 to 9 minutes, turning occasion-ally, until deep brown.

- Let cool 20 minutes, peel and discard skins. then chop.

- In pot cook onion and garlic in butter and olive oil 5 minutes. Add salt, pepper, broth, dried basil, and bell peppers and tomatoes.

- Simmer 10 minutes. Puree with an immersion blender. Add lemon juice; garnish with fresh basil and cheese.

•••• RECIPE VARIATIONS ••••

Roasted Red Pepper Bisque: Make recipe as directed, except use 5 red bell peppers; omit tomatoes. After the soup has been pureed, add 1 cup light cream or evaporated milk mixed with 1½ tablespoons cornstarch. Cook the soup 5 to 10 minutes longer, until thickened and smooth.

Curried Cold Roasted Red Pepper Soup: Make recipe as directed, except add 1 tablespoon curry powder with the onions and garlic; cook 6 to 7 minutes. Omit tomatoes; add another red bell pepper. After soup is pureed, add lemon juice and chill 3 to 4 hours. Serve garnished with chopped fresh red bell pepper.

Roast Vegetables

Simmer Soup

- Never, ever rinse a roasted vegetable, either before or after peeling.

- Water will rinse away a lot of the flavor that you worked so hard to create.

- You can use all olive oil instead of the combination of olive oil and butter, but butter helps reduce the acidity of the tomatoes.

- Don't substitute margarine for the butter. If you want a vegan soup, use all olive oil, preferably extra-virgin.

- This quick-cooking soup is simmered for only a few minutes to help blend the flavors.

- The red bell peppers and tomatoes are completely cooked during the roasting process.

- You can make this soup without pureeing it. Just heat through after adding the lemon juice and serve.

- This soup can be chilled and reheated. Just pour into a saucepan and heat gently until the soup steams.

VEGETABLE BARLEY SOUP

This is a hearty soup, perfect for feeding a crowd or large family

For a hearty vegetarian soup, it's hard to beat the combination of vegetables and barley. Almost any combination of vegetables would be delicious in this soup.

Pot or pearl barley perform equally well in this easy recipe. The pot barley may need to simmer an additional 15 to 20 minutes, until it is tender.

This is a vegan soup because it only uses plant material and doesn't contain dairy products like butter, cream, or cheese.

This is an excellent soup to serve for lunch on a cold winter day. The aroma of simmering vegetables will fill your house, making it warm and cozy. Serve with some grilled cheese sandwiches and hot chocolate.

Yield: Serves 6–8

Ingredients

2 tablespoons olive oil

2 onions, chopped

1 leek, chopped

3 carrots, sliced

2 stalks celery, sliced

4 tomatoes, peeled, seeded, and chopped

2 cups cremini mushrooms, sliced

1 teaspoon salt

$1/8$ teaspoon pepper

1 teaspoon dried marjoram

1 bay leaf

8 cups vegetable broth, homemade or store-bought

1 cup barley

Vegetable Barley Soup

- In large pot heat olive oil. Add onions and leek; cook and stir 5 minutes.

- Add carrots and celery; cook and stir 4 minutes. Add tomatoes, mushrooms, salt, pepper, and marjoram; cook 4 minutes.

- Add bay leaf and broth; bring to a simmer. Add barley and cover.

- Simmer over low heat 55 to 65 minutes, until vegetables and barley are tender. Remove bay leaf and serve.

•••••••••••••• RED●LIGHT ••••••••••••••

Some vegetables have such a strong taste that they are best left out of mixed vegetable soups. These vegetables include brussels sprouts and broccoli. You can make a soup based on these ingredients, but they can overwhelm a mixed vegetable soup.

•••• **RECIPE VARIATION** ••••

Root Vegetable Barley Soup: Make recipe as directed, except add 1 sweet potato and 2 russet potatoes, both peeled and chopped. Omit tomatoes and mushrooms; add 3 cloves minced garlic. Add 1 teaspoon dried thyme; simmer soup as directed.

Cook Vegetables

- Strongly flavored vegetables like onions, garlic, leeks, and shallots are cooked first when making a soup.

- These vegetables need more time to soften and for their flavors to mellow.

- Cooking them in oil also helps impart these flavors evenly to the rest of the soup, as the oil picks up the flavor.

- The remaining vegetables are added according to their cooking time, with root vegetables added before tender vegetables like tomatoes.

Add Barley

- If you'd like the barley to have a nutty, stronger flavor, add it to the onion and leek mixture.

- Cook the barley until it smells slightly toasted. Then add the remaining vegetables and broth and continue cooking the soup.

- This soup freezes and reheats very well. The barley may dissolve; add more cooked barley as you reheat the soup.

- The soup is also a great addition to lunchboxes in a well-sealed thermos.

SQUASH BISQUE
Squash makes a creamy, comforting bisque with a velvety texture

Squash comes in two varieties: hard winter squash and soft summer squash. The type of squash used in this soup is the hard squash.

Hard squashes include pumpkin, butternut squash, acorn squash, sugar pumpkin, Hubbard squash, and turban squash.

Fresh squash may seem intimidating when you pick it up in the grocery store, but it is very simple to prepare. Roast-ing is the easiest method. Just cut in half; remove the seeds; add some oil, butter, or water; and roast until tender. Then remove the flesh and proceed with the recipe.

Other root vegetables like onions and carrots add to the sweetness and flavor of this soup. Serve in white china bowls for a beautiful presentation.

Yield: Serves 6

Ingredients

1 butternut squash, cut in half and seeded

2 tablespoons butter

1 onion, chopped

2 carrots, sliced

1 Granny Smith apple, peeled and chopped

6 cups vegetable broth, homemade or store-bought

$1/2$ teaspoon salt

$1/8$ teaspoon pepper

$1/2$ teaspoon ground ginger

$1/2$ cup light cream or soy milk

Squash Bisque

- Preheat oven to 350°F. Place squash, cut side down, in roasting pan. Roast 1 hour, until tender.

- Meanwhile, melt butter in large pot. Add onion and carrots; cook 5 minutes. Add apple and broth; bring to a simmer.

- Simmer soup 15 to 20 min-utes, until carrots are very tender. Add salt, pepper, and ginger; remove from heat.

- Scoop the roasted squash out of its skin and add to soup. Add cream and puree using immersion blender; heat through.

Pressure Cooker Bisque: Peel the squash, cut in half, remove seeds, and cut into 1-inch chunks. Cook the onions in butter in the pressure cooker, then add everything except the cream. Lock cooker, bring to high pressure, and cook 10 minutes. Release pressure, then puree soup in food processor with light cream.

Curried Squash Bisque: Make recipe as directed, except add 1 tablespoon curry powder when you cook the onions in butter. Just before pureeing the soup, add ½ cup mango chutney with the light cream. Heat soup; serve with toasted coconut and cashews.

VEGETARIAN

Roast Squash

- Roasting squash concentrates its flavor and brings out the nutty and sweet tastes.

- You can roast the squash ahead of time. Refrigerate it until you're ready to make the soup.

- If you do this, add the squash with the apple so it reheats and cooks with the soup.

- You can cut the squash into pieces and then roast it; cook 30 to 40 minutes, until tender.

Add Squash to Soup

- Use a metal spoon to scoop the cooked squash out of the skin. Discard skin or add to your compost pile.

- Other types of squash to try include acorn squash or sugar pumpkin. Use 2½ to 3 pounds squash.

- The soup can be served hot or cold. Chill 3 to 4 hours if serving cold.

- You may need to add more light cream if serving cold, since the soup will thicken in the refrigerator.

TOMATO BASIL SOUP

Fresh summer tomatoes and fresh basil are essential to this easy soup

This is a summer soup, best made with tomatoes fresh from the garden or farmers' market. Don't try to make this soup using tomatoes out of season. The tomatoes you find in the supermarket in the fall and winter have been bred to survive shipping cross-country, not for their flavor.

Use a variety of tomatoes in this soup for easy variations.

The only requirement is that the tomatoes be tender and flavorful, at their peak of ripeness.

This is another soup that can be served warm or cold. To serve cold, chill about 4 to 6 hours, then stir and serve, garnished with more fresh basil and a drizzle of heavy cream.
Yield: Serves 6

Ingredients

6 red tomatoes, seeded and diced

2 yellow tomatoes, seeded and diced

4 cups vegetable broth, homemade or store-bought

2 cups tomato juice

1 teaspoon sugar

1/2 teaspoon salt

1/8 teaspoon pepper

1/2 cup chopped fresh basil

2 tablespoons lemon juice

Tomato Basil Soup

- In large saucepan combine tomatoes with broth, juice, sugar, salt, and pepper.

- Bring to a simmer; simmer 25 to 30 minutes, until tomatoes are very soft.

- Using an immersion blender, partially puree the soup, leaving some tomato pieces if you'd like. Or completely puree the soup for a velvety texture.

- Add basil and lemon juice and heat until steaming; do not boil. Serve immediately.

Uncooked Tomato Basil Soup: Make recipe as directed, except don't cook the tomatoes. Combine all ingredients in blender or food processor and blend or process until smooth. Chill the soup 2 to 3 hours to blend the flavors. Garnish with more chopped fresh basil leaves.

Tomato Rice Soup: Make recipe as directed, cooking the tomatoes. Puree the soup completely using an immersion blender. While the soup is simmering, cook ⅓ cup basmati rice in ⅔ cup vegetable broth until tender. Add to the soup, simmer 2-3 minutes, and serve.

Chop Tomatoes

- Check the skins of the tomatoes before you work with them. If they are tough, blanch the tomatoes.

- To blanch the tomatoes, drop into boiling water 5 to 6 seconds.

- Remove the tomatoes using a strainer or Chinese sieve, and immediately plunge into ice water. The skins will peel right off.

- Remove the seeds for a smoother soup; leave them in for a rustic soup.

Puree Soup

- You can partially or completely puree this soup, either with an immersion blender or in a food processor.

- If you choose to chill the soup, taste it before you serve it; you may need to correct the seasonings.

- Add more salt and pepper if the soup tastes bland, or add some sugar if it's too acidic.

- This is a soup to serve in plain white or glass bowls to enjoy the spectacular color and texture.

QUINOA VEGETABLE SOUP

Quinoa, an ancient grain, adds great texture and flavor to this soup

It's hard to find a soup that's healthier than this one. All of those vegetables give you a nice amount of vitamins and minerals, and the quinoa is a grain that provides complete protein.

This is a fabulous soup to make after a trip through your garden in late summer, or after a journey to a farmers' market or local farm stand. The freshest vegetables are important because they are the stars of this soup.

You can use any combination of your favorite vegetables and herbs in this easy soup. Zucchini, artichoke hearts, tomatoes, and tiny baby peas all would be delicious.

Serve this soup with some hot Cornbread, or crusty multi-grain bread and a green salad.

Yield: Serves 6

Ingredients

2 tablespoons olive oil

1 onion, chopped

3 cloves garlic, minced

1 green bell pepper, chopped

3 stalks celery, chopped

2 carrots, chopped

1 cup sliced cremini mushrooms

1 cup quinoa, rinsed

4 cups vegetable broth, homemade or store-bought

3 tomatoes, peeled, seeded, and chopped

1 cup sliced green beans

1 teaspoon salt

1/8 teaspoon pepper

2 tablespoons minced fresh basil

1 teaspoon fresh oregano

Quinoa Vegetable Soup

- In large pot heat olive oil over medium heat. Add onion and garlic; cook and stir 5 minutes.

- Add bell pepper, celery, carrots, and mushrooms; cook 4 to 5 minutes. Add quinoa.

- Add broth and tomatoes; bring to a simmer. Simmer 10 minutes.

- Add beans, salt, pepper, basil, and oregano; cook 5 to 8 minutes longer, until vegetables and quinoa are tender.

Spicy Quinoa Vegetable Soup: Make recipe as directed, except add 1 jalapeño pepper and 1 habañero pepper, both minced, with the onions. Add 1 cup salsa with the tomatoes, and omit the basil and oregano. Add 2 teaspoons chili powder and 1 teaspoon cumin. Garnish soup with fresh chopped cilantro.

Slow Cooker Quinoa Vegetable Soup: Make recipe as directed, except after the onions and garlic are cooked in oil, combine all ingredients except the green beans, salt, pepper, basil, and oregano in 4-quart slow cooker. Cover and cook on low 5 to 6 hours; add remaining ingredients and cook 30 minutes longer.

Rinse Quinoa

Add Tomatoes and Green Beans

- Quinoa has to be thoroughly rinsed before use. The round beads are coated with a sticky, very bitter substance.

- Called saponin, this coating protects the quinoa from animals and birds.

- This chemical creates "suds" in the water. If you rinse the quinoa until the water no longer suds, all the saponin will be removed.

- You can cook the quinoa until it's just tender, or cook it longer so it starts to thicken the soup.

- These tender ingredients are added at the end of the cooking time so they retain some of their texture.

- The green beans should be cooked until crisp-tender. Taste one at the earliest cooking time.

- At the very end of the cooking time, you could add some tiny green peas for another vegetable.

- Garnish the soup with a dollop of sour cream and some grated Romano or Swiss cheese.

FARMERS' MARKET

WHITE GAZPACHO

This Spanish soup is a nice change of pace during the summer

White Gazpacho is an unusual soup made with nuts, bread crumbs, and cucumber. The soup really is a white color, and it's very cooling on a hot summer day.

For best results make sure the Brazil nuts and almonds do not have any brown skin attached to the nut. If necessary, use a swivel-bladed vegetable peeler to remove the skin from the Brazil nuts.

The soup is forced through a sieve to remove the nut and vegetable pulp. Press down on the solids to remove all the flavorful liquid.

Tiny cooked shrimp or some fresh lump crabmeat is the perfect garnish for this soup, along with a sprinkle of fresh chives or herbs.

Yield: Serves 6

Ingredients

¼ cup skinned Brazil nuts

½ cup slivered almonds

I clove garlic, minced

3 cucumbers, peeled, seeded, and chopped

I cup soft white bread crumbs

I cup vegetable broth, homemade or store-bought

2 cups water

½ teaspoon salt

I teaspoon walnut oil

½ cup thick Greek yogurt

⅓ cup chopped chives

White Gazpacho

- Place Brazil nuts and almonds in dry pan; toast over low heat 4 to 5 minutes, until fragrant; cool completely.

- Place nuts with garlic, cucumbers, bread crumbs, broth, and water in food processor; process until smooth.

- Force mixture through a small sieve. Add salt, walnut oil, and yogurt. Chill 2 hours.

- When ready to eat, stir soup; thin with light cream, if necessary. Pour into chilled bowls and garnish with chives.

Cucumber Pepper Gazpacho: Make recipe as directed, except omit nuts. Substitute 2 yellow bell peppers, seeded and chopped. Add ¼ cup green onions, but only the white parts, chopped. Use 3 cups chicken broth or vegetable broth in place of the water and broth. Stir in ½ cup sour cream instead of yogurt.

Seafood White Gazpacho: Make recipe as directed. Chill 2 to 3 hours, until very cold. Cook 1 cup medium-size raw shrimp in 1 tablespoon butter. Combine with 1 cup fresh lump crabmeat. Whisk ½ cup light cream into the cold soup, pour into bowls, and top with the seafood mixture.

Puree Nut Mixture

Add Walnut Oil and Yogurt

- When you push the soup through the strainer, there will be some thicker liquid that sticks to the bottom of the sieve.

- Be sure to scrape off this layer and add to the soup. It will slightly thicken the soup.

- You can use other nuts if you'd like. Walnuts or cashews would be good substitutes.

- To force mixture through the sieve, use a metal spoon and push firmly on the solids. Discard solids after straining.

- Walnut oil is very perishable and full of flavor. Buy it in small quantities and store it in the refrigerator.

- You can substitute almond or hazelnut oil if you can't find walnut oil.

- Look for Greek yogurt; it's much more flavorful and thicker than plain American yogurt.

- If you can't find Greek yogurt, strain regular yogurt. Place in cheesecloth over a bowl in the fridge overnight. Use the thick yogurt in soups and as a garnish.

CHERRY CAMEMBERT SOUP

Sweet bing and sour cherries combine with slightly melted cheese in this luscious soup

A soup made of cherries may sound odd, but this refreshing mixture is perfect to start a brunch or as an appetizer.

You need a mixture of sweet and sour fresh cherries for the best flavor balance. Fresh cherries are in season in June and July. You can use frozen cherries out of season, but make sure they are dry packed with no sugar. Frozen cherries can be all sweet or a combination of sweet and sour; read labels.

This soup is sweet and tart, so when you taste it before serving, add more sugar or more wine to balance the flavors.

Serve the soup very hot so the cheese melts into it, along with a nice glass of red wine.

Yield: Serves 6

Ingredients

2 cups bing cherries, pitted

2 cups sour cherries, pitted

2 cups cold water

1/2 cup cherry juice

1/3 cup dry red wine

1 tablespoon sugar

Pinch salt

2 teaspoons cornstarch

1 pinch ground cloves

1/2 cup sour cream

1 cup diced Camembert cheese, rind removed

Cherry Camembert Soup

- In pot combine cherries, water, cherry juice, wine, sugar, and salt; bring to a simmer.

- Simmer 10 to 15 minutes, until cherries are tender. Using an immersion blender, puree the soup.

- Combine cornstarch, cloves, and sour cream in small bowl; add a ladle of hot soup and whisk. Stir into soup and heat through until thickened.

- Add cheese to soup and serve immediately.

••••• RECIPE VARIATION • • • •

Frozen Cherry Soup: Make recipe as directed, except omit the fresh bing and sour cherries. Use 1-pound bag frozen cherries, thawed but not drained. Decrease water to 1 cup; increase wine to 1⅓ cups. Simmer and puree soup, then chill. Omit cornstarch, cloves, sour cream, and cheese.

•••••••• RED ● LIGHT •••••••••

Be very careful when you pit cherries. Pit them over a steel or ceramic bowl so you can hear each pit hit the bowl as it comes out of the cherry. If you're using frozen cherries, be sure to carefully examine each one for pits.

Pit Cherries

- You can pit cherries several ways. Use a cherry pitter specifically made for this purpose; you can find them in kitchenware stores.

- Or cut the cherries in half and pry out the pits. You can also push a straw through the cherries to remove the pits.

- Even though the soup is pureed, a cherry pit can add a bitter note.

- Don't pit the cherries ahead of time, as they can develop a brown hue.

Add Sour Cream Mixture

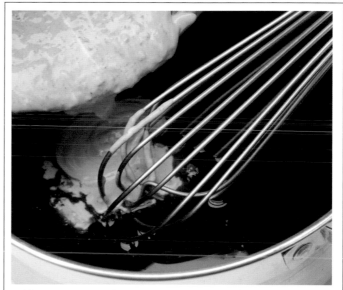

- The sour cream mixture needs to be tempered before it's stirred into the rest of the soup.

- Stir the hot liquid with the cornstarch and sour cream using a wire whisk so it completely blends.

- To serve this soup cold, omit the cornstarch and sour cream mixture.

- Chill the soup 4 to 5 hours. You may need to thin it before serving; add more wine or cherry juice with a wire whisk until desired consistency.

FARMERS' MARKET

COLD PEA MINT SOUP
Fresh mint is the secret to this simple soup

A chilled pea soup is the essence of summer. It doesn't have to be made with fresh peas. If you don't have peas straight out of the garden or from the farmers' market, use frozen baby peas.

Frozen peas are very high quality and have lots of flavor and beautiful color, so don't be afraid to use them. It's easy to shell fresh peas. Rinse off the pods, then use a fingernail to open each pod. Remove the peas gently with the tip of your finger.

This is a great soup to make ahead of time for a summer luncheon. Serve it with a fresh tomato and green bell pepper salad and some Cheese Muffins.

Yield: Serves 6

Ingredients

2 tablespoons butter

3 green onions, sliced

1 clove garlic, minced

1 stalk celery, minced

1 pound fresh peas or frozen peas, thawed

4 cups vegetable broth, homemade or store-bought

1/2 teaspoon salt

1/8 teaspoon white pepper

1/4 teaspoon dried basil

2 tablespoons minced fresh mint leaves, divided

1 cup light cream

Garlic croutons

Cold Pea Mint Soup

- In large pot melt butter over low heat. Add green onions, garlic, and celery; cook 5 minutes.

- Shell peas, if fresh, or drain peas if frozen. Add to pot along with broth.

- Simmer 5 to 7 minutes, until vegetables are tender. Add salt, white pepper, and basil; simmer 2 minutes longer.

- Puree soup using immersion blender. Stir in mint and light cream; refrigerate until chilled. Top with Garlic Croutons and serve.

• • • • RECIPE VARIATIONS • • • •

Cheese Muffins: Mix 2 cups flour, 2 tablespoons sugar, 2 teaspoons baking powder, and ¼ teaspoon salt; set aside. Melt ⅓ cup butter; add 1 cup whole milk; beat in 1 egg. Add milk mixture to flour mixture along with 1 cup shredded cheddar and ½ cup shredded Swiss. Bake at 400°F in 12 greased muffin cups for 15 to 20 minutes until golden brown.

Pure Cold Pea Soup: Make recipe as directed, except use 1½ pounds fresh or frozen peas. Omit green onions and celery. Increase garlic cloves to 3. Continue with recipe and chill as directed. Top with mixture of fresh mint and chopped grape tomatoes.

Shell Peas

- If you're using fresh peas, you can add the pods to the vegetable broth to make it more flavorful.

- Simmer the pods and the broth 15 to 20 minutes, then strain and use the broth in the soup.

- If you use frozen peas, you don't have to thaw them before use.

- Just drop the frozen peas into the broth; simmer another 2 to 3 minutes, until peas and vegetables are tender.

Stir in Cream

- The cream adds a velvety texture and rich flavor to the soup, but you don't have to use it.

- You could substitute whole milk, or you could use soy milk for a purely vegan soup.

- Depending on your taste, you can serve the soup as is, directly out of the fridge, or thin it with more cream.

- Chilling thickens the soup. Stir it well using a wire whisk to blend it before serving.

BERRY BARLEY SOUP

Berries add a wonderful sweet and tart flavor to this easy soup

Berries are usually only used in soup as an accent or garnish. When they are used in soup, it's as an ethnic soup like Scandinavian fruit soup. But berries can make a delicious, nutritious, and colorful soup you can serve at a breakfast or brunch or on a hot day for lunch under a lazily spinning ceiling fan.

This soup can be served hot or cold. The banana pureed with the soup adds a velvety texture and helps moderate the strong flavors of the berries. The barley adds wonderful texture and smoothness and helps thicken the soup.

Whether you serve the soup hot or cold, garnish it with some fresh raspberries and a sprinkle of fresh mint.

Yield: Serves 6

Ingredients

- ¼ cup barley
- ½ teaspoon salt
- 6 cups water
- ⅓ cup sugar
- 2 cups sliced strawberries
- 2 cups frozen raspberries
- 1 cup chopped cherries
- 1 smashed banana
- 1 tablespoon lemon juice
- ¼ teaspoon cinnamon

Berry Barley Soup

- Combine barley, salt, water, and sugar in large saucepan; simmer 50 minutes over low heat.

- Add strawberries, raspberries, and cherries; simmer 20 minutes.

- Using an immersion blender, partially puree the soup. Add banana and puree into the soup.

- Add lemon juice and cinnamon and remove from heat. Serve immediately or chill 3 to 4 hours before serving. You can thin with apple juice if needed.

• • • • RECIPE VARIATION • • • •

Fruit and Rice Soup: Make recipe as directed, except use 1 cup long-grain white rice for the barley. Decrease water to 4 cups; add 1 cup raspberry nectar and 1 cup cherry juice. Increase sugar to ½ cup. Add ½ teaspoon cinnamon. Add ½ cup sour cream as you puree the soup; serve cold.

ZOOM

Berries are very perishable. When you buy them, bring them home immediately and refrigerate as soon as possible. Don't rinse the berries until you're ready to use them, or they could develop mold. Handle them gently so they don't bruise. Use fresh berries within two to three days.

Add Berries

- To prepare strawberries, rinse under cool running water. Use a knife to cut off the leaves and any white part.

- If there are any soft or bruised spots, cut them out with the knife. Then slice the strawberries.

- For the raspberries, just rinse them under cool running water. Sort through the berries and remove any that are soft.

- Rinse the cherries and remove the stems. Remove the pits and discard, then cut the cherries in half.

Add Banana and Puree

- The banana should be quite ripe, with black spots on a yellow skin and no green color.

- Peel the banana and cut it into chunks. Don't prepare the banana until you are ready to use it, or it can turn brown.

- The lemon juice is used to keep the color of the soup bright and to moderate the flavor.

- You can add more lemon juice or more cinnamon if you want a stronger flavor.

FARMERS' MARKET

CREAMY AVOCADO SORREL SOUP

Sorrel is a bitter green that is in season in spring; it is delicious in this soup

Avocadoes are also known as alligator pears because of their pear shape and thick green rippled skin. The flesh is buttery and nutty, perfect for making into a creamy soup.

Sorrel is a bitter green that can usually only be found in spring. It is actually a herb that you can grow in your garden or in pots. Sorrel has a very sharp and tart taste that is modi-

fied by avocado and potato in this soup.

Look for very young sorrel leaves, as they are more tender and the flavor is less pronounced if you want a milder soup.

Older sorrel leaves add a real tang to this soup, so use them if you like the taste.

Yield: Serves 6

Ingredients

1 tablespoon butter

1 shallot, minced

1 russet potato, peeled and diced

1/4 cup chopped celery leaves

4 cups vegetable broth, homemade or store-bought

1/2 teaspoon salt

1/8 teaspoon pepper

1/2 pound sorrel leaves, stems removed

Pinch freshly ground nutmeg

2 avocados, peeled and chopped

1 tablespoon lemon juice

1/2 cup sour cream

2 tablespoons chopped chives

Creamy Avocado Sorrel Soup

- In large pot, melt butter over low heat. Add shallot and potato; cook and stir 5 minutes.

- Add celery leaves, broth, salt, and pepper; simmer 20 to 35 minutes, until potato is tender.

- Add sorrel and nutmeg; simmer 5 minutes. Add avocado and lemon juice; heat through.

- Using an immersion blender, puree the soup. Serve topped with sour cream and chopped chives.

• • • • RECIPE VARIATION • • •

Bacon Sorrel Soup: Cook 5 strips bacon; drain and crumble; pour fat from pan. Add 1 onion and 3 cloves garlic; cook 5 minutes. Add 2 peeled and cubed potatoes and 3 cups vegetable stock; simmer 20 minutes. Add ¾ pound cleaned sorrel; simmer 20 minutes. Season with salt, pepper, and thyme; serve.

• • • • • • • • RED ● LIGHT • • • • • • • •

If you or someone in your family has rheumatism or bladder or kidney stones, avoid sorrel. Its tart taste comes from oxalic acid, which can aggravate these conditions if ingested. Start with a small amount of sorrel if this is your first time using it.

Clean Sorrel

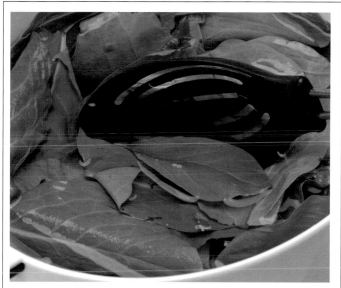

- Sorrel will have lots of grit and sand on it because it is grown in sandy soil.

- Swish the leaves in water, then rinse under cold running water, or immerse the leaves in water to clean.

- Bend each leaf in half lengthwise and pull off the stem along with any tough fibers.

- Chop the sorrel and set aside while you start the base of the soup.

Add Sorrel

- If the sorrel is cooked for at least 15 minutes, it will dissolve into the soup, thickening it.

- You can simmer the sorrel until it's tender or until it has dissolved; it's up to you.

- This soup can be served hot or cold. To serve cold, pour into a bowl and cool 30 minutes in fridge.

- Then place plastic wrap directly on the surface of the soup and chill until cold. Stir in more broth if soup is too thick.

OMELETTE SOUP

Similar to egg drop soup, this recipe is mild and comforting

Soup for breakfast! This easy and delicious soup is mild enough to serve for breakfast or brunch, or it's a good choice for a late-night dinner.

Omelette Soup is filled with all the ingredients of a traditional breakfast, including eggs, sausage, milk, and cheese. Eggs are cooked into an omelette, then cut into strips and dropped into a rich chicken broth.

As in Mushroom Egg Drop Soup, the broth in this recipe must be of the best quality. This is a good place to use your own homemade stock or broth. At the very least, use a boxed stock, which is usually higher quality.

Serve with a warm coffeecake or muffins, along with a fresh fruit salad and lots of hot fresh coffee.

Yield: Serves 4

Ingredients

4 links breakfast sausage

1 tablespoon butter

4 eggs, beaten

$1/4$ cup milk

$1/4$ teaspoon salt

$1/8$ teaspoon pepper

$1/4$ cup shredded Colby cheese

5 cups chicken stock, homemade or store-bought

$1/2$ teaspoon dried basil leaves

2 tablespoons chopped parsley

Omelette Soup

- In small saucepan cook sausage until done; remove to paper towel to drain; cut into small pieces.

- Drain fat from saucepan; add butter and melt. Beat eggs with milk, salt, and pepper; add to pan.

- Cook quickly over me-

dium heat to make a thin omelette. When cooked, sprinkle with cheese, cover, and set aside.

- Heat stock with basil in saucepan. Cut omelette into small strips and add to soup along with sausage; serve sprinkled with parsley.

Omelette Vegetable Soup: Make recipe as directed, except after the omelette is cooked, heat 1 tablespoon butter in soup pot. Add 1 chopped onion; cook 5 minutes. Add 1 cup sliced carrot and ¼ cup green onions with the stock and basil; simmer 10 minutes, then proceed with recipe.

Thai Omelette Soup: Make recipe as directed, except after the omelette is cooked, cook 1 onion, chopped, and 3 garlic cloves, minced, in 2 tablespoons olive oil 5 minutes. Add 1 cup chopped cabbage; 1 carrot, diced; 2 tablespoons soy sauce; and broth. Simmer 5 minutes. Add omelette; garnish with cilantro.

Prepare Omelette

- This is a thin omelette, so don't expect it to puff up. The eggs have to be cooked fairly firm to hold up in the soup.

- The omelette should hold its shape when turned out of the pan, more like a frittata.

- You can season the omelette any way you'd like. Add some dried thyme or marjoram or fresh parsley.

- Don't prepare the omelette ahead of time; make it just before you want to serve the soup.

Add Omelette to Soup

- Don't simmer the soup after the omelette has been added. You don't want it to fall apart in the soup or become too tough.

- Cut the omelette into strips or squares or other designs like triangles or rectangles.

- Any vegetables can be simmered in the stock before the omelette is added.

- Think about using hash brown potatoes, sliced artichoke hearts, green bell peppers, or sliced mushrooms.

SOUPS WITH A TWIST

SPINACH ROOT VEGETABLE SOUP

This hearty soup combines lots of root vegetables with tender spinach

There are many root vegetables that people just don't use any more. Rutabagas, parsnips, and turnips are all delicious and sweet and tender when properly prepared. They are also quite inexpensive, a boon for strained budgets.

You can find these vegetables by the potatoes and onions, usually stacked in bins in the supermarket. These big knobbly roots look inedible, but when peeled and cooked, they are delicious.

Root vegetables are high in fiber and low in calories, free from fat. They have lots of beta-carotene and Vitamin E.

Serve this soup in a stoneware bowl accompanied by a mixed green salad with apples and pears, and some Toasted Garlic Cheese Bread or fresh Cornbread, hot from the oven. *Yield: Serves 6*

Ingredients

2 tablespoons butter

1 onion, chopped

2 cloves garlic, minced

1 shallot, minced

1 bulb celeriac, peeled and chopped

2 carrots, sliced

2 russet potatoes, peeled and cubed

1 bay leaf

1 teaspoon salt

1/8 teaspoon pepper

6 cups vegetable broth, homemade or store-bought

3 cups baby spinach leaves

Pinch fresh nutmeg

1 tablespoon fresh thyme leaves

1 tablespoon lemon juice

Spinach Root Vegetable Soup

- In large pot, melt butter; cook onion, garlic, and shallot 5 minutes.

- Add celeriac, carrots, potatoes, and bay leaf; cook 5 minutes. Add salt, pepper, and broth; bring to a simmer.

- Simmer 25 to 35 minutes, until vegetables are tender. Puree soup using immersion blender, if desired.

- Add spinach, nutmeg, thyme, and lemon juice; simmer 3 to 4 minutes, until spinach wilts.

Bacon Root Vegetable Soup: Make recipe as directed, except instead of the butter, cook 6 slices thick-cut bacon until crisp. Remove, drain, and chop. Pour off fat; do not wipe pan. Continue with recipe as directed, except use chicken broth in place of the vegetable broth. Add bacon to soup with spinach.

Roasted Root Vegetable Soup: Use the same ingredients, but combine celeriac, carrots, and potatoes with onion and garlic in roasting pan; drizzle with olive oil and sprinkle with salt and pepper. Roast at 400°F 1 hour. Combine with broth; simmer 20 minutes, then continue with recipe.

Prepare Vegetables

Add Spinach to Soup

- Peel the root vegetables using a swivel-bladed peeler. Keep going until all the rough skin is removed.

- Any of your favorite root vegetables can be used in this soup, including beets and parsnips.

- For a delicious experiment, try making a variation just of the root vegetables you're unfamiliar with.

- Simmer the soup until the vegetables are tender when pierced with a knife. They will slip right off the knife when done.

- The spinach just wilts in the soup, adding great color and texture to the smooth mixture.

- For a stronger flavor use other dark greens like kale, mustard or turnip greens, or even cabbage.

- Garnish the soup with a dollop of crème fraîche or sour cream and sprinkle with more fresh thyme.

- This hearty soup freezes and reheats well. If you want to freeze it, leave out the spinach until it's reheated.

APPLE CHEDDAR SOUP

Apples and cheddar, combined with curry, make a beautiful soup

Apples add wonderful color, flavor, and texture to this easy soup. The fruit's natural sweetness and tart flavor are perfect cooked with onions and garlic and topped with creamy cheddar cheese.

Even though the apples are sweet, this soup is not. The apples complement the sweetness of the cooked onions and garlic and are the perfect flavor partner with nutty and creamy cheddar cheese.

This is a wonderful soup to serve in the early fall, when the leaves have just started turning and there's a nip in the air.

Curry is a natural partner with these other flavors, but you can leave it out and add herbs like thyme or marjoram instead. Enjoy this unusual soup.

Yield: Serves 6

Ingredients

2 tablespoons butter

1 onion, chopped

3 cloves garlic, minced

2 Granny Smith apples, peeled and chopped

2 tablespoons flour

1 teaspoon salt

1/8 teaspoon white pepper

1 teaspoon curry powder

2 cups chicken broth, homemade or store-bought

3 cups apple juice

1 1/2 cups shredded sharp cheddar cheese

1 tablespoon cornstarch

1 tablespoon lemon juice

Curried Croutons

Apple Cheddar Soup

- In large pot melt butter over medium heat. Add onion and garlic; cook and stir 8 to 9 minutes.

- Add apples; cook and stir 3 to 4 minutes. Sprinkle with flour, salt, white pepper, and curry powder; simmer 5 minutes.

- Add broth and apple juice; bring to a simmer. Simmer 5 to 10 minutes, until apple is very tender.

- Partially puree soup, then add cheese tossed with cornstarch and lemon juice; cook and stir until cheese melts. Serve topped with Curried Croutons.

• • • • RECIPE VARIATIONS • • • •

Apple Carrot Soup: Make recipe as directed, except add 2 carrots, peeled and sliced, with the apples; cook until tender. Increase curry powder to 2 teaspoons. Reduce apple juice to 1 cup and increase chicken broth to 4 cups. Add ½ cup grated Parmesan cheese with the cheddar cheese.

Herbed Apple Soup: Make recipe as directed, except use 3 apples instead of 2. Add 2 stalks celery, sliced. Omit curry powder; add 1 teaspoon dried thyme leaves and 1 teaspoon dried marjoram leaves. Reduce cheddar cheese to 1 cup and add 1 cup shredded Gouda cheese.

Cook Apples

- Peel and chop the apples while the onion and garlic are cooking in the butter.

- You don't want to prepare the apples ahead of time, because they will turn brown, even if sprinkled with lemon juice.

- You can use other apples if you'd like; choose those good for cooking, like Jonathan or McIntosh.

- Add more apples if you'd like a stronger flavored soup that's slightly thicker.

Add Cheese

- Grate the cheese while the soup is simmering. If you grate the cheese ahead of time, it could dry out.

- Don't use prepackaged shredded cheese. It's coated with ingredients that prevent it from melting smoothly.

- Texture is everything in this soup, so it's important that the cheese be soft and fresh.

- Curried Croutons are a nice finishing touch, but you can also use thinly sliced apples or some sour cream.

MOCK TURTLE SOUP

Three kinds of meat replicate the complex flavor of turtle soup

Yes, real turtles are sometimes used to make soup. And not Mock Turtles, as in Alice in Wonderland.

Many turtles are endangered and aren't used as a food source anymore. So creative cooks combine three different types of meat to replicate the complex flavor of real turtle soup. Apparently, turtles have a complex flavor.

You can use other combinations of meat if you'd like. Oxtails are a traditional ingredient in many mock turtle soup recipes, as is ground beef. It all depends on your preference.

Serve this soup garnished with some fresh herbs and crisp croutons. And have a bottle of Louisiana hot sauce on the table to let each diner garnish his or her own.

Yield: Serves 6

Ingredients

½ pound cubed beef sirloin	1 bay leaf
½ pound pork chops, cubed	2 red and 2 yellow tomatoes, peeled, seeded, and diced
¼ pound cubed chicken thighs	3 cups beef broth, home-made or store-bought
1 teaspoon salt	3 cups chicken stock, home-made or store-bought
¼ teaspoon cayenne pepper	1 teaspoon dried thyme
¼ cup butter	1 teaspoon dried marjoram
2 onions, chopped	¼ teaspoon allspice
3 cloves garlic, minced	2 tablespoons lemon juice
2 stalks celery, minced	

Mock Turtle Soup

- Sprinkle beef, pork, and chicken with salt and cayenne pepper; brown in butter 6 minutes; remove.

- Add onions, garlic, and celery to pot; cook 5 minutes. Add bay leaf, both kinds of tomatoes, broth, stock, thyme, marjoram, and allspice.

- Bring to a simmer, then return all the meats to the soup. Simmer 20 to 25 minutes, until meats are tender.

- Remove bay leaf, stir in lemon juice and heat. Serve garnished with sliced hard cooked eggs and chopped cilantro.

Ground Mock Turtle Soup: Make recipe as directed, except substitute 1 pound ground beef for the beef sirloin and 1 pound pork sausage for the pork chops; omit chicken. Continue with the recipe, using all beef broth. Add 2 tablespoons dry sherry in place of the lemon juice.

ZOOM

Real turtle soup was made more frequently back when turtles were plentiful and many people literally had to live off the land. The soup was popular in Cajun and Creole cuisine of the bayous and swamps of Louisiana. You can sometimes find frozen turtle meat in the supermarket if you'd like to try it.

Cook Meat

- You can cook the meat in the butter separately or all at once.

- Use other meat combinations, like pork shoulder, chicken thighs, and ground beef, or pork sausage, sirloin, and chicken breasts.

- Don't overcook the meats in the first step; they should just brown but not cook through.

- Other vegetables you could add to this soup include sliced mushrooms, carrots, or chopped leeks.

Add Tomatoes and Stock

- The tomatoes should be peeled; they will dissolve into the stock and accent the meats.

- Chopped or sliced hard cooked egg is the classic garnish for this unusual soup.

- To make the hard cooked eggs, cover eggs with cold water, bring to a boil, boil 1 minute.

- Remove pan from heat, cover, and let stand 15 minutes. Rinse in cold water until eggs are cold; peel.

SOUPS WITH A TWIST

223

CREAMY PEAR & BRIE SOUP
Creamy cheese melts into this sweet and tart soup

This soup is an excellent starter to a fancy meal. Serve it as an appetizer in tiny cups, or as a first course in white china soup plates.

The most common pears found in the supermarket are Bosc, Anjou, and Bartlett. All pears contain stone cells, which are small hard cells that give the fruit its characteristic gritty texture.

You can use barely ripe or fully ripe pears in this easy soup. The really ripe pears will fall apart in the soup, while the firmer ones will stay in more discrete pieces.

This soup can be served warm or cold. If you want to serve it cold, leave out the Brie and use it as a topping with the Honeyed Pecans.

Yield: Serves 4–6

Ingredients

2 tablespoons butter

1 onion, chopped

1 tablespoon grated ginger root

3 firm pears, peeled and cubed

2 tablespoons flour

$1/2$ teaspoon salt

$1/8$ teaspoon white pepper

1 cup pear nectar

$1 \ 1/2$ cups water

1 tablespoon lemon juice

1 cup cubed Brie cheese without rind

$1/2$ cup heavy cream

$1/2$ cup Honeyed Pecans

Creamy Pear and Brie Soup

- In large saucepan melt butter over medium heat. Add onion and ginger root; cook and stir 5 minutes.

- Add pears; cook and stir 5 to 6 minutes, until tender. Sprinkle with flour, salt, and white pepper; cook 2 minutes.

- Add pear nectar, water, and lemon juice; simmer 10 to 12 minutes, until soup is thickened.

- Add Brie and cream; cook and stir until cheese melts and mixture is smooth. Serve immediately, garnished with Honeyed Pecans.

Pear Blue Cheese Soup: Make recipe as directed, except omit ginger root. Add 2 garlic cloves, minced, to the butter with the onions. Add 1 teaspoon dried thyme leaves with the pears. Omit Brie; add 1 cup crumbled blue cheese.

Honeyed Pecans: On baking sheet, place 1½ cups small whole pecans. Drizzle with 2 tablespoons melted butter, ¼ cup honey, and ¼ cup brown sugar. Bake at 350°F 15 to 20 minutes, until glazed. Sprinkle warm nuts with ½ teaspoon salt and cool.

Cook Onions

Add Cheese

- To prepare the pears, gently remove the peel using a sharp knife or swivel-bladed peeler.

- Cut the pears in half, remove seeds and seed casings, cut out the stem, and chop.

- You can cook the onion just until it's tender, or you can caramelize it for a deeper color and more intense flavor.

- Cook and stir the pears until they are tender. If you cook them until very tender, they will fall apart in the soup, which is also okay.

- Other cheeses can be added besides Brie. Use peeled and cubed Camembert or shredded Gouda.

- Think about cheeses that are served with pears, like Gruyère, Roquefort, Gorgonzola, or Stilton.

- Save some of the cheese to garnish the soup along with the pecans.

- Serve this soup with a nice wine, either a dry white or a sweet red, with some toasted baguettes or water crackers.

SOUPS WITH A TWIST

MELON BERRY SOUP

This soup tastes of the essence of summer

Melons and berries are natural partners, usually served in salads. This is one of the few totally uncooked soups in this collection.

It's important that the melons and berries be at their peak of ripeness in this soup, because their flavor is critical to the success of the soup.

You can use cantaloupe, honeydew melon, or watermelon in this recipe. Watermelon soup will not be as smooth as the soup made with the other two types.

This soup should be served well chilled, so make it at least three hours ahead of time. Prepare the berries just before serving so they are perfect, then enjoy the taste of summer. *Yield: Serves 6*

Ingredients

2 ripe cantaloupes, peeled, seeded, and chopped

1 cup mango nectar

¼ cup orange juice

1 tablespoon lemon juice

Pinch salt

1 teaspoon vanilla

1 cup raspberries

1 cup blueberries

1 cup blackberries

1 tablespoon chopped fresh mint

Melon Berry Soup

- Combine cantaloupe, nectar, orange juice, lemon juice, salt, and vanilla in food processor.

- Process until mixture is smooth. Cover and chill 4 to 5 hours before serving.

- To serve, combine raspberries, blueberries, blackberries, and mint in chilled bowl.

- Pour soup into chilled bowls and serve topped with berry mixture.

・・・・ RECIPE VARIATIONS ・・・・

Mixed Melon Soup: Make soup as directed, except use 1 ripe cantaloupe and 1 ripe honeydew melon. Puree them separately with the evenly divided nectar, orange juice, lemon juice, salt, and vanilla. Chill, then pour the soups at the same time into serving bowls. Garnish soup with Honeyed Pecans.

Curried Melon Soup: Make soup as directed, except add 1 teaspoon curry powder when you puree the cantaloupe. Omit the berry topping. Arrange these garnishes on the table: toasted coconut, chopped pecans, mango chutney, and chopped fresh mint.

Prepare Cantaloupe

- To prepare the cantaloupe, first wash it under cool running water.

- Cut the cantaloupe in half and carefully remove and discard the seeds. Cut the fruit into fourths.

- Use a knife to cut along the base of the cantaloupe, in between the fruit and rind. Then cube the flesh.

- You can find prepared, cubed melons in the produce aisle of the supermarket.

Process Soup

- Process the soup just until it's smooth. Don't overprocess the mixture.

- You can serve the soup as soon as it is made, but it will be better if given some time to chill and blend.

- For a creamier soup, add ½ cup light cream or heavy whipping cream just before serving.

- Use your favorite combination of fresh berries and herbs to garnish the soup.

SOUPS WITH A TWIST

WEB SITES, TV SHOWS, & VIDEOS
Information for making soup

Soups are ubiquitous around the world, so are featured on many TV shows and Web sites. Online there are lots of videos, recipes, and tips and hints to make your soup experience perfect.

Product manufacturers, books, magazines, and catalogs can also help. You'll be able to find information about products, many recipes, soup making and serving tips, and where to find special ingredients, tools, and equipment.

Online message boards and forums are wonderful resources as well. On popular boards you will get an answer to your questions very quickly. Don't be afraid to ask for help!

Soup Web Sites

AllRecipes.com
- allrecipes.com/

- AllRecipes.com, which features reader-submitted recipes that are rated by members, is a reliable source of hundreds of soup recipes.

BH&G
- www.bhg.com/recipes

- *Better Homes and Gardens* offers hundreds of simple and interesting soup recipes, all tested in their test kitchens.

Campbell's Soup
- www.campbellsoup.com

- This site, run by the maker of Campbell's, has lots of soup recipes for soups from scratch, as well as uses for other canned soups.

Crockpot@CDKitchen.com
- crockpot.cdkitchen.com

- This Web site features recipes submitted by bloggers. More than 4,200 old-fashioned and updated recipes are reliable and delicious.

Home Cooking at About.com
- homecooking.about.com

- This time-tested site is full of information and recipes about everything from chicken broth to mock turtle soup.

RecipeZaar
- www.recipezaar.com

- Thousands of soup recipes are submitted by readers and rated by viewers.

Soup Making Videos

About.com Food Videos
- video.about.com/food

- Dozens of sites offer hundreds of videos teaching you how to make every kind of soup.

AllRecipes Videos
- allrecipes.com/

- AllRecipes.com has a lot of excellent videos that show how to make soup in their test kitchen.

Expert Village
- www.expertvillage.com

- You'll learn how to make everything from Chinese Corn Soup to Chicken Artichoke Soup at this site.

iFoods.tv
- ifoods.tv/soups/Tomato-Soup/68/

- iFoods TV offers lots of informative videos that will teach you how to prepare every soup in the world.

- Vegetarian Cooking at About.com

- video.about.com/vegetarian/Vegetable-Soup

- Videos show you exactly how to make easy and delicious soups.

You Tube
- www.youtube.com/watch?v=AKyiF0kWEFc

- Thousands of videos will teach you how to make lots of soup recipes.

Soup TV Cooking Shows
America's Test Kitchen
- *Cook's Illustrated* is responsible for this show on PBS that teaches you how to cook. There are lots of excellent soup recipes.

Robin Miller on the Food Network
- Robin Miller in her show *Quick Fix Meals* uses soups as primary recipes and as ways to use up leftovers.

Semi-Homemade Cooking with Sandra Lee on the Food Network
- Sandra Lee developed the concept of "30 percent fresh food, 70 percent prepared food." She often includes soup recipes.

RESOURCES

BOOKS & MAGAZINES
Hundreds of slow cooker cookbooks and magazines are here to help

Druker, Marjorie, and Clara Silverstein. *New England Soup Factory Cookbook.* Thomas Nelson, 2007 Nashville, TN
- This book offers one hundred recipes for regional soups; the best that Boston has to offer.

Jonath, Leslie, and Frankie Frankeny. *Soup's On!* Chronicle Books, 2007 San Francisco, CA
- Book offers seventy-five soup recipes, with lots of practical advice.

Reader's Digest. *Biggest Book of Soups.* Reader's Digest, 2007 Louisville, KY
- Delicious, classic soup recipes include family favorites and kid-friendly choices.

Soup Books

Better Homes & Gardens. *Biggest Book of Soups and Stews.* Wiley, 2005 Hoboken, NJ
- Kitchen-tested recipes for the best soups and stews, including lots of kid-friendly recipes.

Betty Crocker's Soups and Stews. Betty Crocker, 2009 Minneapolis, MN
- This is an excellent collection of triple-tested soup recipes from the giant of cooking.

Culinary Institute of America. *Book of Soups.* Lebhar-Friedman Books, 2001 New York, NY
- One hundred recipes for perfect soups, from the school that creates the world's best chefs.

Slow Cooker Soups

- By the editors of *Slow Cooker* magazine, this little volume offers lots of soup recipes and tips.

Taste of Home

- This venerable magazine focuses on reader-submitted recipes, tested in their test kitchens.

Woman's Day

- There are lots of soup recipes in each issue of this magazine, along with cooking lessons and tips.

Rosbottom, Betty, and Charles Schiller. *Sunday Soup.* Chronicle Books, 2008 San Francisco, CA
- A year's worth of soups that range from Roasted Pear Soup to Shrimp Gumbo, along with salads and sides.

Soup Magazines

Better Homes & Gardens

- This magazine has tons of soup recipes that follow the seasons.

Family Circle

- This magazine offers lots of soup recipes and menus, seasonal recipes, and tips.

EQUIPMENT RESOURCES

Find equipment through these resources to stock your kitchen

Catalogs for Cooking Equipment

Brylane Home
- This catalog has lots of kitchen equipment, including specialty tools, utensils, and dishware.

Solutions
- You'll find lots of new equipment and tools to make cooking quick and easy.

Sur la Table
- This catalog offers lots of kitchen equipment, along with dishes, serving utensils, and flatware.

Williams-Sonoma
- This catalog showcases top-of-the-line equipment, along with cookbooks and many appliances, tools, and accessories.

Soup Equipment Web Sites

Chefsresource.com
- www.chefsresource.com
- Cutlery, flatware, gadgets, tools, knives, and brands like Cuisinart are featured on this site.

Cooking.com
- www.cooking.com
- Kitchen fixtures, large appliance, cutlery, cookbooks, and tools can be found at this site.

Crockpot.com
- www.crock-pot.com
- The Web site for Rival slow cookers, this site offers customer service, replacement parts, and recipes.

KitchenManualsonline.com

- kitchen.manualsonline.com
- This Web site offers contact information for dozens of slow cooker manufacturers.

FIND INGREDIENTS

There are many resources for ingredients other than the grocery store

Catalogs and Online Resources

Amazon Grocery
- www.agrocerydelivery.com

- Amazon.com has a grocery delivery service that offers general foods and hard-to-find items.

The Baker's Catalog
- From King Arthur's Flour, this catalog offers cooking equipment and baking ingredients, including specialty flours and flavorings.

Schwans
- Home-delivery service for groceries, serving parts of the United States.

Peapod
- www.peapod.com

- Online grocery store serving some areas of the United States.

Safeway.com
- Grocery chain that offers delivery of food items, as well as recipes and tips for healthy living.

Farmers' Markets

Farmers' Markets
www.farmersmarketla.com
This is the Los Angeles Farmers' Market Web site—the original farmers' market.

Farmers' Market Search
apps.ams.usda.gov/FarmersMarkets
This USDA site lets you search for a farmers' market by state, city, county, and zip code, as well as methods of payment.

National Directory of Farmers' Markets
farmersmarket.com
Site has index of U.S. Farmers' Markets listed by state.

234

METRIC CONVERSION TABLES

Approximate U.S. Metric Equivalents

Liquid Ingredients

U.S. MEASURES	METRIC	U.S. MEASURES	METRIC
¼ TSP.	1.23 ML	2 TBSP.	29.57 ML
½ TSP.	2.36 ML	3 TBSP.	44.36 ML
¾ TSP.	3.70 ML	¼ CUP	59.15 ML
1 TSP.	4.93 ML	½ CUP	118.30 ML
1¼ TSP.	6.16 ML	1 CUP	236.59 ML
1½ TSP.	7.39 ML	2 CUPS OR 1 PT.	473.18 ML
1¾ TSP.	8.63 ML	3 CUPS	709.77 ML
2 TSP.	9.86 ML	4 CUPS OR 1 QT.	946.36 ML
1 TBSP.	14.79 ML	4 QTS. OR 1 GAL.	3.79 L

Dry Ingredients

U.S. MEASURES	METRIC	U.S. MEASURES		METRIC
⅟₁₆ OZ.	2 (1.8) G	2⅘ OZ.		80 G
⅛ OZ.	3½ (3.5) G	3 OZ.		85 (84.9) G
¼ OZ.	7 (7.1) G	3½ OZ.		100 G
½ OZ.	15 (14.2) G	4 OZ.		115 (113.2) G
¾ OZ.	21 (21.3) G	4½ OZ.		125 G
⅞ OZ.	25 G	5¼ OZ.		150 G
1 OZ.	30 (28.3) G	8⅞ OZ.		250 G
1¾ OZ.	50 G	16 OZ.	1 LB.	454 G
2 OZ.	60 (56.6) G	17⅗ OZ.	1 LIVRE	500 G

RESOURCES

HOTLINES & MANUFACTURERS

Find help with cooking problems and equipment manufacturers

RESOURCES

Hotlines

Butterball Turkey Holiday Line
- 1-800-323-4848

- Hotline available year-round; answers questions about turkey cooking and preparation.

Empire Kosher Poultry Hotline
- 1-800-367-4734

- Year-round hotline answers questions about poultry.

Perdue
- 1-800-473-7383

- Year-round hotline helps with cooking questions, especially poultry products.

Reynolds Turkey Tips
- 1-800-745-4000

- Year-round hotline answers consumer questions about turkey preparation; also offers free recipes.

USDA Meat and Poultry Hotline
- 1-800-535-4555

- Year-round line offers information about food safety and answers consumer questions about meat preparation.

Manufacturers of Equipment

All-Clad
- www.all-clad.com

- This was one of the first manufacturers to make metal inserts for the slow cooker.

Cuisinart
- www.cuisinart.com

- This company can completely outfit your kitchen, with ranges to stockpots.

GE Appliances
- www.geappliances.com

- Outfit your entire kitchen with GE appliances. The company offers online service and customer support.

Kitchenaid
- www.kitchenaid.com

- This company offers lots of high-quality appliances, from refrigerators and stoves to slow cookers.

Rival
- www.rivalproducts.com

- This is the Web site of the manufacturer of the original Crock-Pot; it offers product information, recipes, and an online store.

GLOSSARY
Learn the language first

Al dente: Italian phrase meaning "to the tooth" describes doneness of pasta.

Beat: Manipulating food with a spoon, mixer, or whisk to combine.

Bisque: A soup thickened with cream and sometimes egg, pureed to velvety smoothness.

Borscht: A soup from Eastern Europe, usually made with beets, served hot or cold.

Broth: Liquid extracted from meats and vegetables, used as the basis for most soups.

Brown: Cooking step that caramelizes food and adds color and flavor before cooking.

Coat: To cover food in another ingredient, as to coat chicken breast with bread crumbs.

Chill: Refrigerate a soup or place it in an ice-water bath to rapidl cool.

Chop: To cut food into small pieces, using a chef's knife or a food processor.

Chowder: A soup thick with vegetables and meats, usually seafood thickened with cream and cheese.

Deglaze: Adding a liquid to a pan used to sauté meats; this remove drippings and brown bits to create a sauce.

GLOSSARY

Dice: To cut food into small, even portions, usually about ¼-inch square.

Flake: To break into small pieces; canned meats are usually flaked.

Fold: Combining two soft or liquid mixtures together, using an over-and-under method of mixing.

Gazpacho: A cold soup, usually made of tomatoes, that is pureed without cooking.

Grate: A grater or microplane is used to remove small pieces or shreds of skin or food.

Grill: To cook over coals or charcoal or over high heat.

Marinate: To stand meats or vegetables in a mixture of an acid and oil to add flavor and tenderize.

Melt: To turn a solid into a liquid by the addition of heat.

Mulligatawny: Meaning "pepper water," this hearty soup comes from India via the British Isles.

Pan Fry: To cook quickly in a shallow pan, in a small amount of fat, over relatively high heat.

Shred: To use a grater, mandoline, or food processor to create small strips of food.

Simmer: A state of liquid cooking, in which the liquid is heated to just below boiling.

Slow Cooker: An appliance that cooks food by surrounding it with low, steady heat.

Soup: A mixture of solids and liquids, served hot or cold, as a main dish or part of a multicourse meal.

Toss: To combine food using two spoons or a spoon and a fork until mixed.

Whisk: Both a tool, which is made of loops of steel, and a method, which combines food until smooth.

INDEX

Library Resource Center
Renton Technical College
3000 N.E. 4th St.
Renton, WA 98056

Renton Technical College
3000 N.E. 4th St.
Renton, WA 98056